Revolutionaries in the Theater
Meyerhold, Brecht, and Witkiewicz

Theater and Dramatic Studies, No. 49

Oscar G. Brockett, Series Editor

Leslie Waggener Professor of Fine Arts
and Professor of Drama
The University of Texas at Austin

Other Titles in This Series

Revolutionaries in the Theater
Meyerhold, Brecht, and Witkiewicz

by
Christine Kiebuzinska

U·M·I Research Press

Ann Arbor / London

Produced and distributed by
UMI Research Press
an imprint of
University Microfilms Inc.
Ann Arbor, Michigan 48106

Library of Congress Cataloging in Publication Data

Kiebuzinska, Christine Olga.
Revolutionaries in the theater.

(Theater and dramatic studies ; no. 49)
Bibliography: p.
Includes index.
1. Theater—History—20th century. 2. Experimental
theater—Europe—History. 3. Meierkhold, V. E.
(Vsevolod Emilevich), 1874-1940—Aesthetics. 4. Brecht,
Bertolt, 1898-1956—Aesthetics. 5. Witkiewicz,
Stanislaw Ignacy, 1885-1939—Aesthetics. 6. European
drama—History and criticism. 7. Formalism (Literary
analysis). 8. Semiotics and literature. 9. Semiotics
in the arts. 10. Theater and society. I. Title.
II. Series.
PN2193.E86K54   1988   792'.09'04   87-25516
ISBN 0-8357-2019-5 (pbk.)

British Library CIP data is available.

Dedicated to Gregory, André, and Ksenya

Contents

Acknowledgments

This study began at the University of Maryland with the support of Professors Roger Meersman, Peter Beicken, and Carla Peterson, and in particular Professor John Fuegi, to whom I am grateful for his continued support and insightful criticism.

Introduction

Traditionally, discussions of drama have been polarized along lines of binary opposition: the dramatic work versus the performance text or *mise-en-scène*. Literary scholars and teachers often state that a play only "lives" when seen on stage. Yet, at the same time, these scholars insist on the purity of the dramatic work and on the need for directors and actors to remain faithful to it. In this manner, the work has acquired an authority over those performing it. Some dramatic works, such as the plays of Shakespeare, have acquired a sacred value, and all that is needed is to dust them off by getting rid of deposits of history and hermeneutic sediment left on the pure work.[1] Frequently such dusting off entails a staging of *Hamlet*, for example, in modern dress and setting. Yet, as any student of the theater knows, Shakespeare was first and foremost a practitioner who understood that the problem of making a play accessible to his audience consisted not of presenting *Julius Caesar* in the dress of the Elizabethan period but rather in presenting a *mise-en-scène* open to interpretation ad infinitum.

I find Roland Barthes's distinction between *work* and *text* particularly useful in examining the criteria separating the dramatic work from its concretization in the *mise-en-scène*. According to Barthes, while the work is concrete, and in the case of the theater would entail the heritage of theatrical usage, the focus on the theatrical text opens up "a methodological field," an activity, or production of the text's plurality of meaning. The plurality of possible meanings is not so much dependent on the possibility of several meanings arising from the ambiguity of the dramatic work, but is rather more a product of a simultaneity, or "explosion," or dissemination of meanings found in the signs of the *mise-en-scène*.[2]

This shift from *work* to *text* also disrupts the role of the reader, or in the case of the *mise-en-scène*, the spectator. Rather than demanding an interpretation from the spectator, the *mise-en-scène* engages the spectator into an "active collaboration"[3] which culminates in what Barthes calls "pleasure." This "pleasure" is not the satisfaction a spectator may gain from the consumption of dramatic works, but rather the enjoyment of participating in the concretization of theatrical discourse.

What has radically changed since the avant-garde theater of the 1920s disrupted theatrical conceptions is the relationship between the director and the work. Vsevolod Meyerhold, Bertolt Brecht, and Stanislaw Ignacy Witkiewicz opened up the dramatic work to theatrical experimentation by focusing on the plurality of signifieds, the simultaneity of theatrical enunciators, and the intertextual use of codes and conventions drawn from theatrical heritage, but now appearing in a new way. Most importantly, the idea of ownership of the dramatic work was put into question, as well as the theatrical practices of institutions like the Comédie Française, which have as their mission the preservation of the dramatic work and a mode of performance that keeps that work in the frame of the dramatist's ownership rights. Thus, the theatrical avant-garde of the twenties were radical not only because they introduced innovations in theatrical practice, but, more importantly, because they turned against the institutionalization of art as an autonomous mode. As Peter Bürger explains, while the modernists and the avant-garde artists both shared the attitude that art calls attention to its own material, the social roles of the modernist and avant-garde artist were radically different since "modernism may be understandable as an attack on traditional writing techniques, but the avant-garde can only be understood as an attack meant to alter the institutionalized commerce with art."[4]

Contributing to the general changes in the focus on art as an institution and the course of its development in bourgeois society were concepts brought into general discourse by the Russian formalists, in particular their view of "defamiliarization" as an artistic technique. "What was claimed," as Bürger explains, "is no more than a connection . . . between the principle shock in avant-gardiste art and the recognition that defamiliarization is a category of general validity."[5] The Prague structuralists took the idea of defamiliarization further into the study of the norms and values inherent in the reception of a work of art. In particular, the members of the Prague Linguistic Circle also contributed to a systematic analysis of theatrical signs and their reception. With these ideas in mind, the purpose of this study is to explore the contributions of the three avatars of the avant-garde, Meyerhold, Brecht, and Witkiewicz, to new directions in the theater.

As Jiří Veltruský writes, the basis of drama is action. Although events in real life are also shaped by action, the properties of an action directed toward a practical objective are determined by this objective, irrespective of perceivers, unless the objective of the action is communication. In the theater the action is an end in itself and lacks an external practical purpose outside of being understood by its audience as a coherent meaningful event. While in real life actions are decoded by an intuitive understanding of both intentional and unintentional signs, since the action on stage has no practical function, the spectator's understanding of the stage presentation is shaped exclusively by intentionally presented signs.[6]

The study of signs in theatrical performance begins not with the semiotics of the dramatic work but rather with a semiotics of everything that makes up the reality of the stage—the dramatic work, the actor's acting, the stage design, costume, lighting, and sound effects. Notwithstanding a close adherence to the dramatic work, an absolute congruence between a play as read and a play as acted is not possible. Paradoxical in nature, the dramatic work first precedes a performance and later accompanies it. A clear distinction must therefore be made between a theatrical presentation and the dramatic work. Since most theatrical performances are based on dramatic works, an analysis of the relation between the two is desirable.

Unlike the unfolding of signs of dramatic works, which subsist through time and are inexhaustible, since new contexts provide them with constantly renewed possibilities of interpretation, such gradual unfolding of the richness of cultural signs is impossible in a theatrical performance. As a result, fewer signs exist and are perforce more conventionalized and more strongly coded than signs in real life. Since theater uses elements not from one but from many domains, the theatrical performance has a more polysemous character than the other arts, one which enables it to appeal to a wider and more varied audience, with different types and degrees of education, with different cultural backgrounds and different expectations, who may respond with varying degrees of intensity to the different sign patterns that combine to form the theatrical performance.

While the dramatic work is an important component of most theatrical performances, it is equally legitimate to consider theater as an art in its own right—one in which a dramatic work may have a place but which is not dependent on the work, and which may even be, to some extent, independent of language. A circus performance, for example, is almost entirely independent of language; however, messages are conveyed in specifically theatrical ways. In the *commedia dell'arte* tradition a predetermined dramatic work does not exist; instead, dialogue is elaborated in the course of the performance rather than prior to it.

The essence of theater lies in the act of presentation. As such, it necessitates a spatial dimension, the spectacle occupying its realm, the spectators theirs. These two realms may be constant, as in traditional theater, where spectacle is confined to the stage and spectators to the auditorium, or they may shift through the creation of other realms for the sake of exaggerating the particular tensions inherent in each play. Moreover, for the purposes of this study a dramatic work providing a story-line which recounts or reenacts a sequence of past, present, future, or potential actions or events based on the utilization of language is necessary. This type of presentation also involves an actor's assumption of a role or roles, or the assignment of a role to an object; role is here understood to mean a fictive identity. Since a theatrical presentation differs from the dramatic work in its fundamental concretization, we cannot define that which occurs between a dramatic work and a theatrical performance as simply a translation but rather as a distinctly separate methodological activity in which verbal signs are communicated by means of signs from nonverbal systems.

A detailed history of the opposition to the dominance of the dramatic work might be interesting and would find ample documentation in the writings of Mic, Tairov, Appia, Craig, or Artaud. It could be argued that the moment the written word is read aloud it is translated into another language. Pitch, intonation, inflection, loudness, and paralinguistic utterances substantially alter the written text. Roman Jacobson quotes the famous example of the actor from the Moscow Art Theatre who was asked by Stanislavsky to produce some forty variations on the single phrase *"Segodnja vecerom"* (this evening) by modifying the expressive tone.[7]

Equally, gesture can be read as a language in its own right, and Artaud in fact saw the gestural or kinesic as the fundamental code of theater, a view that has been widely shared. Meyerhold's bio-mechanical system incorporated both the gestural and kinesic with attention to the proxemic code, the system of interaction between groups of six figures, and the actor's use of space. Both kinesics and proxemics can be related to the written text but are in no way subordinate to it. As Jiří Veltruský explains, the linguistic system both combines and conflicts with the physical systems that comprise acting.[8]

Brecht's position in this movement was an original one. Whereas some of the other theoreticians of the theater seem to have envisaged an almost total sweeping away of the word, Brecht aimed at a kind of counterpoint in which gesture, song, and decor would comment on the spoken text and be commented on by it. Brecht speaks of a *Literarisierung* of the theater, and even if he intends different effects from those desired by Meyerhold or Witkiewicz, he too emphasizes that the theatrical presentation differs from the dramatic work; he too pays considerable attention to gesture, music, and the multiplicity of signs. There is even a place for the printed word in Brecht's presentations, where slogans and captions serve as a commentary upon the action, a device used before Brecht by Meyerhold, particularly in his constructivist productions.

Visual signs which can refer loosely to shades, tones, colors, brushstrokes do not provide the coherence that linguistic signs do, but may, as in the theory of pure form in the theater presented by Witkiewicz, communicate, through the possibilities of combination, the analogical character of scenic design, costumes, and props, which may be combined in unusual ways to extend their contradictions to spoken dialogue, thus obliging the audience to move toward an interpretation that does not necessarily rely on the logical breakdown of the dramatic work.

The greater the extent to which the presentational elements of theatrical productions are codified, the more the affective experience in the theater tends to be individualized. Each spectator draws on his own "language." Theater semiotics, then, must take into account the wide range of decoding of texts and necessarily must pay attention to signs as being culturally determined. The classical theater solved the problem of semantic discrepancies by respecting a fixed and rigid system of conventions. The naturalistic theater attempted to dissimulate the discrepancies in various ways, primarily by adhering as closely as possible to the conventions of the novel and psychological motivation of characters, while the avant-garde theater used semantic discrepancies deliberately as a means of opening meditation about its own medium. "Those codes on which the aesthetic sign-function is based" writes Umberto Eco, "release a process of code changing" which "frequently produces a new type of awareness about the world insofar as the aesthetic labor aims to be detected and scrutinized repeatedly by the addressee," ultimately producing a network of diverse communicational acts "eliciting highly original responses."[9]

A text (and hereby a performance becomes a text) may become open to several semiotic practices, which, as Julia Kristeva explains it, can be designated as "translinguistic."

> The text is therefore a productivity, and this means: first, that its relationship to the language in which it is situated is redistributive (destructive-constructive), and hence can be better approached through logical categories rather than linguistic ones; and second, that it is a permutation of texts, and inter-textuality: in the space of a given text, several utterances, taken from other texts, intersect and neutralize one another.[10]

Most deliberations on theatrical presentations ignore the capacity of the theater for polysemic organization. Piscator writes that the theater should be a radar—"a detecting device that emits and focuses a powerful scanning beam on the universe."[11] Such an analogy calls attention to the ability of the theater to both pick up signals and to emit them. Appropriate decodification of a given theatrical presentation derives above all from the spectator's familiarity with other theatrical presentations. The genesis of the performance itself is necessarily intertextual, writes Keir Elam. "It cannot but bear the traces of other performances at every level, whether that of the written text (bearing generic, structural and linguistic relations with other plays), the scenery (which will 'quote' its pictorial or proxemic influences), the actor (whose performance refers back . . . to other displays), directorial style, and so on."[12]

The ideal decoder of a theatrical presentation is a spectator with "a sufficiently detailed and judiciously employed textual background to enable him to identify all relevant relations and use them as a grid for a correspondingly rich decodification."[13] This approach focuses attention on the spectator rather than on the aesthetic concretization. Aesthetic response, according to Wolfgang Iser, should be viewed "in terms of a dialectic relationship between text, reader and their interaction," while aesthetic reception deals with readers "whose reactions testify to certain historically conditioned experiences of literature. A theory of response has its roots in the text; a theory of reception arises from a history of readers' judgments."[14]

Every spectator's interpretation of a text is a new construction of it according to the cultural and ideological disposition of the spectator. The Prague structuralists, particularly Felix Vodička and Jan Mukařovský, formulated a theory of reception which took into account Roman Ingarden's aesthetic concretization but which also included aesthetic functions, norms, and values as social facts to be taken into account in the evaluation of the activity of reception. While aesthetic response, according to Ingarden, should not interfere with the intersubjective intentionality of the text, the Prague structuralists focused both upon the subject-object interaction in the reception of aesthetic objects as well as on the shared codes conditioning this interaction.[15] Thus, while Ingarden's position is invaluable in reconstructing the process of cognition, or response, as based on the object's form, its material endowments, and its existence in a certain determinate mode,[16] the Prague structuralists' focus on the semiotic components renders the aesthetic object as subject to social determinants, thus shifting from a concern with solely aesthetic qualities to extra-aesthetic qualities as well. Its leading theorist, Jan Mukařovský, takes the position that works of art are always perceived against the background of artistic norms that differ from those which gave birth to them:

> From a single work several different structures with different dominants and hierarchies of components can be realized depending on the period (or milieu). The work therefore is not an unambiguous structure. It becomes so only if perceived against the background of a particular immediate tradition from which the work deviates and against which it is reflected. If the background tradition shifts, the structure changes as well as the dominant, and the work acquires a totally new appearance.[17]

Despite the revolution in the theater against the tyranny of the dramatic work, most deliberations on drama, even today, deal exclusively with works and deal with them in the way works are usually dealt with—that is, from the point of view of literary interpretation, disregarding that in its "concretization" on stage the work constantly changes under changing temporal, local, social, and even individual considerations.

As established by the Russian formalists, the literariness of literature is conditioned not only synchronically by the opposition between poetic and practical language, but also diachronically by the opposition to the givens of the genre and the preceding form in the transition of that genre. When the work of art is "perceived against the background of other works of art and in association with them" as Viktor Shklovsky formulates it,[18] the interpretation of the work of art must also take into consideration its relation to other forms that existed prior to it. According to Shklovsky and Jurij Tynjanov, there exist in each period a number of literary schools "wherein one of them represents the canonized height of literature." The institutionalization of a literary form leads to its automatization and demands the formation of new forms that "conquer the place of the older ones," then grow to be a mass phenomenon, and finally are themselves in turn pushed to the sidelines:[19]

> The more light you shed on a literary period, the more you become convinced that the images you had considered to be the creation of a certain particular poet had been borrowed by him from other poets, virtually unchanged. All that the work of poetic schools amounts to is the acquisition and demonstration of new devices for deploying and elaborating verbal materials; in particular, it amounts more to deploying images than creating them. Images are handed down; and poetry involves far more reminiscence of images than thinking in them.[20]

In this manner the Russian formalists refuted the principle of artistic autonomy and countered by advancing the device of "making strange" (*ostranenie*) by means of which art is conceived of as a way of breaking down automatism in perception. The aim of defamiliarization is not to make a meaning more accessible but to bring about the "seeing," and not just "recognizing."[21] It follows that the reception of art can no longer exist in the naive enjoyment of the beautiful, but rather demands a differentiation of form and the recognition of the process. This attitude prevents the work from the past from being naively assimilated to the prejudices and expectations of meaning of the present, and thereby allows the work to be seen in its alterity.

The question that the process of deautomatization of drama ultimately raises is whether there exists an unbridgeable division, or even opposition, between the dramatic work and a performance of the work. Is there something genuinely "theatrical," different in kind from what is inherently "literary"? For the playwrights and directors under consideration in this study, the dramatic work serves as a point of departure for works of art that by their nature are ephemeral, productions rather than ultimate products.

The distinction between dramatic and narrative plots was explained by Hegel as one between action and event. Jiří Veltruský explains that both action and event consist in the character's carrying out some purpose. When this is presented as an action, everything is reduced to the character to include his mentality, duty, opinions, and purpose; when it is presented as an event, the outer circumstances which favor or hamper or in any way affect the carrying out of the purpose are equally important. In dramatic plot the motifs emerging from the dialogue tend to be related to the conflict or the purpose of the action, while in the narrative plot the motifs emerging from the dialogue may not be necessarily "related to and marked by conflict."[22]

The progression of a narrative plot depends on the reader's ability to take in the simultaneity of actions that are presumably taking place at the same time, often generating tension which may be increased by relegating the decisive action into the background while a secondary action is presented. In the dramatic plot, progression does not unilaterally depend on the way the language proceeds and is not retarded or obstructed by descriptions as in narrative plots. Instead, dramatic plot is characterized by its momentum, which constantly drives it forward, comprised not only of meanings emerging from the dialogue but also tied to the corresponding extralinguistic signs of theatrical presentations.[23] Brecht's attempt to make theatrical discourse narrative rather than dramatic focuses on the relationship between narrative texts and readers that allows the plot to go on as if the dialogue had stopped, allowing the reader to sit back and reflect on the "outcome."

Reading a dramatic work calls attention to the components that differentiate it from other literary works—dialogue and stage directions. The dialogue ultimately serves as the verbal component of the dramatic work and presents the voices of the characters. Stage directions appear as mostly visual components, although they can be acoustic as well, taking into account sound effects, voice quality, and paralinguistic utterances. In addition, stage directions serve to indicate the identity of the dramatis personae and to place them into a structure of place and time. Consequently, more than the dialogue, the stage directions present the direct authorial voice, which, in a production of the dramatic work, may develop into a subsidiary text—that of the director or producer staging the text. The presentation of a dramatic work produces an additional text, particularly since every dramatic script is to some degree incomplete and contains gaps that must be filled in by the director. Thus, the distinction between the mode of existence of the dramatic work as read and as performed is that the former is purely verbal while the latter is both verbal and nonverbal.

Even where there is narrative dialogue, this can be considered as distinct from dramatic dialogue, since it emphasizes, as Jiří Veltruský writes, "the succession of speeches rather than the simultaneous unfolding and interplay of the contents from which they spring." Having made this distinction, Veltruský goes on to explain the function of stage directions or the dramatist's comments. Since these notes are eliminated in performance, the resulting gaps in the unity of the work are filled in by other than linguistic signs. This process is not arbitrary but is "essentially a matter of transposing linguistic meanings into other semiotic systems."[24]

The semiotics of theatricality focuses on the work's potential for staging—the study of the necessary interaction of verbal signs and signs that compose the *mise-en-scène*, whereby the latter transform the former. The essential nature of theatricality is thus located in the process or activity of transformation, and it is this potentiality of the dramatic work to undergo transformation that designates the dynamic relationship between the work and the performance.

The distinction between dramatic performance and the dramatic work became a general theoretical reflection around the turn of the century. Perhaps the most fundamental aspect of theatrical reform in the twentieth century has been the devaluation of the written theatrical work. The attention of critics and dramatists has focused on the understanding that the full implications of a dramatic work are only to be discovered in performance. Thus, dramatic criticism of even poorly staged performances produces a more valid judgment than a merely literary reading, since performance serves as evidence of the viability of the work in the genre's own medium.

The physical elements of theater do not need the support of a work in order to be read as meaningful signs. What the spectator must learn to "read" in the theater is not the dramatic work from which each production is derived but rather "the irreducible and immediately perceived language of movement, sounds, shapes, and colors."[25] Words in the play, as Peter Brook has observed, are "an end product which begins as an impulse. This process occurs inside the dramatist; it is repeated inside the actor."[26] Since the performance is designed expressly to touch and involve and audience, "a study of the passage of signals and responses in the theater like that of semantics, cybernetics, or any other system of communication, must be descriptive before it is prescriptive."[27]

Thus, it is attention not to words but the communicative activities in the theater that determines the machinery of the theater, as Bernard Beckerman insists:

> Unfortunately, dramatic theory has not sufficiently addressed itself to a close analysis of theatrical activity, primarily because it has seen theatre as a composition of words rather than of activities. It has tended to split motion from action, and then to concentrate upon the discussion of action. This seems to be a serious error, because, in failing to concern itself fully with activity before examining the concept of action, dramatic criticism and theory are ignoring the foundation of theatrical art.[28]

What Beckerman describes as "activities" Barthes describes as "messages" or "signals" that are received by the spectator simultaneously from the scenery, costumes, sound effects, lighting, actors, their gestures, enunciations, and facial expressions. While some of these messages or activities remain fixed in their spatial qualities, others change and are purely temporal, as speech and gestures for example. The study of theatrical presentations is the study of how the stage compels the audience to be involved in its actual processes. The spectator interprets the signals presented on stage and thus contributes to the activity known as theatrical art. An awareness that everything that appears on stage is "a sign of a sign"[29] is fundamental to viewing theatrical performances as special kinds of communicative events. Consequently, theatrical perception involves an activity that does not necessarily take into account a familiarity with the dramatic work but rather projects a sensitivity to the density of signs and the relationship among them.[30]

Ultimately, the repudiation of the dominance of dramatic works over theatrical performances had to do with the reaffirmation of the physical immediacy of the theater. Within the new attitude fostered by a rebellion against the arbitrary control of theatrical art as a branch of literature, with directors and actors as mere servants to the dramatic text, Meyerhold, Witkiewicz, and Brecht, as well as many of their predecessors and contemporaries, called attention to the multiplicity of signs in the theater that designate its essential theatricality. The often violent attacks on the sanctity of the work served to call attention to a theater whose significance, as Artaud writes, was contained in "a new physical language with its basis in signs and no longer words."[31]

Attention to the literariness of the work was discerned as emblematic of a certain repressive elitism, rationalism, pragmatism, even spiritualism, and anthropocentricism. Literariness came to be considered as an extension of mimetic realism and both attitudes exerted pressure to make dramatic presentations as real and natural as possible. In the conception of the playwrights and directors under discussion in this study, mimetic realism in its most limited sense was that which the theater needed to escape, or as Eugène Ionesco observes: "Realism, socialist or not, never looks beyond reality. It narrows it down, diminishes it, falsifies it, and leaves out of account the obsessive truths that are most fundamental to us: love, death and wonder."[32] Thus, the emphasis on the actor, on gesture, and all that surrounds the actor and signifies along with him: on decor, lighting, sound effects, and so on, was at least in part an implicit criticism of a tradition in which the physical elements of the theater were intended to realize a literary work, to serve it, to illustrate it, and to adorn it.

To accomplish the theatricalization of the theater the effects of the *mise-en-scène* were to be magnified, underlined, and stressed to the maximum, writes Ionesco. "To push drama out of that intermediate zone where it is neither theatre, nor literature is to restore it to its own domain, to its natural frontiers. It was not for me to conceal the devices of the theatre, but rather make them still more evident, deliberately obvious."[33]

Attention was called to the signifying function of all performance elements and to the understanding that "all that is on stage is a sign."[34] The object was to draw the spectator's attention to the sign-vehicle and its theatricality, rather than to the signified and its dramatic equivalent.

In reaction against "slice of life" representations, the impulse was to return the theater to its earlier modes, expanding its anti-illusory tactics by obvious tricks of switching conventions, thus allowing for the more open link of communication between the stage and the audience. "There is a theatrical reality going on at each moment," writes Peter Handke. "A chair on the stage is a theatre chair."[35] Consequently, existing signs from the semiotic codes of quotidien life enter onto the stage as "signs of signs and not as signs of material objects."[36] Although theatrical signs are commonly themselves material objects, on stage they are intended as signs of material objects, or as a sign of a sign, but not as an object itself. The important, immediate consequence of their status as signs of signs is that theatrical signs are almost always abbreviated, bearing only those marks and elements "which are necessary for the given dramatic situation." This is true both for material objects represented by signs (costume, scenery) and also for language presented on stage. Ultimately, "The dramatist and actor select only a small part of the system of signs which practical language possesses."[37]

In addition to the abbreviated, multifunctional, and transformable signs that constitute each semiotic system employed on stage, the theatrical presentation is characterized by the multiplicity or polyphony of semiotic systems that together make up the structure of theatrical expression, a structure to which belong both fixed sign systems, such as the set, costumes, and lighting, and also changeable structures, such as speech, gestures, and musical accompaniment or sound effects. In their simultaneity, and in the plurality and interchangeability of their functions, intentional signs on the stage produce a vital tension,[38] the focus of which is the actor or a figure representative of the actor, such as the puppet, shadow, or ultimately "a piece of wood." By virtue of the actor's inescapable materiality writes Petr Bogatyrev,

> we see in him not only a system of signs but also a living person. . . . This dual perception of the actor by the spectator is of great importance. In the first place, thanks to it, all signs expressed by the actor are made animate. Second, at the same time this dual perception of the performance affirms that it is impossible to identify the player with the role he plays, that no equation can be made between the actor and the character whom he represents, that the costume and mask and gesture of the actor are only a sign of a sign of the character portrayed by him.[39]

This antinomy between sign and object is characteristic not only of obvious-ly artificial signs, such as sets, costumes, or masks, but also of other semiotic systems used on stage. On the one hand, their status as signs and sign systems is self-evident, but on the other hand the irreducible and unavoidable materiality from which the signs are constituted is also apparent. Volosinov's insight that "every ideological sign is not only a reflection, a shadow, of reality, but is also itself a material segment of that very reality"[40] is especially useful. Consequently, the theatrical presentation must keep that dual nature ever in the forefront. This emphasis on artificiality ultimately results from the basic semiotic antinomy focused in the actor:

> Neither the spectator nor the actor should have the sensation of complete transformation . . . the action on stage must not be sensed as reality but as theater. . . . Sometimes actors and spectators do experience a sensation of a complete transformation, but this sensation must be a temporary not a lasting one; it must come and go . . . perception of the theater as real life through the whole performance must inevitably lead to results violating the theater.[41]

The main thrust of the avatars of the revolution in the theater was to deemphasize the illusion that what appears on stage is an imitation of reality.

Max Frisch writes that one must remember that the only reality on the stage lies in the fact that the action is played on a stage:

A play permits what life does not. Life does not permit us, for example, to ignore the continuity of time; to be in several places at once; to interrupt the action (with songs, choruses, commentaries, etc.) and to proceed only after we have grasped the cause of it and the possible consequences; to eliminate what is simply repetition, etc. In real life we can perhaps through a later action make good some mistake that has occurred, but we cannot wipe it out, cannot cause it not to have happened, we cannot select some other behavior for a time that is past. Life is historical, definitive moment by moment, it allows no variations. A play allows these things. Flight from reality? The theater reflects it, but does not copy it. Nothing is more nonsensical than an imitation of reality, nothing more superfluous: there is reality enough already. The theater of imitation is a misunderstanding of the theater's function. There are producers who are very good at it, turning audiences into voyeurs and then deceiving them. In order to be a voyeur I must set aside my own consciousness and forget that it is only a play I am watching, and when I do not succeed, it is doubly embarrassing. The original theater (with cothurnus, masks, verse, etc.) was, of course, never a theater of imitation: the audiences of those days were always aware that the ensemble contained no real gods. . . .[42]

"I come forward pointing at my mask." It was thus that the actors in the Roman theater emphasized to the audience that they were playing traditional roles and not representing real people.[43] The opposite was true of naturalistic theater that dominated the European stage when Jarry, Maeterlinck, Craig, Appia, Jessner, Copeau, Fuchs, Meyerhold, Tairov, Vakhtangov, Reinhardt, Witkiewicz, Artaud, Piscator, and Brecht sought to free the theater from imitating reality. Within the conventions of naturalism, dramatists and directors commented on real life in a mimetic manner, using accurate and detailed sets and realistically costumed actors and actresses to draw the spectator into the illusion that that which was presented on stage indeed constituted reality. Theater purported to imitate reality, not to transcend it or complement it. The peephole stage with the nonexistent fourth wall served to draw the spectator into the role of a voyeur spying on characters (not actors) who were to behave (rather than act) exactly as if the curtain had never risen. To sustain this illusion, the actor was trained not to play a part but rather to become the part, to live the part. Likewise, not only costumes, but furniture, props, and whole settings were to be as genuinely observed and as significantly real as the actor.

The scene was to loom up before the spectator "with the same vividness, solid, palpable, substantial as if plucked from the stream of life itself."[44] The setting in particular was given a great deal of studied attention in order to give significance and vital meaning by establishing a background for the spectator by means of which he could interpret the environment's influence on the characters.

To correspond with the carefully drawn psychological development of the motivations of characters, new acting and staging techniques were introduced, not to project a new theatricality but rather to deny it. The stage's essential theatricality was disavowed by producers such as Antoine of the Théâtre-Libre and Stanislavsky of the Moscow Art Theater, who attempted to reproduce on the stage, photographically, "in toto, the whole body of environment with all its details, relevant or irrelevant."[45]

Elaborate and over-detailed stage directions reflected the demands of the naturalistic school of drama. To achieve the proper atmosphere in his stagings, Stanislavsky slavishly followed all of the allusions in dramatic works, to the point that for his production of Tolstoy's *The Power of Darkness* a visit was required to the distant province of Tula, where actors and scenic designers were to document the environment through a close study of the local architecture, costumes, and festivals.

Too often, the quest for absolute veracity in details became an end rather than a means. That a chair was made of soft wood, that a man had a wart on his nose, or that the beer served in a tavern came from Bavaria, was of little consequence for either the development of action or the immediate stage effects. However, as in Hauptmann's *The Weavers*, the stage directions were held to be sacred: every facet of the dismal lot of the Silesian weavers had to be reproduced, producing a play which in production strained for a subtextual significance.

The well-wrought naturalistic style was both a method and an end: it had to seem real and at the same time be purposeful. Thus, the naturalistic drama was fraught with contradictions which arose from having to do two things simultaneously: to reproduce reality and to stay true to a larger purpose, a direction which socialist realism took on with a vengeance. The demands for presenting naturalistic drama were dangerously limiting, for they denied the stage its traditional quality of generalized and universal reference. The actor playing in a naturalistic drama, as if in a picture frame, lost the direct contact with his audience that had existed for hundreds of years; he was set apart in a magic box and in another world, divided from the spectator by a wall of darkness.

In this context the spectator lost his role in what is an essential aspect of all theatrical performances—the role of participant. The main purpose became to act upon the spectator, to make him gasp in awe. For that reason, the theater's function "to make the spectator's participation in the stage performance as direct as possible"[46] was totally negated.

Symbolist drama, although opening and introducing new possibilities in staging and lighting, closed the channels of theatrical communication even further due to its adherence to a dramatic work. The methods of symbolism sought to conjure up the more mysterious world that lay beyond, behind, or beneath apparent reality. Instead of detailed sets, symbolist drama depended on the creation of mood through poetry, visual effects, silences, and symbolic gestures. Maeterlinck was symbolism's leading proponent, and his plays *Pelleas and Melisande* and *The Blue Bird* conveyed a world that lay beyond reality by means of background music, long silences, mime, and heavily draped backdrops. An atmosphere was created suggesting dark forces that appeared to manipulate the characters, turning them into puppets. The intent of these effects was to elicit a feeling in the spectator that spiritual forces and emotions existed which were beyond his control.

To portray the realm of the soul, symbolist drama emphasized verbal and scenic poetry, often attenuating the status of the actor to a marionette-like figure whose strings were controlled by external forces. From a theatrical point of view, symbolist drama reflected a static quality of acting balanced by an introduction of innovative forms of staging and lighting. In the province of acting, the emphasis shifted away from the delineation of character, an essential characteristic of naturalism, and moved toward the projection of personalities. Instead of searching for the appropriate motives for character preparation, the actor sought the mood and atmosphere or the spiritual essence of the character.

The verbal elements of the play were of the essence, and staging and lighting assisted as mere symbolic adornments. The actor came to serve as a purely symbolic figure who could just as easily be replaced by Gordon Craig's *Übermarionette:* "It does not matter whether he is a human being; an actor could be a piece of wood, as well. If the wood moves about and its movements are accompanied by words, then such a piece of wood can represent a character in the play, and the wood becomes an actor."[47]

Craig propounded a new slogan to supplant the "slice of life" doctrine of the realists: "not realism, but style." Style, however, became as much of a dogma for the symbolists as realism had been for the naturalists. The theater of the future, as Craig envisioned it, was to be founded on "action, scene, and voice":

And when I say ACTION I mean both gesture and dancing, the prose and poetry of action. When I say SCENE, I mean all which comes before the eye, such as the lighting, costume, as well as the scenery. When I say VOICE, I mean the spoken word or the word which is sung, in contradiction to the word which is read, for the word written to be spoken and the word written to be read are two entirely different things.[48]

Reducing the stage figure to a "voice" changed the dynamic relationship of the actor and the acting space. When the dramatic action was relegated to the imaginary action space and signified to the audience by offstage speeches, as in Maeterlinck's conception of the theater, everything on stage turned into pure immaterial meaning except the actor's voice performance. In addition, certain crucial segments of the plot were presented in narrative form. These literary procedures restrained the actor's movement, largely immobilizing the actors and drastically reducing the depth of the stage.[49]

Perhaps one of the most influential notions about theater at that time was Wagner's conception of a synthesis of the arts. In the *Gesamtkunstwerk*, music, drama, poetry, and all the visual arts of the theater were to function together without respite. What Wagner sought to capture was the movements of the soul, which would flow on in "endless melody," enfolding the entire drama in a rich fabric of closely woven musical motifs. To these ends, Wagner's music-dramas reduced motivation in order to explore a single strong emotional situation. It was jealousy or love itself, and not the complicated actions in everyday life that give rise to them, that Wagner desired to present.[50]

To make the spectator utterly responsive to these movements of the soul, Wagner had to hypnotize him. He used every means at his disposal. First, music became a medium between the spectator and the larger, profounder world on stage. Then plot development was reduced in order to let the action revolve around one or two crucial scenes. In Bayreuth, the orchestra was placed in a sunken pit in a totally darkened house as a means of transporting the spectator out of himself:

> In the presence of the dramatic artwork, nothing should remain for the combining intellect to search for. Everything in it must come to an issue sufficient to set our feeling at rest thereon. . . . In the drama we must become knowers through feeling. In drama, therefore, an action can be explained to us only when it is completely vindicated by the feeling . . . thus it is the dramatic poet's task, not to invent actions, but to make an action so intelligible through its emotional intensity that we may altogether dispense with the intellect's assistance in its vindication.[51]

Wagner believed that his word-tone drama should tend toward the representational rather than the presentational, toward the "expressive" rather than the intellectually meaningful. The tendencies toward "pure" art and toward merging with other art forms were heightened to an extreme degree in Wagner's musical dramatic works. Ultimately, however, their characteristic recurring motifs were more directly influenced by literature than by theatrical practice.

In Wagner's concept of theater as "collective art" the multiplicity of theatrical devices is organized in such a way that individual components unite, providing a "collective effect," as Jindřich Honzl writes: "Thus the dramatic character is present not only on the stage, but also in the orchestra; we experience its inner state, development, and fate not only from words and actions we see on the stage but also from the tones we hear. Here it is matter of the parallelism of the musical stream, the dramatic action, the words, scenery, props, lighting, and all other factors."[52]

Wagner's dramatic characters appear upon the stage not only as actors but also as "leitmotifs." The character's gesture is repeated in the orchestra, and props also acquire symbolic stature as "leitmotifs" in their own right. As Honzl points out, Wagner's principle of the *Gesamtkunstwerk* assumes that the intensity of the spectator's impressions is directly proportional "to the number of perceptions that synchronically flood the senses and mind of the spectator at any given moment."[53] Despite his attention to a total art form, Wagner's formulation indirectly claims that specific, unitary dramatic material does not exist but that separate materials exist which must be kept apart and treated side by side in parallel form. Thus, dramatic art results as the sum of all other arts.

Wagner's aesthetics ignore the positive aesthetic effect of the internal dialectal contradictions among the components of a theatrical presentation. The modern stage text is too complex a structure, eagerly absorbing everything that contemporary developments in theater arts offer and that other arts provide, to be conceived of as merely the interplay of individual elements complementing one another. Deautomatization of perception consists of an awareness of the constant regrouping of stage components and "in an agitated replacing of the dominant one, in an obliteration of the boundaries between the drama and kindred form."[54]

Whenever an attempt is made to declare some element of the theater as basic and indispensable, one can always find a dramatic form lacking this element. There are nevertheless certain components which are more characteristic of the theater than others and to which falls the role of the unifying process. It is the purpose of this study to view the transformation of the single system of signs from the dramatic work into a work which exploits simultaneously several systems of signs. It is to these signs, their nature, and the way they combine to create the theatrical work of art that I should like now to turn.

I have already mentioned that the theater uses elements drawn not from one but from many domains, and it is very probably this polysemous character of the theater that enables it to appeal to a more varied audience than literature does. The form of a dramatic text must be perceived as a dynamic entity, and its unity not as a closed symmetrical whole "but an unfolding dynamic integrity; between its elements stand, not the static sign of equation and addition, but always the dynamic sign of correlation and integration."[55]

In order to better understand the multiplicity of sign systems in the work of the directors and playwrights in this study, I intend to discuss the work of the Russian formalists and Prague structuralists in this area. Although many subsequent studies have been written discussing the sign systems inherent in theatrical art, among them those of Barthes, Mounin, Pavis, Elam, Kowzan, and others, the work of the Prague structuralists still remains the best systematic study of signs in the theater.

The Prague structuralists were able to place literary development and social influence in a logical perspective, acknowledging that society can and does exert influence on art. Ultimately, the perceiver often deals with aesthetic material while in nonaesthetic situations, and, simultaneously, the material being perceived presents to him both its extra-aesthetic values associated with the world of experience and its aesthetically valid norms.[56]

Viktor Shklovsky's *ostranenie* in effect describes the violation of existing aesthetic norms. While the Russian formalists were primarily interested in the effects of such a violation on literary styles and genres, the Prague structuralists were concerned about the change resulting from deautomatization as basically a social and not a literary mechanism. As Mukařovský explains it:

> Extra-aesthetic values in art are thus not only properties of the work itself but also of the perceiver. The latter, of course, approaches the work with his own system of values, with his own attitude toward reality. It frequently happens that a part, often a significant part, of the values which the perceiver obtains from the work is in conflict with the system which he himself holds. The manner in which such a conflict and its resulting tensions can arise is clear. The artist who created the work was from the same social milieu and the same period as the perceiver. In this case, the conflicts between the values of the work of art and the perceiver result from a shift in the artistic structure intended by the artist.[57]

This attention to extra-aesthetic values inherent in the codes that comprise the polysemic quality of theatrical presentations is particularly important in the discussion of the work of the three men under consideration in this study. The theater and arts of the period between 1918 and 1939 has a distinctive character. The plays of this time not only look backward to the catastrophe of World War I but seem to anticipate even greater upheaval. These years saw the flourishing of the one and only great period in Soviet theater, with Meyerhold as its leading director and Brecht and Witkiewicz their countries' greatest dramatists. They were determined to break with the past, to create something entirely new. No other theatrical avant-garde has been as colorful and flamboyant, none has made so violent an attack on existing society and prevailing conventions of the stage, and none has been so rich in new ideas and theories about art and theater. To be sure, the playwrights and directors of the 1920s and 30s owed much to their precursors, Strindberg, Maeterlinck, Wedekind, and Fuchs, among others. However, what distinguishes the interwar period is concern not only with a new aesthetics of theater but also the theater's relationship to society.

In the plays of Mayakovsky, staged by Meyerhold, the remnants of dying but not quite dead revolutionary ideals are often projected into the future to provide a frame of reference for a highly questionable present. Brecht shows capitalism in embattled turmoil. However, since his plays have the ability to generate questions about a postcapitalistic society as well, this suggests that meaning in Brecht's plays is shaped by the social context and that the significance of plays such as *Galileo* or *Mother Courage* will never be exhausted. Witkiewicz examines the hopelessness of communication through language which no longer imparts meaning since his characters, being pragmatists, no longer have anything to impart. In his plays love is perverted into boredom, creation into destruction.

In the background of the work of Meyerhold, Brecht, and Witkiewicz lurks the Russian Revolution. In *Literature and Revolution*, Leon Trotsky defined two kinds of revolutionary art—those works "whose themes reflect the Revolution, and the works which are not connected with the Revolution in theme but are thoroughly imbued with . . . the new consciousness arising out of the Revolution."[58] Trotsky saw art as the organic culmination of the Revolution rather than a simple service to the Revolution, and thus he makes a distinction between art with a revolutionary subject matter and one motivated by a new consciousness resulting from social changes.

For Meyerhold, the revolution provided new metaphors and new dynamics for revolutionizing theatrical presentations. For Brecht, the imagination of revolution provided the perception that human action will totally alter the structure of society and dialectically produce the radically new. For Witkiewicz, the imagination of revolution derives in part from the imagination of prophecy and the imagination of apocalypse inherent in the aftermath of the revolution and the destruction of class society as he knew it. Witkiewicz's catastrophic view makes public what was essentially a private vision of the way he saw the world.

Notwithstanding the social facts of the revolution that are part of the work of Meyerhold, Brecht, and Witkiewicz, the view that extra-aesthetic values, often designated as content, are separate from stylistic elements, or form, has been shown to be false by the Russian formalists. For that reason, to view the Russian Revolution as content in the work of these dramatists and directors would be an injustice. All elements of a work are, without distinction, components of form. It must also be added that all components are equally the bearers of meaning, and thus are de facto components of content. Within this understanding, a discussion of the work of Meyerhold, Brecht, and Witkiewicz must not be narrowed to a mere formal analysis. However, it must also be made clear that the entire construction of the work, and not just what we designate as content, is a vital part of the values and norms that are the governing features of art.

Whereas naturalistic drama was intent on attaining social significance and symbolist drama a murky cosmic relevance, the drama of the between-wars period was social as well as metaphysical, and more often than not irreverent and mocking—as in Mayakovsky's *The Bedbug*, tough-minded and flippant—as in Brecht's *Threepenny Opera*, and ironic and absurd—as in Witkiewicz's *The Water Hen*.

The revolt of the theatrical avant-garde artist was not a mere reaction to society as a last-ditch effort to break down prevalent styles, but also represented an energetic attempt to reintegrate art into life. In fact, even though the avant-garde theater rejected the stranglehold of naturalism and its theatrical conventions, it did not reject reality as such. Brecht, for example, opened up a wider concept of realism as "a confronting of a many-sided, contradictory (and often hidden) historical reality"[59] using new formal means of facilitating an awareness in the spectator of the constantly shifting social reality.

Witkiewicz in his theory of pure form in the theater, based on an analogy with painting, while rejecting realist mimesis, focused on objectifying and depersonalizing functions of language to open up an awareness that language is dominated by political and economic systems and consequently has become closed and static. The surrealist montage of images in his plays was often intended to help remake the social world on the model of the life of dreams. Since the Russian Revolution and Freudian psychoanalysis had torn down conventional ways of viewing both social and inner worlds, the surrealists sought to balance and connect "'surrender to the unconscious' and psychic automatism with social revolution."[60] The images of the dynamic collision of the world of dreams with social reality were intended by Witkiewicz to deepen his understanding of reality by shocking the spectator from his habituated automatism of perception.

Brecht's dialectical realism and Witkiewicz's surrealism stand in contrast to the simultaneity, juxtaposition, and montage of scenes in Meyerhold's theater. His theater, rather like cubism in art, most clearly registered the technical innovations of the machine and cinematic montage. In the plays directed by Meyerhold in the 1920s, constructions such as scaffolding, cubes and arches become dynamic parts of the action as actors set various pieces of stage machinery into action. While the sets and movements of actors dressed in industrial work uniforms suggest a contemporary industrial world, they did not merely "represent" it; instead, the spectator was never allowed to forget that he was a productive force in Meyerhold's dynamic theatrical workshop.

The theater of Meyerhold, Witkiewicz, and Brecht calls attention to itself as theatrical play, often irreverently fusing popular arts and popular culture—circus, cabaret, jazz, and sports—into the theatrical process. Although the approaches to theater of these avatars of the avant-garde differ, they nevertheless draw on a theatrical "intertexuality" whose aim it was to reveal the theatrical construction of dramatic works and, as a consequence, to reveal that the wide social world represented on stage is neither unalterable nor rigid.

1

Semiotics in Theater:
The Prague School Contributions

Between 1926 and 1948, a prolific group of linguists and theoreticians of literature, known as the Prague School, or the Prague Linguistic Circle, established the first systematic structuralist approach of the study of art. The antecedents of Czech structuralism were Husserl's phenomenology; Bühler's theory of *Sprechakt* and *Sprechgebilde* (speech act and language structure); the literary studies of the Russian formalists; and the linguistic studies of A. Meillet, A. Marty, V. Mathesius, F. de Saussure, and R. Jakobson.[1] The Czech structuralists were interested in the phenomenology of language, as well as in the study of its structure, and, in particular, in the distinction between poetical and practical language, as well as in the connection between culture and these two types of language.

Although initially the Prague structuralists were strongly under the influence of Russian formalism, a problem exists in designating them, as Victor Erlich has done in *Russian Formalism*,[2] as merely an outgrowth of the earlier aesthetics of the Opojaz group, the later so-called formalist group. While the aesthetics of the Opojaz group represented an "anti-positivist revolt," the Prague structuralists, developing their aesthetic theories as a revolt partially against Herbartian Czech formalism of the nineteenth century, concluded that the techniques of art cannot be studied in a vacuum, artificially isolated from related systems, particularly social systems. The purest of the Russian formalists concentrated on literary facts, focusing exclusively on the primary features of poetic language. Everything which did not fit into the category of poetic language was considered to be a secondary feature and therefore dismissed. The Prague structuralists's leading theoretician, Jan Mukařovský, ultimately took Viktor Shklovsky's exclusive interest in the material aspects of verbal art, what material is used and how the work is made, as a means of contradicting the formalist excesses inherent in the formal method of Shklovsky. Using the analogy Shklovsky had presented in the introduction to his *Theory of Prose*—that he was solely interested in the types of yarn and techniques of weaving and not in the situation on the international wool market or in the politics of wool trusts—Mukařovský claimed that "the techniques of weaving with their figurative implications for art, necessarily reflect the needs and pressures of the market in accordance with the law of supply and demand."[3]

The inherent contradiction in the methods of Russian formalism and Prague structuralism does not negate the fact of the two movements being closely related. Many members of the Moscow Linguistic Circle participated in the founding of the Prague Linguistic Circle. Of these the most prominent and influential were Roman Jakobson, Petr Bogatyrev, Nikolaj Trubeckoj, and Sergej Karcevskij.[4] However, even in light of this extensive contact, the relationship between the two groups should not be treated as a mere transfer of ideas. The issue of literary development, raised but unsolved by the Russian formalists, particularly Jurij Tynjanov, became the center of the concern of the Prague Linguistic Circle. They insisted that being a social structure, verbal art should not be analyzed solely with regard to its autonomous properties but also in its relationship to other structures, to "structures such as science, politics, economy, social stratification, language, ethics, religion, each having its own imminent development."[5]

Prague structuralism and Russian formalism both shared an antispeculative, empiricist outlook, and it is this common understanding that allowed for the absorption of some of the principles of Russian formalism by the Czech structuralists. The most important contribution for poetics was the use of linguistics as a tool for the study of verbal art. Russian formalists refused to accept Saussure's dichotomy *langue-parole,* because of their aversion to signs as being too palpable. In contrast to the formalist attitude, the Prague structuralists were intrinsically semiotic in outlook. "Unless the semiotic character of art is adequately elucidated," Mukařovský insisted, "the study of its structure will remain necessarily incomplete."[6]

A second contribution to structuralist aesthetics by Russian formalism was the functionalist approach, which inspired the formalists to differentiate between practical and poetic language. The functionalist approach was later to be extended by the Prague structuralist beyond linguistics and poetics into such areas as folk theater and folk costume. They saw the notion of function as "the basic working hypothesis of modern culture," permitting a grasping of things as events without a denial of their materiality.[7] Accordingly, the investigation of poetic function is expected to take into account that art principally calls attention to its sign structure and in this manner obliquely imparts information relevant to the social content.

The Russian formalist principle of "making strange" also became a crucial notion for the Prague structuralists. Deautomatization, according to Mukařovský, referred to the peculiar hierarchical organization in a work of art in which one element becomes dominant, or is foregrounded, and subordinates all the other elements within the work to its own needs. In contrast to the Russian formalists, who limited their field of inquiry to literature, the Prague structuralists attempted to apply the principle of deautomatization to other arts as well, particularly in studies on the folk theater and folk costume by Petr Bogatyrev, the Chinese theater by Karel Brušák, and a study of Chaplin's acting by Mukařovský.

Another important formalist principle which became the foundation for the Prague structuralists' concept of signs was Tynjanov's system picturing literary texts as realizations of a socially shared literary system, or a literary tradition. Paralleling Saussure's *langue*—a system of linguistic rules shared by the users of a language which is the basis of every utterance—Tynjanov's concept underlined the importance of viewing both literary production and literary reception as a sharing of the same system of rules or codes. This aspect was later to serve as the foundation of *Rezeptionstheorie* in Germany, particularly in the work of Hans Robert Jauss and Wolfgang Iser. Certainly, a similarity can also be determined in Roland Barthes's studies of *the fashion system* or other cultural idiolects as well as in Umberto Eco's *Theory of Semiotics*, where Eco clearly establishes that all sign systems are culturally determined.

Tynjanov's studies on literary evolution were central to the development of the Prague structuralists's view that "the problem of the sign is one of the most pressing philosophical problems of the cultural rebirth of our era" since "all reality, from sensory perception to the most abstract mental construction, appears to modern man as a vast and complex realm of signs."[8]

Ultimately, it was the establishment of the sign as an organizing principle which opened the path for the Prague structuralists to the treatment of a work of art as composed of both material and immaterial bonds. From the semiotic point of view, culture and cultural objects appear as complex interplays of signs mediating among the members of the same collectivity. Thus, the semiotic approach did not deny the necessity of studying the organization of sign vehicles, but the description of this organization ceased to be an end in itself; instead, the meaning and significance of the organization became as prominent.

Jan Mukařovský's programmatic paper, "Art as a Semiotic Fact," presented at the Eighth International Congress of Philosophy in Prague in 1934, served as the theoretical basis for investigating the properties of signs in the study of art. In this fundamental study, Mukařovský attempted to show that the objective study of a work of art must regard art: (1) as a semiological fact (i.e., signans); (2) as an internalized signification (i.e., signatum); and (3) as a relationship of an oblique kind to which the binary character of signs refers (i.e., designatum).[9] The structure proper of the work lies in the second of the constituents, that is, in its system of internalized signification. However, besides its function as an autonomous sign, the work of art, according to Mukařovský, has another function, that of a communicative sign, the latter "being reserved especially for the representational arts."[10]

Mukařovský's functionalist approach is concerned not only with the objective structure of the work of art but equally with the social structure in which it is received. Mukařovský notes that the perceiving public comes to anticipate certain structural or organizational qualities from art and thereby exerts a normative influence on art. Just as aesthetic function inevitably finds itself regulated by these norms, so do these norms depend on value judgments for their validity. However, since the aesthetic function is the dominant function in a work of art, aesthetic values, according to Mukařovský, are also dominant values, placing other values, which are always present, into a subordinate position.[11] The aesthetic function makes the very structure of the sign the center of interest and pushes the practical functions into the background.

The Prague Linguistic Circle referred to this "foregrounding" process in the aesthetic examination of a work of art as deautomization of the act: "The more an act is automatized, the less it is consciously executed; the more it is foregrounded, the more completely conscious it becomes."[12] This concept of defamiliarization had been defined by Shklovsky in the programmatic statement entitled "Art as a Device":

> And art exists that one may recover the sensation of life; it exists to make one feel things, to make the stone stony. The purpose of art is to impart the sensation of things as they are perceived and not as they are known. The technique of art is to make objects "unfamiliar," to make forms difficult, to increase the difficulty and length of perception, because the process of perception is an aesthetic end in itself and must be prolonged. Art is a way of experiencing the artfulness of an object; the object is not important.[13]

Although the Russian formalists themselves did not apply the the concept of defamiliarization to the study of a theatrical work of art, later developments in the theater, as for instance Brecht's theory of the *Verfremdungseffekt*, took over this concept. For the Prague structuralists the binary opposition of Shklovsky's "unfamiliar/familiar" was understood as a mutual relationship of foregrounded and unforegrounded elements.

While continuing to concentrate primarily on the problems of poetry and literature, the Prague structuralists gradually expanded their interest to include theater, film, the visual arts, music, and folk art. Most studies on the theater have examined the dramatic work of art exclusively from the angle of literature. However, members of the Prague Linguistic Circle, among them Petr Bogatyrev, Karel Brušák, Jindřich Honzl, Jan Mukařovský, and Jiří Veltruský,[14] observed that the units of meaning found in the text of a dramatic work ultimately form, in the presentational aspect, a complicated structure consisting of two interrelated systems of sings: one visual, the other acoustic. Visual signs are associated with dramatic space and its utilization of both static and kinetic properties, while acoustic signs incorporate dialogue, music, and sound effects.

In the development of a structuralist approach to the study of theatrical presentation, the dichotomous concept of language/speech was also applied. The primary object of a linguistic approach to the study of theatrical form was to investigate language as a synchronic semiotic code. While it was difficult to pin down a semiotic code in the avant-garde theater due to the inherent breaking down of conventions as part of its intrinsic form, the Prague structuralists found a fertile field of study in the strongly codified theatrical forms of the Oriental and folk theater. In particular, Bogatyrev applied Saussure's linguistic model to the study of recurrent codes in the Czech folk theater, a model study which later served as a basis for further elaboration and application:

> We can carry over the concept of *la langue* and *la parole* from the field of language phenomena to art. Thus, just as the hearer, in order to comprehend the individual utterance of the speaker, must have command of the language, that is, language as a social fact, so also in art the observer must be prepared to receive the individual performance of the actor or any other artist—his special speech acts, as it were—in terms of his (the observer's) command of the language of that art, its social norms. This is the point of congruence between the field of language and the field of art.[15]

Theatrical productions are distinguished from all other artistic works and from material objects by their great abundance of signs. Jan Mukařovský writes that "the essence of the theater is a changing flux of immaterial relations which constantly regroup."[16] The *mise-en-scène* projects a multiplicity of signs, among them signs that are purely visual in nature, such as the theatrical set, costumes, makeup, gestures, and movements, and signs that are acoustic in essence, such as music, sound effects, intonations of voice, silences, and paralinguistic utterances. The most difficult aspect of the semiotic approach to the performance of a dramatic work ultimately has to do with not only the pointing out of signs but with the demonstration of their unfolding and their syntagmatic relationships. Too often, as Patrice Pavis rightly points out, semioticians are "too intent on static descriptions of scenic systems and fixed signs to take into account the rhythm and phrasing of the scenic discourse."[17] The scenic discourse of the theatrical component (i.e., dramatic action, dramatic character, dramatic plot, and dramatic place)[18] influences the parallel arrangement of the scenic systems: how they are brought together during the performance, the structuring design of each of the individual systems, and, in particular, their reciprocal relationships of divergence and reconciliation.

While on the surface a semiotic analysis of a dramatic work appears to resemble in theory the *Gesamtkunstwerk* approach of Wagner, the contribution of the Czech structuralists to the study of the theater has to do with the rejection of Wagner's view that the theater was a sum of several independent arts and the redefinition of theatrical art as an art in which "the individual arts renounce their independence, penetrate one another, contradict one another, and substitute for one another," ultimately "dissolving" and merging into a new form.[19]

In their analysis of theatrical art, the Prague structuralists intended to show that despite the material tangibility of theatrical means (i.e., sets, props, machines), the theater represents "a dynamic interplay of all its components, a unity of forces internally differentiated by intertensions, and a set of signs and meanings."[20] The theoretical preconditions of such a view were based on a study of aesthetics in the theater conducted by Otokar Zich, whose work, *Estetika dramatického umění (Aesthetics of Dramatic Art)*, published in 1931, played an important role in the development of structuralist theory. Zich's work contributed to the elaboration of a methodological framework for the structuralists in much the same manner as Roman Ingarden's work, *Das Literarische Kunstwerk (The Literary Work of Art)* contributed to the understanding of the active relationship between the units of meaning and the context.[21] Zich approached the theatrical work from a phenomenological point of view by concentrating on the interrelationship of the dramatic components and by stressing equally the dual aspects of performance: the technical and the imaginary. Moreover, Zich's detailed discussion of "things representing other things"[22] in the realm of theater lent itself to reinterpretation by the structuralists as a framework for the study of signs in the folk theater as well as in the highly codified Chinese theater.

In his study of the Chinese classical theater, Brušák called attention to the strongly codified form of that theater in which "the elaborated system of signs enabled the Chinese actor to give a comprehensive portrayal of the most varied actions without having to re-create reality on the stage."[23]

> The conventional action signs never aim at imitation of reality. They naturally take this as their starting point, but in most cases they are so constructed as to divorce themselves from realism as much as possible. The player for example suggests the action of drinking tea by raising an imaginary cup to his lips, but in order to avoid being realistic, masks the hand executing the gesture with a special movement of the other hand. To illustrate someone sleeping, he does not lie down but sits leaning the fingers of one hand lightly on his temple. An action sign thus owes its final form to a tension between the aesthetic function and other functions, communicative, expressive, and so on. The relationship of action signs to reality is variable: conventional sequences of movements which relate to the scene even at their most artificial are in fact in closer contact with reality than actions expounding thought processes and character relationships.[24]

In the Chinese theater, various aspects of reality are linked together through a highly conventionalized system of signs which forms a language, the acquisition of which is a necessary precondition to the understanding of that form. The Chinese theater acts as a medium in which one lexicalized structure is transformed into another system of lexicalized signs, which though autonomous in their own right, develop spontaneously one from another.

This transformational quality of signs due to contextual changes was also studied by Bogatyrev in the area of folklore and folk culture. In his study of the components of folk culture—as, for example, folk costume, Bogatyrev discovered that while the costume itself is simultaneously a material object and a sign, or more precisely, the bearer of a structure of signs which in their semiotic multifunctionality carry not only aesthetic, but also magic, ritual, religious, and erotic functions as well as various practical functions,[25] on the stage that costume becomes, in Bogatyrev's formulation, "a sign of a sign."[26] The theater for Bogatyrev is a medium that transforms everything into a sign and in which even real objects become for the spectator a sign of a sign or a sign for a real object.

Zich suggested that theatrical signs have two functions. The first and most characteristic one is to give a graphic depiction of the characters and the place of action; the second one is to take part in the dramatic action as icons or symbols. The spectators behold real objects appearing on stage not as real material objects but merely as signs of material objects. "If an actor," Bogatyrev elucidates, "representing a millionaire wears a diamond ring, the audience will take it as a sign of his great wealth and not care whether or not the diamond is a real or false stone."[27] The diamond ring thus performs the function of assisting in characterizing the dramatic figure and appears in its own right as a symbol of wealth.

Conversely, the most schematic signs can signify the material object. For example, a column on stage may signal that the structure it represents is a temple, a building of state, a great hall, and so on. These signs ultimately gain connotation only within the limits of the particular context or within a particular performance tradition, and only then are they able to represent and denote significance without the aid of other signs.

In addition to a multitude of elements that are nothing but signs, there are objects, for example, in the Chinese theater, that are not "signs of particular objects but of objects in general." These signs are also able to represent all aspects of the scene without assistance from other signs.

> The most important of these are a table and chair that are almost never absent from the Chinese stage. If the table and chair are standing in the usual manner, then the set is an interior. On the other hand, a chair placed side on the ground or on its back signifies an embankment or earthwork; overturned it signifies a hill or mountain; standing on the table, it signifies a city tower.[28]

Thus, the more conventionalized the signs, the more the audience is conscious of them as signifiers. Ultimately, signs used in this manner can convey a broader range of meanings, in contrast to naturalistic presentations where "the more acting resorts to natural delivery, gestures, etc., the more the distinction between the sign and what it stands for is blurred and can be overlooked by the audience."[29]

As the relations between stage figures and characters are projected into dramatic space, the text, according to Veltruský, provides the verbal component of theatrical performance, which allows for the emergence of subtexts and extratextuality. In the end, the text not only predetermines intratextual relations but also predetermines the fundamental relationship between stage figures and audience.[30]

The actor on the stage can never fully escape the obligations imposed on him by the dramatic text. While it is true that the actor creates all the extralinguistic components of the stage figure, even in theatrical forms that rely on improvisation, the actor's freedom in the choice of both verbal expression and gesture is restricted by the particular norms of that theatrical tradition. For example, in *commedia dell'arte*, in the classical Chinese theater, in Japanese Kabuki, and in the Balinese theater, the extralinguistic resources at the disposal of the actor are subject to strict conventions imposed by that theatrical tradition, and ultimately the *mise-en-scène* predetermines the stage figure in all its aspects.

In his analysis of the components of the theatrical structure, Veltruský places the dramatic figure at the center of the binary sign systems that are invariably present in the presentation of a dramatic work, language and acting:

> Since the semiotics of language and the semiotics of acting are diametrically opposed in their fundamental characteristics, there is a dialectial tension between the dramatic text and the actor, based primarily on the fact that the sound components of the linguistic sign are an integral part of the voice resources drawn upon by the actor. The relative weight of the two poles of this antinomy is variable. If the linguistic sign prevails, there emerges a tendency to strip the sign embodied by the actor of its materiality. If, on the contrary the linguistic sign is outbalanced, its semantic potential diminishes. However, both sign systems not only check but also enrich each other. The actor gives more weight and punch to the language he voices and, in return, receives from it the gift of extremely flexible and variable meanings.[31]

At this point it is important to make a distinction, as Zich suggests, between the stage figure and the dramatic persona, who ultimately is represented by the actor and also by relevant information about the persona conveyed by other codes: costume, props, lighting, the set, and sound effects. "In semiotic terms," explains Roberta Reeder, "the dramatis persona would be the signified, while the stage figure might be only one element in the set of signs that signify it."[32] The actor figures as a carrier of signs, which emerge both from the dramatic work and dramatic space, and who accumulates other signs around himself. Other signs outside the actor are perceived only in relation to him; the actor, as a result, appears as the most real of the realities on the stage. The figure of the actor ultimately is the dynamic unifier of an entire set of signs, the carrier of which may be his body, voice, gestures, movements, as also various other signs, such as the costume and parts of the set.[33]

The closer to the stage action the actor is, the greater the number of signs at his disposal. In addition, Veltruský explains that the more complex the action of the actor, the greater is "not only the number of his purposeful signs, but also of those without purpose."[34] A figure whose actions are more simple is by its nature more schematic. Hence, as Mukařovský points out, the difference between the major and minor characters. A hierarchy of parts is thus created, with the figure of the lead at the center of the attention functioning as the regulating focus of the other sign. The spectator may still perceive the other figures in the more removed position from the action, as acting subjects, but their subordination is evident. Ultimately, when certain actions become totally schematized, the function of the stage figures becomes similar to props.[35] Such figures carry few signs beyond those to designate their particular action. Thus, for example, when an actor dressed in the costume of the livery of a servant enters, the spectator assumes that he is there in that function and perceives only those signs that designate that function: his costume and the schematized gestures of the servant.

Human props represent the lowest denominator in the hierarchy of stage figures, for, as Veltruský points out, when the action level of stage figures falls to the "zero level," these figures are absorbed into the signs of the set. They may be used to designate the place of action, for example, as guards in front of a palace. The constituent signs of such figures are limited to posture, stature, makeup, and costume, and it follows that the actors in such roles could easily be replaced by lifeless dummies.[36] In the Japanese Kabuki theater, *kurogos* (stagehands dressed completely in black, black signifying "nothingness" or protective cover) function as assistants to the actor, handing him props or unfolding his costume. They slide along sideways on the stage as inconspicuously as possible, and to perceivers well versed in the conventions of the form, appear not to exist. Although they are moving props, their constituent signs are virtually nonexistent. In the end, actors used as part of the set "form the transition between the sphere of man and the sphere of the object."[37]

Ultimately, the hierarchy of actors differs according to period and milieu and, in part, in relation to the dramatic text. Sometimes actors create a structurally sound whole in which no one has a dominant position and no one is the focal point of the relations among the characters of the work. For example, it would be difficult to determine a hierarchy of characters in such plays as Mayakovsky's *Mystery-Bouffe* since all the characters appear to be equal in terms of carrying the action. However, sometimes all the characters appear to be equal yet lack structural relations. Often their relationship is merely compositional, as in Robert Wilson's plays, where each of the various figures on stage moves in his own world, part of the whole but separate.

Notwithstanding the hierarchical standing of the actor in the action of the play, he has certain objects at his disposal that assist him in moving his particular action. The actor who appears at the axis of the other stage figures has more objects to manipulate; yet, all stage figures rely on the semiotic values of costumes, makeup or masks, and props to convey their semantic meaning.

Costumes, particularly those subject to strong convention, may reveal not only the wearer's social status and age, but also his worth, character, and interests. Convention may also link a specific costume with a traditional or famous character, as for example, Harlequin's or Pierrot's costumes, which have perpetuated that link far beyond their conventional use in *commedia dell'arte*. However, and this is important to remember, theatrical costumes do not have as many constitutive signs as real clothing would have: "Theater uses only those signs of costume and construction," writes Bogatyrev, "which are necessary for the given dramatic situation."[38]

While costumes usually denote the rank, stature, and circumstances of the dramatis personae, they sometimes acquire their own semantic charge. For example, Stanislavsky relates that after watching his performance in *The Seagull*, Chekhov asked him to play Trigorin in torn shoes and checkered trousers:

> Trigorin in *The Seagull* was a young writer, a favorite of women—and suddenly he was to wear torn shoes and checked trousers! I played the part in the most elegant of costumes—white trousers, white vest, white hat, slippers, and a handsome makeup.
>
> A year or more passed. Again I played the part of Trigorin in *The Seagull*—and during one of the performances I suddenly understood what Chekhov had meant.
>
> Of course, the shoes must be torn and the trousers checked, and Trigorin must not be handsome. In this lies the salt of the part: for young, inexperienced girls it is important that a man should be a writer and print touching and sentimental romances, and the Nina Zarachnayas, one after the other, will throw themselves on his neck, without noticing that he is not talented, that he is not handsome, that he wears checkered trousers and torn shoes.[39]

An actor who was particularly aware of the semantic properties of costume was Chaplin, who used a costume ordinarily denoting a particular class as a means for heightening and sharpening the social paradox of his situation. "The formal attire which is ragged, the gloves without fingers, yet the cane and black derby, project both self-assurance and superiority combined with the expressive gestures of the inferiority of the beggar with social aspirations."[40]

The use of makeup or a mask contributes to the characterization of the stage figure by either exploiting or neutralizing the facial characteristics of the actor. Makeup, in the same manner as costume, serves to denote a character's age, personality, intelligence, temperament, background, and state of mind. To neutralize or to distance the semiotic qualities of the face, an immobile mask is used in some theatrical traditions to indicate that the actor is in the theatrical world and functioning as a representative sign of the character. "In the theatre reality can be represented in a factual or a fantastic form" writes Brecht, "the actors can do without (or with a minimum of) makeup, appearing 'natural,' and the whole thing can be a fake; they can wear grotesque masks and represent the truth.''[41]

Since one of the prime characteristics of the theater is the transformation of signs, an actor appearing with a minimum of makeup may be considered to be artificial, while one hidden behind a mask to be real. In some highly conventionalized theatrical traditions, as in the Japanese Kabuki, makeup is highly stylized, and colors as well as painted patterns are commonly used to reveal qualities that the character possesses. Red, for example, indicates strength; blue denotes demons, spirits, and evil characters; and rust suggests animal spirits or imaginary beings. In addition, changes are sometimes made in makeup during the progress of a scene, to mark some change in character. This use of colors and patterns in makeup to denote characters substitutes for the facial expressions that a character in European theater has at his disposal, and who depicts changes in character by adopting a particular facial expression to express his change in mood or feelings.

Additional objects at the disposal of the stage figure are characterizing signs, or props, those articles worn visibly and continuously by the actor, such as swords, daggers, whips, and so on, which form a point of transition to costume. These signs are ultimately associated with particular dramatic gestures, and often their movement from stage figure to stage figure represents the movement of the action in the play.

In addition to characterizing signs, the actor may make use of signs that have a transformable quality and acquire significance through the function which the actor assigns them. Bogatyrev and Mukařovský both discuss the famous shoes of Charlie Chaplin as examples of this type of connotative sign which performs a variety of hitherto foreign functions. In *The Gold Rush,* for example, these shoes are transformed by his acting into food, with the shoelaces transformed into spaghetti.[42] In the Chinese classical theater, the actor is able to portray the most varied actions using only one or two props that have acquired significance through repeated actions:

To act riding on horseback he uses a whip that represents a horse. The color of the whip denotes the color of the horse. Thrown at random on stage, the whip represents a horse grazing. Riding by carriage is indicated by an assistant carrying a banner on both sides of the actor, usually a yellow banner marked with a circle, the sign of a wheel; to indicate alighting the assistant raises the banner.[43]

Another type of visual sign that the actor uses is the gesture. Gestures, or movements, assist in conveying meanings contained in the written text and, as Veltruský points out, are "hardly conveyable by the vocal resources on which spoken language relies."[44] Veltruský illustrates this need for a graphical sign as a supplement to language within the text by an example from a speech in Ibsen's

John Gabriel Borkman: "'You deserted the woman you loved! Me, me, me!' wherein intensity of emotion can no longer be conveyed by voice intonation since the peak of loudness is reached at the end of the triple exclamation that follows."[45]

By the same token, ironical meanings in words or phrases usually cannot be adequately expressed by voice coloring and demand completion by a shoulder shrug, a grimace, and so forth. Deictic gestures also belong to extralinguistic situations, as for example in utterances like: "He was the one!" As Veltruský suggests, it would be very odd if this utterance were not accompanied by a deictic gesture. In addition, lexicalized gestures often accompany linguistic cliches, as when a glass is lifted to the words: "To your health."[46] Instinctive movements accompanying certain actions often also serve to underline the significance of the action. Thus, Helene Weigel in Brecht's *Mother Courage* bites a coin to see if it is genuine before stowing it away in her purse.

In the highly stylized form of the Kabuki theater a gesture may also serve to suspend the action, allowing the spectators to take in the beauty of the moment. This gesture, or *mie,* is used by the actor to halt action when he wants to make the character particularly impressive to the audience, as for example, in a scene announcing his true identity, or in a scene in which the hero slays his attackers, prolonging the effect by a string of *mie* poses. An example of a *mie* pose used effectively in Western theater is Helene Weigel's silent scream as the anguished mother in *Mother Courage.*

In addition to having at his disposal visual signs to assist in moving the action of the play, the actor also has the sound components of his own voice to project the semantic qualities of the dramatic text. Intonation, voice coloring, and intensity aid in giving substance to the visual gestures that may accompany them. Intonation reveals unexpected semantic shifts and brings into focus barely perceptible connotations, "generating all kinds of faint and fleeting connections between words."[47] Often, an actor may be recognized by the coloration of his voice even if the spectator does not see him. He may also project by his voice color such mental dispositions as "angrily," "joyfully," "ironically," and so on.[48] Coloration of voice offers so many semantic possibilities that the choice of a particular actor can become a significant factor in the director's instrumentation. The actor also uses intensity of voice to stress certain meanings by either raising the pitch of his voice or by lowering it to a stage whisper. "When voice intensity is in the dominant position," writes Veltruský, "the distinction between single contexts tends to be very pronounced and every single speech is formulated in such a way as to recall the context to which it belongs."[49] However, none of the sound components of the actor's voice remain dominant for long, and while they may assume a leading role during the course of development, they are, nevertheless, subject to the dramatic discourse of the text.

The shifting relationships of the various components used by the actor during his presentation and demonstration of the action within the dramatic text converge within the boundaries of what can be designated as dramatic space, a construction which, in the sense that Sergei Eisenstein gives the term, "serves to embody the author's relation to content while at the same time compelling the spectator to relate himself to content in the same way.[50] Rather like the stage figure, dramatic space functions as a "mode-effector" for the interpretation of the other scenic signs.

The demarcation of dramatic space varies from theatrical tradition to tradition. Although the use of a stage curtain as a convention denoting that dramatic space exists behind the curtain, once it is opened, is commonly used in modern European theater, dramatic space exists wherever there is space to mount a play. While the Chinese theater uses a rectangular platform to suggest architectural space, dramatic space itself is denoted by a conventionalized system of signs, as for example the different positions of a chair and table signifying changes of locality. In Elizabethan theater, dramatic space was often indicated by inscriptions: the terrace below the castle, the throne room, a battlefield, and so on. Similarly, Brecht often designated dramatic space by projecting announcements upon a screen to designate both temporal and scenic changes. He also did away with the convention of the stage curtain, often not using one at all, or using a half curtain to maintain the essence of theatricality.

In the European theater, dramatic space has usually been contained within the architectural construction of a stage upon which scenery made of wooden frames and painted canvas designated dramatic place. Not until the freeing of the stage by the stylized theater of such innovators as Fuchs and Appia in Germany and the constructivists Meyerhold and Tairov in Russia was dramatic space released from its confinement from behind the proscenium. The constructivists departed completely from realistic representations of space; instead, they used constructions made of planks to represent a factory yard, a park, a wheat field, or a flour mill: "Indeterminate in shape and color they became signs only when used for the actor's actions. It can be said that a representative function was not expressed by means of form and color but by the actor's actions on the stage construction, on the bare floor, on the suspended planes, on the staircase, on the slanting surface, and so on."[51]

With the freeing of the stage, other aspects of theatrical productions, such as the theatrical set, were released from the confines of tradition. Instead of adhering to the restrictions of a representational set, stage designers produced scenic metonomies to suggest, rather than to represent, dramatic place. For example, an English coat of arms on a silken banner was enough to represent a royal court, or the same banners carried by soldiers could represent a battlefield. Not only was a part used to represent a whole, but it could be used to represent several different wholes.

In addition, with the introduction of technology into the theater, light and sound techniques were used to extend or to limit dramatic space at will. Sound effects projected from speakers at all corners of the auditorium encompassed the spectator in a dramatic space which was as much in back of him as in front of him. Sound effects, or "acoustic scenery" as Honzl refers to them, are signs that may be exemplified "by the sound of the tapping of typewriters used to denote an office, the rattling of a pneumatic drill and the rumbling of wagons to represent a coal mine, and the like."[52] Another example of nonspatial denotation of the stage occurs in the last act of Chekhov's *The Cherry Orchard*. Although we do not see the orchard, it is represented acoustically as the blows of the axes cutting down the orchard are heard by spectators.[53]

Similarly, lighting may also expand or limit dramatic space. When the spotlight catches only one actor the dramatic space is limited entirely to him. The other theatrical components, although present on stage, no longer contribute to the action. Or two spotlights may focus on two dramatic figures, signalling to us their isolation from each other and the breaking up of dramatic space into two distinct areas. When the light is diffused, dramatic space expands. Comparably, different colors in lighting denote the extension of mood created by the actors into dramatic space.

Music has a similar function to lighting in extending both dramatic action and dramatic scenery. The use of music may either serve as an accompaniment to dramatic action or as counterpoint to it. For example, Brecht used music as a means of bringing out the "gestic" qualities within his *Mahagonny* and *The Threepenny Opera*:

> This music's character as a kind of gestic music can hardly be explained except by a survey to establish the social purpose of the new methods. To put it practically, gestic music is that music which allows the actor to exhibit certain basic gests on the stage. So-called "cheap" music, particularly that of the cabaret and the operetta, has for some time been a sort of gestic music. Serious music, however, still clings to lyricism, and cultivates expression for its own sake.[54]

As a participant in denoting scenery, music may present the singing of birds, the burbling of a brook, the whistling of the wind, and the like. Or it may announce the entrance of the hero or the villain through repetition of a theme that has a connotative association with the dramatic figure.

Perhaps one of the most valuable contributions by the Czech structuralists in their analysis of dramatic space was the distinction they made that "dramatic space is not identical with the stage or with three-dimensional space in general since it originates in time through gradual changes in the spatial relations between the actor and the stage and among the actors themselves."[55] Since the disposition of the actors within dramatic space produces changes in the dynamic relationship of the space, Zich explained that dramatic space could be best described as a set of forces, which on account of their energetic nature often transcended the stage and its physical properties:

> The characters represented by the actors are certain centers of power of various intensity according to the significance of the characters in the given dramatic situation; their dramatic relations provided by this situation are then like lines of force which unite and disunite among the characters. The dramatic stage, filled out by a net of these lines of force and by the motor paths caused by them, is a kind of power field, changeable in its shape and in the force of its individual components.[56]

Zich's description of dramatic space brought out the variable nature of the intratextual relationships among the dramatic figures. In addition to Zich's contribution, the Prague structuralists also contributed to the analysis of how "the effects deriving from the dynamic field of dramatic space are transferred to the auditorium."[57] Even if the stage is separated from the auditorium by footlights, it does not have an independent existence; instead it takes over the entire theater and is created in the spectator's consciousness during the production. Through the means of narrative dialogue, dramatic space extends beyond the stage and is projected to an imaginary stage. This shift in dramatic space may occur for purely technical reasons—for example when actions are too difficult to stage; or due to conventions that designate certain actions as being unsuitable for stage presentation, or for artistic reasons—for example, to attenuate tension.

As a result of the extension of dramatic space into the auditorium, a great deal of attention was also directed toward investigating the psychological space of the perceiver. The spectator, according to the Prague School, "has a summarizing role in the theater in the sense that everything which happens there is addressed in one way or another to the audience."[58] Frequently, the dialogue is conducted in such a way that the audience understands it differently than one of the dramatis personae, or knows more or less about the situation at a given moment than the stage figures. Due to this interaction, the audience is omnipresent in the structure of a stage production. In recent years, returning to conventions that were a standard part of the practice of Shakespeare, a constant effort has been made to make the spectator's participation in the stage performance as direct as possible. Actors have been placed among the spectators, they have made their entrances down the aisles onto the stage; often, certain characters have been designated as mediators between the stage and the auditorium.

One seeming problem of theatrical semiotics has provoked much discussion, but in light of the elucidations by Mukařovský, Bogatyrev, and their colleagues, the problem disappears. I refer to Georges Mounin's challenge to the notion that a theatrical performance which involves any sort of communication must involve an ability to transmit messages in two directions, using the same code and channel in both directions. If we concede this not-undebatable position, we must still view his conception of theater as deficient, since, as he contends, reciprocal communication does not exist in the theater:

> If there is communication, it is in a special sense, different from what happens in linguistic communication. The spectators can never respond to the actors. One could argue about the murmurs and sighs, bravos and whistles, some other gestural and mimic indices, which are the only observable and the only possible responses of the public to the actors: but these responses are part of another system of communication than that which constitutes the play itself. We repeat, the spectators can never respond to the actors "through theater."[59]

Those who have disputed Mounin[60] have done so from an equally restricted conception of theater. Thirty years before, the Prague Circle semioticians had extensively described instances of direct participation by audience members in the performances of folk theater and folk puppetry, participation that satisfies Mounin's demand for reciprocal, one-code, one-channel communication in every respect. They had also analyzed other types of audience response as well. Veltruský discusses "actors becoming spectators," a concept later used by Grotowski in his Poor Theater, and also the institutionalization of an actor-turned-spectator who remained among the audience and served as an intervening member representing the collective of spectators. "It suffices" writes Bogatyrev, "that one spectator contribute actively to the performance; he fills the role of public representative."[61] Invoking Bogatyrev's examples of overt audience participation, Mukařovský suggests that "the theater also exhibits a constant effort to make the spectator's participation in the stage performance as direct as possible."[62]

Not only does Mounin fail to understand theatrical communication as being by its nature dependent on the participation of the audience, but he also assumes that the real communication in theater is between dramatic characters. What he fails to note is, as Ervin Goffman explains, that the overall task in a stage performance concerns the performers who project characters, not these characters themselves. "A character, note, cannot forget his lines."[63]

Goffman goes on to discuss staged productions where it is quite clear that the performers know all the secrets and outcome, and yet the character each actor projects must necessarily act as if he did not know some of the relevant matters and obviously does not know the final outcome. Communication is thus totally directed toward the spectator. In addition, out-of-frame activity by the actors involves the spectator in differentiating what is meant as text from what is meant as comment on the text. Direct address may be used as a means of awakening the audience, expanding on a moral point, explaining an intricate twist in the plot, apologizing for having to play two parts, or providing a summary of what has happened. In this manner, theatrical framing allows out-of-fame activities specifically designed to involve the spectator in the collective activity of theater.[64]

Perhaps the most conscious investigator of the phenomenology of acting and its effect on the consciousness of the spectator has been Jerzy Grotowski, who writes:

> Every performance built on a contemporary theme is an encounter between the superficial traits of the present day and its deep roots and hidden motives. The performance is national because it is a sincere and absolute search into our historical ego; it is realistic because it is an excess of truth; it is social because it is a challenge to the social being, the spectator.[65]

The aim of his Poor Theater is to provoke an encounter between the text and the actor, and between the text and the spectator. To provide an environment suitable for this type of self-encounter, Grotowski has included the spectator as a participant not only within the dramatic space but also within the dramatic action. For example, in his staging of Slowacki's *Kordian* the entire auditorium is built up to suggest the interior of a mental hospital, and the spectators are worked into the scenic arrangement as patients within the asylum.[66]

An important requirement for understanding the relationship of the various components projected into dramatic space is that the individual components are by their nature closely related. "For example," writes Mukařovský, "it is sometimes almost impossible to distinguish an actor's movement from a gesture (his walk is at the same time a movement and a gesture), or a costume from the actor's physical appearance."[67] Although their relationship is intrinsic, components may also substitute for one another. For example, the rich costumes, makeup, and highly stylized gestures of the Kabuki or the classical Chinese theater serve as substitutes for the lack of an expressive verbal depiction. Conversely, in Elizabethan theater a richly developed verbal depiction substituted for the sets and scenery which that theater lacked. In their study of the different forms of the folk theater, the classical Chinese theater, and the Czech theater, the Prague structuralists observed that precisely because of the constantly shifting relationships in the presentation of dramatic action, theatrical components do not exist as diverse materials which are to be treated side-by-side, but rather as a system emcompassing all theatrical signs, which constantly regroup.

The Prague structuralists have provided a methodological approach to the study of theatrical art and observed that the theatricality of dramatic characters, action, plot, and place corresponds to the changeability of their constituent theatrical signs. In light of the conclusions made by the Prague structuralists that aesthetic signs are subject to culturally determined norms and values, the work of Meyerhold, Brecht, and Witkiewicz assumes particular significance, since the period during which they created was one in which social change was highly volatile and dramatic. To study the creativity of Meyerhold, Brecht, and Witkiewicz without taking into account the highly charged signs as social facts would ultimately create a gap in our understanding.

2

Meyerhold:
The Aesthetics of Presentation

There are several reasons why semiotics is a vital area of study for the aesthetics of theater during a period of social change. Any criticism necessarily depends upon knowing what a text means, being able to "read" it. Unless we understand the code or mode of expression which permits meaning to emerge in a theatrical presentation, we may miss the essential nature of theatrical play. In order to isolate all the phenomena which fit into the semiotic field of the *mise-en-scène*, it is essential to recognize that on stage there are only signs. All is sign. Moreover, the signs in the theater are simplified, conventionalized, and selected in relation to those found in real life. Thus, a theatrical presentation represents "a sort of summary and laboratory model of sign-function" found in the world. Due to the manipulation of the expression of the various subcodes used in theatrical play, "a new type of awareness about the world" is activated in the spectator.[1] The more aware the spectator becomes of the code-changing process of theatrical signs, the more aware he becomes of the relationship between the theater and reality. This is no doubt what has made the metaphor of the world as a stage so common.

The main task of the critic is to determine the quality that can be defined specifically as theatricality, for as the Russian formalists insisted, the task of literary criticism is to study not literature but "literariness." Unfortunately, the whole drift of modern thought about the theater has been to submerge it into general discussions on communication, whether psychological or sociological, or to treat theatrical presentations like any other work or message, thus denying theater the specific aesthetic qualities by which it can be distinguished.

In the 1920s Russian directors like Meyerhold, Tairov, and Vakhtangov concerned themselves with the elimination of the traditional relationship between the stage and the spectator which in the theater of illusion was perhaps best represented in the style of Stanislavsky at the Moscow Art Theater. Instead, Meyerhold, Tairov, and Vakhtangov, each in his own way, sought to establish a theater that was highly theatricalized in nature. To bring about a revolution in the theater, the Russian avant-garde theater became the arena where a vital synthesis of the arts occurred, with the collaboration between Russian artists, poets, dramatists, and composers, on the one hand, and critics, theater and film regisseurs, on the other. For many Russian artists, composers, and dramatists, the theater became an important link between their art and the public, as for example the collaboration of cubists and constructivists, such as Malevich, Rodchenko, Popova, and Stepanova, as well as composers such as Glazunov and Shostakovich in the stagings of Meyerhold's theater.

The theater reflected the general trend of the Russian avant-garde to turn against art as an institution and against the mode in which art functions autonomously. The attack of the Russian avant-garde on established traditions in art was not so much directed toward a subversion of traditional art forms but was meant more to alter the institutionalized commerce with art. In his discussion of the avant-garde, Peter Bürger writes that "when the avant-gardists demand that art become practical once again, they do not mean that the contents of works of art should be socially significant" but rather that art should be directed toward the way it functions, "a process that does as much to determine the effect that works have as does the particular content."[2]

The theater was obviously affected by the dynamics of these exchanges. The breakdown of the old political order and its academic censorship gave impetus to an intensification of intellectual and aesthetic inquiry. The fruition of this was the crystallization of an artistic intelligentsia, which, not tied to an earlier academic hierarchy, issued manifestos, wrote broadsides, and collaborated in many areas: theater, mass spectacles, and film.

The new role assigned to the theater reflected a growing concern with the role of culture and art in a mass industrial society. What qualities constituted a workers' culture, and to what extent the workers' immediate environment needed to be reflected by the arts, became central questions. The entertainment provided for workers was created by artists who were not necessarily workers themselves but who embodied those qualities that would ennoble the workers, which was also considered a function of art in the new society. Ultimately, it was hoped that a culture actually created by workers, rather than for workers, might evolve from these attempts to create a theater of "rapid action, major passions, rare contrasts, whole characters, powerful, suffering and lofty ecstasy," a theater that would at the same time be "noisy, rapid-flying and crude."[3]

This attitude is reflected as early as 1913 in Vladimir Mayakovsky's first writings on theater, which despite the overtones of futuristic harangue reflect serious considerations about art as an institution: "Having fed its machines with thousands of horsepower, the city for the first time made it possible to satisfy the materials needs of the world employing only six to seven hours of daily labor. Now the intensity and tension of contemporary life have stimulated a colossal necessity for the kind of free play of cognitive aptitude which is art."[4]

Prior to the revolution in the theater, the theater, according to Mayakovsky, "served only as an artificial cloak for all types of art" and appeared only "as an uncouth oppressor of art." This was because theatrical decor in the traditional theater was purely decorative, and the artist in stooping "to a utilitarian view of art" had forgotten his own freedom. The text, or "The Word," in the theater had also been subsumed to express "moral or political ideas which are incidental to art," a category to which Mayakovsky relegated Gorky and Ibsen.[5] These early explorations into the nature of theater by Mayakovsky reflect a relationship to F. T. Marinetti's manifesto, *The Variety Theatre*, written in 1913, which became the common ground for many experiments in the theatrical revolution of the 1920s. Two points in particular seem to have influenced Mayakovsky's ideas on the nature of the theater: Marinetti suggested that the theater of the future had the potential to destroy "the sacred, the serious, and the sublime" by introducing new dynamism of color and form through the "simultaneous movements of jugglers, ballerinas, gymnasts, colorful riding masters, and spiral cyclones of dancers spinning on the points of their feet." In addition, the sanctity of dramatic works could be destroyed by "plagiarizing them, parodying them, making them look commonplace by stripping them of their solemn apparatus as if they were mere attractions."[6] This concept of Marinetti's gave rise to an interest in a theater that was to free the stage from the power of literature, the psychological motivation of characters, and the domination of the dramatic text. Drawing on these ideas, Mayakovsky conceived theatrical presentations as presentations of attractions, an idea usually credited to Eisenstein in his theory of montage as "a collision of attractions" and likewise ideas anticipated by Meyerhold in his prerevolutionary stagings such as *Don Juan* and *Masquerade*.

The first years immediately following the Revolution allowed for a wide range of theatrical expression, particularly since the Soviet regime soon recognized the theater as a potent means for natural education. Anatoly Lunacharsky, the newly appointed head of the Commissariat of Public Enlightenment, realized that to build up the theater he must allow "the fellow travellers" such as Stanislavsky and Tairov to continue the theatrical tradition, hoping in time to build up a new and more politically conscious repertoire that would promote the goals of the revolution. For that reason, since the Soviet Union had not yet evolved social and political institutions capable of incorporating the philosophy of its new leaders, many attitudes were allowed. However, by the late twenties the decision was made to build up socialism with "the methods employed by the Pharaoh for building pyramids," and art was, henceforth, to be subject not just to party censorship but to the mysterious requirements of a greater purpose.[7] Socialist realism, publicly pronounced in 1934 at the First Congress of the Union of Writers by Zhdanov, Stalin's spokesman in cultural affairs, was a doctrine, as James Billington explains, which called for two mutually exclusive qualities: revolutionary enthusiasm and an objective depiction of reality.[8]

Before the turn to positive heroes and positive messages that marked the literature, film, and theater of the 1930s, Soviet avant-garde art encompassed both radical innovation and a revolution in form, on the one hand, and a reworking or deformation of old conventions, on the other. At one extreme, the period exhibited the shocking novelty of the avant-garde experiments that included such artists as Diaghilev in his Paris ballet season, the abstract paintings of Larionov and Goncharova, the constructions of Gabo and Rozanova, and the self-dramatizing poetry of Mayakovsky.

One of the most representative figures of the artistic intelligentsia, Meyerhold was already a successful theatrical director before the Revolution and emerged after it as a leader of the avant-garde. His theatrical presentations, even before the Revolution, differed substantially from Stanislavsky's. Meyerhold's original antipathy to naturalism, in part an inheritance from his early involvement with symbolism, which until the futurists, such as Mayakovsky, burst upon the scene, was the leading movement that ran counter to the dominant domestic drama on civic and social themes, going back to Chernishevsky's *What Is to Be Done?*, to Belinsky's "literary evangelism," to Tolstoy's morality plays. The sense of social responsibility, political commitment, and moral vision in the critical writings of Belinsky, Chernishevsky, and Dobrolyubov helped mold the climate for a literature that emphasized social and political commitment, largely at the expense of aesthetic expression. Rather than continuing the didactic, social consciousness inherent in Russian nineteenth-century literature, the Russian avant-garde's aesthetics provoked a dislocation and deformation of assumed aesthetic values.

The aim of the concepts of dislocation and distortion introduced by the Russian formalists was to force the public into a position of self-reflection, to make it discover its own discontent. A discussion of the dialectic between Meyerhold and other figures from the Soviet avant-garde over whom he exerted a great influence—Eisenstein, Okhlopkov, Shostakovich, Mayakovsky, Vakhtangov, Stepanova, Popova, and Rodchenko—and their audience is particularly relevant, since what all the members of the avant-garde shared was the intention of using new forms to create a new society in which "art and literature would play a seminal and organizational role."[9] This, of course, had to do with restructuring basic aesthetic codes that would fulfill the dramatic expectations occurring in the wake of the Revolution. However, these codes refer more to shifts in expression than to an ultimate destruction of old forms, or as Umberto Eco explains: "Man is continually making and re-making codes, but only insofar as other codes already exist. In the semiotic universe there are neither single protagonists nor charismatic prophets. Even prophets have to be socially accepted in order to be right; if not, they are wrong."[10]

The avant-garde, inspired by political and social cataclysm, strove to embody Soviet social values not only in literature and the theater but also in painting, sculpture, architecture, and industrial design. This break with traditional aesthetics, however, did not represent a total break with the past, as Shklovksy explains:

The defeated line is not annihilated, it does not cease to exist. It only topples from the crest, drops below for a time of lying fallow, and may again arise as an ever-present pretender to the throne. Moreover, in practice, things are complicated by the fact that the new hegemony is usually not a pure instance of restoration of an earlier form, but one involving the presence of features from other junior schools, even features (but now in a subordinate role) inherited from its predecessor on the throne.[11]

Shklovsky's analysis of the assimilation of stylistic elements from older traditions serves as an appropriate introduction to Meyerhold, whose work epitomizes what Tynjanov describes as a "struggle involving a destruction of the old unity and a new construction out of old elements."[12] In Meyerhold's case, the destruction of the conventions of naturalism, as espoused by Stanislavsky in the Moscow Art Theater, where ironically Meyerhold received his training as both actor and director, represents the break with the immediate past. His attention to the stylistic elements of the *commedia dell'arte,* the medieval mystery plays, the cabotin player, and the Japanese theatrical tradition serves as a point of departure for his particular theatrical style. However, the development of Meyerhold's style cannot be seen as a succession of styles flowing directly into one another in a linear manner. Rather, the multiplicity of his interests together with the dynamics of the political environment contributed to that development.

Although his symbolist productions at the Komissarzhevsky Theater differed in style from his later Soviet productions, Meyerhold's general direction toward experimentation with nonrepresentational stage techniques is clearly evident. Symbolism's greatest contribution to stage design was to remove the clutter of detail that pervaded the naturalist theater. Disassociating himself from the Moscow Art Theater, Meyerhold, like Tairov, rejected an attitude that "would allow both the audience and the actor himself to believe that they were dealing not with the stage, but with real life."[13] Much like Tairov, Meyerhold introduced stylized settings, gave attention to the significance of gestures and objects, and introduced exaggerated lighting and draping of the stage to create sculptural effects. It was, however, in his elimination of the stage curtain, in his use of multiple levels to offset the actor in theatrical space, and in his method of area lighting in order to eliminate scene changes, that Meyerhold anticipated what were to become the essential characteristics of his style.[14]

An important influence on Meyherhold's theatrical aesthetics was the work of the German theorist Georg Fuchs, whose suggestion in *Die Schaubühne der Zukunft (The Stage of the Future)* that dramatic art is "primarily the rhythmic movement of the body in space"[15] became central to Meyerhold's arrangement of the actor in an appropriate spatial context.

Fuchs stressed the importance of unity between actor and audience, and to these ends he broke up the stage into several planes, projecting the actor's body upon them by use of electric spotlights and by bringing the action of the proscenium right down to the audience. In addition, in Fuch's model theater, side walls were to be eliminated, exposing the actual machinery of the theater. Fuchs sought to create a theater that would involve the audience more by visual and aural effects than by the spoken word. According to Fuchs, modern technology, in destroying traditional culture, was necessitating a reappraisal of the theater. In order for the theater to maintain contact with the new technological world, it would have to master the new machinery of that age.[16] Fuchs's ideas were a revelation for Meyerhold, since they gave him theoretical justification for what he was already attempting to do in his revolt against the tenets of naturalism.

This attitude was embodied in Meyerhold's plans for a theater in which there were to be no architectural barriers between spectators and actors, no proscenium arch or wings. The stage was to be set in the middle of the space with the audience banked around it. As Huntley Carter puts it, "Stanislavsky told the actor he must forget that he is on the stage. . . . Meyerhold told him he must remember that he is one of the audience."[17] Anticipating Brecht in his *Verfremdungseffekt*, Meyerhold wanted to bring about a new relationship between the stage and audience by focusing on the theater as a mirroring device by means of which other codes—social, political, cultural—and not only aesthetic ones—could be reexamined. Eco explains that the close dialectical interrelationship between messages and codes creates an awareness in the spectator "of new semiotic possibilities," compelling him to reconsider the usual codes and their interpretation. According to Eco, to change semantic systems means "to change the way in which culture 'sees' the world."[18] This was precisely Meyerhold's attitude. The dramatist and the director were to prepare the ground on which those two vital theatrical forces, the actor and the spectator, were to work daily:

> Nowadays, every production is designed to induce audience participation: modern dramatists and directors rely not only on the efforts of the actors and the facilities afforded by the stage machinery but on the efforts of the audience as well. We produce every play on the assumption that it will be still unfinished when it appears on the stage. We do this consciously because we realize that the crucial revision of a production is that which is made by the spectator.[19]

It is with the spectator, in brief, that theatrical communication begins and ends. In order for this communication to be meaningful, "all devices which are at the disposal of the other arts must be used as an organic fusion to affect the audience."[20] Theater must be accepted as theater, and the signs of the *mise-en-scène* and/or their various combinations function not only to communicate information, but also to transmit to the public their supplementary values.[21] Through the introduction of nonverbal means of expression, theater also gains a dimension of communication which is also important in everyday life. In a theater which does not conceal the means of production, the spectator does not forget for a moment that he is in the theater, nor does he lose sight of the actor as a master of his profession who is only playing a part. The selection of materials for use in the theater is meaningful because of their particular stimuli. Much attention was given by Meyerhold to their intrinsic value: "In art it is always a question of arrangement of material,"[22] he declared. Accordingly, the point of departure for an analysis of his productions should be the designation of material and the definition of the relation between material and sign value.

Perhaps the best example of a contrast in the use of materials and their signifying means is between the 25 February 1917 premiere of Meyerhold's production of Lermontov's *Masquerade*, and his production five years later of Crommelynck's *The Magnanimous Cuckold*. The production of Lermontov's play, with sets designed by Alexander Golovin, was the pinnacle of Meyerhold's prerevolutionary career. This monumental production, although it was put on at eighteen days' notice, had been in preparation and rehearsal since 1912. The production was overlong in preparation partly because of Meyerhold's and Golovin's research in the archives of St. Petersburg and in the antique shops of Paris for materials that were aimed at presenting the romantic splendor that masked the passion and sense of grotesque which Meyerhold viewed as central to the play.

The intent on Meyerhold's and Golovin's part was not to reproduce the period with historical exactitude in the manner of Saxe-Meiningen, but to underline the essence, or *gestus*, of Lermontov's play. To accomplish this, Meyerhold made the ominous figure of the Unknown Man central to Lermontov's drama. Clad in a black Venetian costume, with his face covered by a white *bauta* from carnival time, with a sharp beak, the Unknown Man was present throughout the play, holding all the threads of intrigue. As the demonic shaper of events, he cast his terrible shadow on everything, even behind the transparent fabric of the curtain in the final scene.

Meyerhold broke up the four acts of *Masquerade* into ten scenes. The technical problems of brief scenes in swift succession were solved by painted curtains, before which some of the action took place forward on the stage apron. Together with Golovin, Meyerhold considered the stage to be an architectural continuation of the auditorium at the Imperial Alexandrinsky Theater. A semicircular proscenium was pushed into the auditorium and was fenced off by bannisters, with two staircases leading down to the orchestra. On the sides of the proscenium, above sculptured portals, were loges shut off by closed red silken curtains, suggesting mysterious spectators to the events taking place. Numerous curtains of a different color served as symbolical background for emphasizing the moods of the various scenes, permitting the stage to be rearranged without the use of intermissions. In addition to curtains, Meyerhold used screens allowing him to deal freely with stage space. "This changeability of stage space," writes Konstantin Rudnitsky, "supplemented the overall impression of shifting mystery and ghostliness."[23] Mirrors on both sides of the portals reflected the auditorium, thus strengthening the connection with the stage and making the actors part of the audience as self-reflecting objects.

Only twice was the enormous stage of the Aleksandrinsky revealed in depth: in the masquerade scene of the first part and the ball scene in the third part. In these scenes, in particular, music composed by Alexander Glazunov served the purpose of providing commentary. The satanic waltz at the masquerade emphasized the irony between the superficial gaiety and the demonic subtext. At the final ball, a musical leitmotiv underlined the contrast between the purity of Nina and the corruption of society. With the music as background, Meyerhold choreographed each step of the production, including the masked ball scene, in which over a hundred and fifty guests took part. This was Meyerhold's first use of the "crowded setting" forming a single composition, a device he was to use later in his production of *The Inspector General.*

Meyerhold developed the small scene of the masquerade into a picture of grotesque irony. The scene, for which Golovin designed all the furniture, china, crystal, candelabras, swords, walking canes, and even playing cards, served to heighten the feeling that Meyerhold wanted to portray. Nothing was taken from stock, and everything that had a signifying value was made slightly oversized to intensify the effect on the spectator. To increase the effect that what the spectator was seeing on stage was all illusion, the auditorium was illuminated throughout the play with bright chandeliers, the lights of which were reflected in the mirrors flanking the proscenium. "The mask, the candle, and the mirror—that is the image of eighteenth-century Venice," writes Meyerhold, quoting from Muratov's *Italian Images,*

> Isn't it masks, candles and mirrors, the passions of the gaming tables where the cards are scattered with gold . . . those intrigues born of tricks played at masked-balls, the halls "gloomy despite the glitter of candles" in Lermontov's *Masquerade*? Isn't it this very Venetian life imbued with the magic which always lies hidden in cards and in gold which shows through the images of *Masquerade*, "hovering on the borderline of delirium and hallucination."[24]

There was something dark and prophetic about this production of *Masquerade*, which opened as the first shots of the Revolution were booming out at a distance. Unsurpassed in the luxury of its costumes and sets and in the number of actors, the masked ball with the glitter of its images "echoed like a grim requiem for the empire, like a stern, solemn, tragic, fatal funeral rite of the world which was perishing in those very days," writes Rudnitsky.[25] Znosko Borovsky also viewed Meyerhold's production as an ominous, prophetic leave-taking of a world which had lost its reality and was reduced to phantoms and masked shadows of the past:

It was as if fate itself hounded the jealous husband as he thrashed about in the circle of his suspicions and in the circle of the dancers. The masks became bent. The horns were frightening. The fateful circle that surrounded him kept growing smaller. There was general rejoicing, joking intrigues, and spontaneous dancing which acquired a strange and foreboding aspect, as the danger kept growing greater; a whirlwind and a windspout spun about the stage. It was as if we were among some unlikely monsters created by the sick, troubled imagination of a husband who has a blameless wife and does not believe in her innocence. He handed the poison to her himself in order to kill not her, but rather his own dark thoughts which had acquired such frightening reality.[26]

Although the premiere on 25 February 1917 was the theatrical event of the decade, on that same day "the world was extinguished"[27] when the tsarist regime was forced to a final confrontation with the Petrograd proletariat. Another critic of the period, Alexander Kugal, saw the production from a different perspective:

At the entrance to the theatre stood tight black lines of automobiles. All the rich, all the aristocratic, all the prosperous Petrograd pluto-bureau, and homefrontocrats were present in force . . . and when that Babylon of absurd extravagance was unveiled before us with all the artistic obscenity of a Semiramis, I was horrified. I knew—everybody knew—that two to three miles away crowds of people were crying "bread" and Protopopov's policemen were getting seventy rubles a day for spraying those bread-starved people with bullets from their machine guns.[28]

The production of *Masquerade* was Meyerhold's farewell presentation as director of the Imperial Theater. However, the discoveries that contributed to the development of his style between 1905 and 1917 had an enormous influence on the development of the Soviet theater. First and foremost, Meyerhold believed that theater was not subject to the same laws as reality. The language, signs, materials, and time and space of Meyerhold's productions differed in spirit from those of naturalism. He effected a renascence of theatricality, bringing back the magic of the theater of masks and the forms and conventions of the *commedia dell'arte*, the cabotin player, and the Japanese Kabuki theater. Meyerhold destroyed the footlights that cast shadows on the stage and separated the audience from the stage with a wall of darkness. He bared the stage, constructed bridges into the auditorium, introduced constructions to set the actor into a three-dimensional perspective, and made lighting a new device for dividing scenes and individualizing episodes and details of the set.

Meyerhold, at this time, also introduced a new discipline to the study of gesture and motion, based on devices used by older theatrical traditions and the training of gymnasts and circus performers. This attitude differed significantly from Stanislavsky's in that the goal was to train the actor to study the conventions of gesture rather than the psychological motivation for these same gestures.

In addition, he also declared that the director was the author of the production and had the right to revise classics or to interpret dramatic material freely, a right which Brecht was to later use with even more freedom. Above all, it was Meyerhold's attention to the spectator as the coequal creator in the process of theatrical productions that made him an enormous influence on the work of the new, revolutionary age in the Soviet theater. This ability to adjust his creative ideals to the needs of a new audience can be best illustrated by his production of Crommelynck's *The Magnanimous Cuckold*, a production light years away from the decadent elegance of Golovin's set and materials for *Masquerade*.

Theater played a crucial role in the Soviet life of the 1920s, and Meyerhold, who had embraced the Revolution almost immediately, joining the Communist Party in 1918, established his reputation under the new political order with the first production of Mayakovsky's *Mystery-Bouffe* in 1918 and Verhaeren's *The Dawn* in 1920. In these and other productions of the 1920s, Meyerhold introduced a number of innovations on the stage that related to the industrial energy of the machine, so foregrounded in the discussions of five-year plans. Cars, machine guns, cameras, movie projectors, a revolving stage, and mechanically moveable projection screens were employed. For *The Magnanimous Cuckold*, Meyerhold introduced ramps on which his actors moved in accordance with his "bio-mechanics." For Ilya Ehrenbrug's *Trust D. E.* (1927), he placed an entire jazz band on stage. Even when performing the Russian classics, such as Ostrovsky's *The Forest* (1927), Gogol's *Inspector General* (1926), or Gribodeov's *Woe from Wit* (1928), Meyerhold experimented with moveable sets workers's overalls for eighteenth-century characters, flashing neon lights, and a montage-like cutting up of action into scenes. At the same time, the circus, the music hall, and vaudeville all provided Meyerhold with new means to show his audience that what they were watching was a theatrical spectacle.

The shattering of political, social, and economic structures, part of the historical process set into motion by the Revolution, related to artistic movements as well. From an aesthetic point of view, Meyerhold's early productions of the Soviet period seem at first glance to be almost irreconcilable with those of *Masquerade, Balaganchik, The Scarf of Columbine*, or *Don Juan*, produced before 1917. His easy transition to the political pronouncements of the *Proletkult* and the Futurist's fascination with the machine aesthetic appears as a contradiction of his earlier dedication to the Symbolists, to Appia, Fuchs, and Maeterlinck. Yet it is important to remember that even in his early productions, and certainly in his production of *Masquerade* that Meyerhold's attempts were always focused on bringing the audience into a mental dialogue between the action occurring on stage and their own values and beliefs. With the Revolution, the audience changed, but Meyerhold's interest in the theater as an expression of society did not. In Meyerhold's view, the theater of the revolutionary period was a theater conceived for great masses of spectators, an explosive theater without the halftones of psychologism.

The first Soviet drama to be staged by Meyerhold was Mayakovsky's *Mystery-Bouffe* written to honor the first anniversary of the Revolution and presented on 7 November 1918 at the Petrograd Theater of Musical Drama. It was revived with great acclaim in Moscow for the 1st of May festival in 1921, before many members of the Party.

Mayakovsky's brilliant farce in six acts can be called a twentieth-century version of a medieval morality play. In posters announcing the production, Meyerhold called it a "heroic, epic, and satiric representation" of the class struggle. This loud, crude, cartoon-like parody of a biblical mystery play based on the Flood demonstrated, as Nikolai Gorchakov aptly states, the noisy transition of the brilliant director to Bolshevism.[29]

The Revolution of 1917 also gave Mayakovsky a new life, and he was one of the first artists to mythologize the revolution with *Mystery-Bouffe,* adopting the revolution as something entirely his own. Above all, Mayakovsky was intent on creating a revolution in the theater:

> Today
> over the dust of theaters
> our motto shall light up:
> "Everything anew!"
> Stand and wonder![30]

Implicit with the revolution in the theater came the tearing down of "the relics of the old theater," and, symbolically, at the premiere of *Mystery-Bouffe,* Meyerhold had the actors tear posters from Petrograd theaters to shreds. "This was no longer a discussion of 'old theater,' " writes Rudnitsky, "but of specific, near, and well-known theaters."[31]

In the prologue to *Mystery-Bouffe,* one of the proletarian characters steps forward and discusses the function of the theater in the new society:

> Why is this playhouse in such a mess?
> To right-thinking people
> it's a scandal, no less!
> But what makes you go to see the show?
> "You do it for pleasure—
> isn't that so?

He continues to explore the idea that theatrical space needs to be extended and not limited to the stage

> But is the pleasure really so great, after all,
> if you're looking just at the stage?
> The stage, you know
> is only one-third of the hall. . . . [32]

In his prologue, Mayakovsky also attacks the attitude that the theater's function is to create illusion by acting on the spectator through the manipulation of the psychological identification with characters. The actor playing in the naturalistic dramas, which Mayakovsky so disparaged, lost direct contact with his audience; he was set apart in a magic box and in another world, separated from the spectator by a wall of darkness:

> For other theatrical companies
> the spectacle doesn't matter:
> for them the stage
> is a keyhole without a key.
> "Just sit there quietly," they say to you;
> "either straight or sidewise
> and look at a salience of other folks' lives."
> You look—and what do you see?
> Uncle Vanya
> and Auntie Manya
> parked on a sofa as they chatter.
> But we don't care
> about uncles and aunts:
> you can find them at home—or anywhere!
> We, too, will show you life that's real—very!
> But life transformed by the theatre into a spectacle
> most extraordinary![33]

Clearly, the prologue focuses on the idea that theater should above all be pleasurable, nonillusionistic, and relevant to the audience. The word "relevant," however, took into account political messages that were part of the program of the Theatrical October, a slogan introduced by Meyerhold as a sort of cultural Red Army war cry which aimed not only at rousing the masses to fight revolutionary battles over again, but also at destroying the conventions of the decadent theater, thus clearing the ground for a "new theater" emerging from the ashes. Nor was the sanctity of Mayakovsky's play held to be inviolate; the preface to a revised version exhorts that, "henceforth everyone who performs, stages, reads or prints *Mystery-Bouffe* should alter the contents in order to make it modern, up to date, up to the minute."[34]

In both content and use of materials, Meyerhold's production of *Mystery-Bouffe* was the first Soviet political review. Posterish and coarsely propagandistic as the production appeared, Meyerhold nevertheless made broad use of his prerevolutionary experiments, but in a new and purely Bolshevik way. He used farce, elements of the grotesque, and buffonade to aid him in unsparing satire and ridicule of the "clean" people in the ark scene. In order to stress the working-class solidarity of the "unclean," the actors were dressed in identical blue overalls and uttered their lines in the elevated style of political oratory, and both the costume and oratorical style were later adopted by the agit-prop Blue Blouse theater.

In terms of style, Meyerhold stripped the stage bare, focusing on cubist elements which, based on the geometric principles of the "machine," served as symbols of the new age of industrialization. As in his pre-Revolutionary productions, Meyerhold collaborated with an artist, in this case K. S. Malevich, a suprematist, to create for his production a huge blue hemisphere for the world, a few cubes for the ark, and a geometrical backcloth. On the stage a series of platforms of differing levels, interconnected by steps with a broad ramp sloping down to the first row of seats, brought the action right into the audience. Unfortunately, no pictures of the 1918 or 1921 productions survive; however, Malevich describes the set as a condensation of cubist elements:

> My approach to the production was cubist. I saw the box stage as the frame of a picture and the actors contrasting elements. . . . Planning the action on three of four levels, I tried to deploy the actors in place predominantly in vertical compositions in the manner of the latest style of painting; the actors' movements were meant to accord rhythmically with the elements of the settings. I depicted a number of planes on a single canvas, I treated space not as illusionary but as cubist. I saw my task not as the creation of associations with the reality existing beyond the limits of the stage, but as the creation of a new reality.[35]

Meyerhold's awareness of antiillusionistic devices of staging, as well as the biting satire, the exaggerated theatricalism, the disregard for plot suspense, and constant interruptions and asides—were characteristics that would remain associated with all future collaborations with Mayakovsky. At the opening night of the second staging of *Mystery-Bouffe* for the Third Congress of the Communist International, the response of the spectators was feverish and enthusiastic. And at the conclusion of the last act, the playing and singing of the "Internationale" was followed by stomping and cheering as Mayakovsky and Meyerhold bowed continuously to the cheering crowds. However, success in the theater, as James Symons points out, is marked in two ways: by acclaim as a "hit" and by continuity in the repertoire.[36] Although a loudly acclaimed hit, *Mystery-Bouffe* proved unable to establish a place for itself in the repertoire of later seasons. Perhaps having had an opportunity to digest the message, the spectators were able to see that the blue-uniformed proletariat did not appear entirely favored in contrast to the highly individualized, although caricatured, "clean" antiheroes.

Meyerhold's premiere production to open at the First Theater of the R.S.F.S.R. was his Sovietized version of Emile Verhaeren's *The Dawn*. In this Bolshevik production, Meyerhold inflated the role of the masses, words and phrases were inserted about the "dictatorship of the proletariat and a "worldwide proletrian revolution," and the finale contained a radio broadcast about the victory of the Revolution. To bring Verhaeran's play even closer to the audience, at every performance a messenger appeared to read the latest dispatches from the civil war front. At this point also, the orchestra chimed in with the strains of the Internationale. A public meeting followed, initiated by actors dressed in ordinary street clothes who were placed among the spectators to begin a dialogue between the public and the actors on stage.[37] This was clearly Meyerhold's attempt at the agit-theater.

Agit-art sought contact with the public in all areas, and making use of the traditional media, the artists engaged in the painting of agit-prop streetcars, posters, and, in the case of Mayakovsky, propaganda posters commissioned for ROSTA, and called "the windows" since they were displayed in empty store windows. New and more dynamic ways of intensifying visual, motive, and audio sensations were introduced creating a new street theater of sorts.

The political poster influenced both theater and film, as for example the frequent use of placards and screen projections in Meyerhold's theater. Posters also became a part of the scenography in agit-prop theater. The Window Rosta posters usually consisted of a series of images demonstrating a slogan in progression, an attitude that pervaded the Soviet theater as well as influencing the theater of Piscator and Brecht. In 1928, Mayakovsky wrote:

> Window ROSTA was fantastic thing. . . . It meant telegraphed news immediately translated into posters and decrees into slogans. . . . It was a new form that spontaneously originated in life itself. . . . It meant men of the Red Army looking at posters before a battle and going to fight not with a prayer but a slogan on their lips.[38]

The Dawn was staged at the former Zon Operetta Company theater. The unheated auditorium with its flaking plaster and broken seats resembled a meeting hall more than a theater. This was, however, the effect that Meyerhold desired. To exaggerate the effect, he removed the curtain and the cornices and hung the walls with propagandistic placards. B. Alpers describes the hall:

> It was an ordinary meeting hall, with damp spots on the walls, and a damp and bluish atmosphere. There were no ticket collectors at the doors of the theater. . . . They were wide open and, in the winter, snowstorms would sometimes invade the lobby and the corridors of the theater and make the audiences turn up their overcoat collars. . . . The railings were stripped off the loges. The seats and benches for the audience had been greatly knocked about, and they were no longer arranged in rows. One could crack nuts or smoke cheap tobacco in the lobby. Red Army units and groups of young workers constituted the new audiences. They received their tickets by allotment, and they filled the theater with noise and excitement.[39]

The Dawn was also crude in terms of staging. Cables, reaching from the floor to the flies, divided the stage. In addition, *contre-reliefs* consisting of triangles, bits of bent tin, and a pair of red and gold disks, abstract in form, hung in the air. The overall picture projected a tawdry composition of materials made to look even harsher by the white light of military searchlights.

Critics viewed the production as a conglomeration of theatrical trinkets. Defending his choice of Vladimir Dmitriev as stage designer, Meyerhold insisted that the functional aspects of the production were more important than effects:

> We are building just as they are building. . . . For us the art of manufacture is more important than any tediously pretty patterns and colours. What do we want with pleasing pictorial effects?
>
> What the modern spectator wants is the placard, the juxtaposing of the surfaces and shapes of tangible materials! . . . We are right to invite the Cubists to work with us, because we need settings which resemble those which we shall be performing against tomorrow. The modern theatre wants to move out into the open air. We want our setting to be an iron pipe or the open sea or something constructed by the new man. I don't intend to engage in an appraisal of such settings; suffice it to say that for us they have the advantage of getting us out of the old theatre.[40]

In addition, the program for the acting company underlined team effort on revising plays to fit the needs of the new man. Improvisation rather than training were stressed:

> The psychological makeup of the actor will need to undergo a number of changes. There must be no pauses, no psychology, no "authentic emotions" either on the stage or whilst building a role. Here is our theatrical programs: plenty of light, plenty of high spirits, plenty of grandeur, plenty of infectious enthusiasm, unlaboured creativity, the participation of the audience in the corporate creative act of the performance.[41]

To project the political, revolutionary, and scientific concerns of the new society, Meyerhold worked out techniques for actors which he called "bio-mechanics." He considered this theory to be a projection into the theater of the scientific spirit motivating the life of the Soviet Union at a time when the "machine" had become a symbol of a new society. In Meyerhold's training for actors, the actor's expression was to be projected more through control of the body rather than through psychological motivation, a movement more towards Pavlov than towards Freud, towards "mechanics of the brain" rather than "secrets of the soul."

Attention to physiology rather than psychology had to do with the movement away from the monistic concept of the individual toward the collective view, the notion that the individual lives on in the memory of the collective. The constructivist artists of that period strove to project this ideal into their work. As Robert C. Williams describes, in the constructivist period of the 1920s conductorless orchestras performed in Moscow,[42] Meyerhold transformed the chorus into gymnasts dressed in worker's coveralls, and Eisenstein made the masses themselves into a new collective hero in such films as *Strike* and *Potemkin*. The aim of the constructivist was the formal organization of a social utopia. As the generation that reached maturity only after the end of the civil war, they saw the task at hand no longer as destruction of the old society but celebration and construction of a new one. Meyerhold, although in terms of generations belonging more to the symbolist aesthetes of the late nineteenth century, appropriated the youthful spirit of the constructivists as a fitting one for the building of the new theater in the new society. He particularly favored the transformation of art into revolutionary propaganda by the repetition of a single idea or slogan for political effect. For this reason, his utilization of bio-mechanics was similar to the cartoons intended for mass consumption. His theater was to be a visual newspaper for the illiterate masses, a demonstration of the motor efficiency of the workers in the new society.

The fascination with the motion and rhythm of work found its way into early Soviet culture based on the study of workers's movements by the American efficiency expert Frederick Winslow Taylor, whose time-and-motion analyses included the use of stopwatches and film. In part, this interest was manifest also in a revival of gymnastics and dance, particularly in the free-flowing movements of Isadora Duncan, who found her way to the Soviet Union, and in the eurhythmics of Emile Dalcroze. As Meyerhold envisioned it, bio-mechanics would enable the actor to control his movements with steel nerves and an engineering exactitude as a demonstration of the ideal collective and its mechanization. The machine idea is, of course, not an exclusively Soviet dramatization of the worship of the machine but can be related to similar endeavors by Marinetti to regard society "as a great industrial machine, of which each individual is a functional part."[43]

Attraction to the machine was not confined to the constructivists. The futurists also appropriated the machine as part of the great movement for the resurrection of cultural values, the creation of a new idealism, and a new acceptance of the world. The futurists took the city, the skyscraper, and the machine as well as the noise, the bustle, the smoke, and traffic as central images. For Mayakovsky, New York and Chicago and the Brooklyn Bridge were symbols of man's triumph over his environment. In Meyerhold's stagings, motorcycles and automobiles appear on stage, and Tatlin's reliefs, Rodchenko's mobiles, and Kuleshov's montages also influenced the abstraction of the setting and movement of the presentations.

Above all, the viewer's response was an essential part of the work, and Meyerhold took the machine as a "law unto itself and as the starting point of new culture." Thus, machine and science, the discovery of the atomic nucleus, and the publication of Einstein's *Theory of Relativity* all played a role in the new attitude towards theater. Nick Worrall writes:

> The invention of the internal combustion engine and the mass production of motor cars, for example, can be seen to have affected Futurist verse production, as well as Futurist stage forms, in the directest of ways. In reflecting a revolt against the passive, contemplative world

of the Symbolists, the Futurists aimed at a dynamic reconstitution of reality. In terms of versification, this meant the re-substitution within the poetic structure of that which had been absent from Symbolist verse—namely the verb. The verb is nothing less than a motor. The restoration of the verb meant the introduction of the engine into what had become an etiolated form.[44]

Within this context, Meyerhold's system of bio-mechanics, developed as an exercise system to stress the supremacy of motion in actors, can be directly related to the emphasis on the part of futurists, such as Mayakovsky, "on a technology of artistic production which was to be harnessed to the 'verb' as engine."[45]

The possibilities of film also influenced Meyerhold's stage presentations; this was particularly evident in the speeding up of action and in the cutting of acts into scenes "montaged" together for effect. Between scenes, placards or even film projections announced the coming scene. Aware of the possibilities of film, Meyerhold called for a "cinefication" of the theater not by equipping the theater with "all the technical refinements of the cinema," but by revolutionizing the form and content of the theater to create certain effects that would make the spectator's viewpoint more mobile, as it is in the cinema.[46] Frequently, the effects produced in Meyerhold's constructivist productions have to do with the fragmentation of action into scenes or frames, now generally referred to as "montage."

The term montage was brought into wide use in the arts by Soviet films: by Eisenstein's *Potemkin* and later by such films as Pudovkins's *Mother* and Dovzhenko's *Earth*. Before this time, montage was associated with the principle of building and construction in the field of engineering and of photography in the word "photo-montage." Eisenstein's engineering training in the building of bridges struck him in retrospect as being essentially "a course in the art of *mise-en-scène*," involving a precise time-space relationship—factors he later identified as basic to film montage.[47] The theory of montage attraction assembly then did not refute but rather gathered together centuries of theatrical experience from Shakespeare, *commedia dell'arte* and the Kabuki theater.

The word *monter* means, simply, to construct, and its cinematic derivative had been used for some time to describe the process of film editing. Pioneered by Kuleshov and Vertov as a cinematic technique, its basic principle was to juxtapose dissimilar objects for effect. Although in Eisenstein's films the theory of montage was based on aesthetic principles already envisioned in the scenario, the roots of the idea lay in an attempt to overcome practical problems facing the newly emerging Soviet film industry.

For Eisenstein, however, the value of montage lay in the "conflict" within frames or juxtapositioned frames. "If montage is to be compared with something," he wrote, "then a phalanx of montage pieces, of shots should be compared to the series of explosions of an internal combustion engine, driving forward its automobile or tractor: for similarly, the dynamics of montage serve as impulses driving forward the total film."[48] Eisenstein's notion of "collision montage," according to Sergei Yutkevich (a fellow student in Meyerhold's school), came about during their work on a schema for pantomime which they dedicated to Meyerhold and called a "montage of attractions." "It was the same kind of daring," writes Yutkevich, "as when Picasso or Braque introduced bits of coloured paper or fragments of newspapers into their pictures, when 'collage' made its appearance" and people dared to introduce new elements into art, the theater, and film.[49]

In the theoretical justification for the use of a montage of attractions, Eisenstein defined an attraction as an "aggressive moment" which shocks the audience through a combination or "colliding" of actions or the juxtaposing of dissimilar objects.[50] The basic principle of juxtaposing dissimilar objects for effect was also the principle used by Russian futurist poets and formalists who argued that words should be "made strange" by unusual combinations and juxtapositions to make the reader take notice.

If the Moscow Art Theater imitated life and was primarily interested in showing its continuous course, Meyerhold's theater was more intent on selecting dynamic moments, episodes, fragments, or "attractions" and presenting them without seemingly paying attention to connecting meaning to the preceding or subsequent scene. The disjointedness of action was thus a way of underscoring its relativistic nature. Fragmentation then marked a new, fundamentally important aesthetic approach by Meyerhold's theater to deny "the flow of life," and break down illusion. To achieve these ends, Meyerhold diminished the individual psychological development of characters and concentrated on the principle of "social mask" to be later pushed to the idea of social type projecting not the specificity of character but rather the specificity of social class.

Stage constructions, actors moving in accordance to bio-mechanics, and the breaking up of dramatic texts into a series of montaged episodes reflected the fascination of the artists and critics of that time with new structures. Meyerhold directed his productions in such a way that the action never stuck on one plane, but moved over the width and the depth of the stage—not only in the horizontal plane but also in the vertical. The culmination of his workshop experiments was the production of Crommelnyck's *The Magnanimous Cuckold*. The production was staged with utmost economy, not just because Meyerhold at the moment lacked a budget and a theater but also because he wanted to create a model people's theater: "We wanted with this show to lay the foundation for a new kind of theater requiring neither an illusionistic set nor complicated properties, theater which could get along with the simplest objects at hand and progress from the spectacle acted by professionals to the free play of workers during their free time."[51]

This was the beginning of a revolution in the theater. The staging of *The Magnanimous Cuckold* was one of pure theatricality, as much as the pre-Revolutionary staging of *Masquerade* had been. The set designed by Liubov Popova cost only 200 rubles, but this construction, as silhouetted against the red brick walls of the theater, with its combination of platforms, stairs, and ramps, marked the beginning of one of the most exciting periods of artistic innovation in the theater. It also introduced a radical change in the role of the vocabulary of stage design, as Alma H. Law explains:

> Scenery (*dekoratsiia*) was replaced by the more aptly descriptive "object formulation" (*veshchestvennoe oformiennie*), from the word *veshch* (object or thing), which by the early 1910s became one of the most widely used terms in aesthetics. A construction was a *veshch*. A production was a *veshch*, not a representation of something. And talk was no longer of "props" (*butaforiia*), but of "requisitions," objects purchased or ready-made.[52]

The name given to this new movement was "Theatrical Constructivism," and brought into close relationship to the theater as a laboratory for developing artistic concepts such artists as Kazimir Malevich, Alexandra Exter, Liubov Popova, Vladimir Tatlin, Varvara Stepanova, and Alexander Rodchenko who shared the common goal of using new forms suitable for the new society in which "art and literature would play a seminal and organizational role."[53]

With its emphasis on functionalism, constructivism gave the theater a new ideal of aesthetics based on simplicity, proportion, and the use of real materials. It also gave the theater new flexibility and an awareness that a theatrical performance can take place almost anywhere, with a minimum of stage props. "Let's hurry up and find formulae for working with the materials on hand," writes Liubov Popova, "whether in two dimensions, in three, or in four."

> Only with such precise calculations can we even think of working in the field of so-called 'artistic' material design—until that happy moment when the very principle of 'artistry' (in contrast to whatever seemingly is 'unartistic') will be studied only as part of this history of superstition and prejudice. . . . So in vain do aesthetes take shelter behind the visual, poetic, and theatrical arts by talking about *formal* and *aesthetic* "searches and achievements" (such as "the problem of form and color in studio painting' or the construction of scenic space"). Their "art for art's sake" days are numbered. . . . [54]

Indicative of this interest was the exhibition "5 × 5 = 25" organized in Moscow in September 1921 presenting the work of the five contributors—Alexandra Exter, Popova, Rodchenko, Stepanova, and Alexander Vesnin—who set as their task the examination of "color construction based on the laws of color itself."[55] A few months later, at the plenary session of Inkhuk, inspired by Stepanova's statement that "technology and industry have confronted art with the problem of 'construction' not as a contemplative representation, but as an active function," the group declared "the absoluteness of industrial art and constructivism as its only form of expression."[56]

This attitude was expanded by Rodchenko in his *Constitution of Constructivism*: "The abundance, variety, and many-sidedness of the phenomenon of constructivism prove that it is not some kind of abstract method having limited applicability. On the contrary, we are convinced that constructivism encompasses and penetrates into, an extremely wide area of man's creative work. Consequently, it is possible to speak of constructivism as a world view."[57]

The new aesthetics, with its functional and machine-oriented constructions, gave the actors 'acting instruments' with which to interact: a system of staircases, ladders, trapdoors, and shifting screens intended to engulf the audience in the swirl of theatrical activity in much the same way as the circus acts on its audience. The actors in *The Magnanimous Cuckold* wore, instead of costumes, work clothes (*prozodezhda*) designed by Popova to facilitate the relationship between the actors and the stage constructions, and also to bring out "antics proper to the theater" with attention to the actor as a functional, well-trained physical machine.

To assist his audience in decoding the theatrical text, Meyerhold worked out a system of training actors which he called bio-mechanics, conceived of as a combination of military drill with algebraic functions. This was to be a *commedia dell'arte* tradition mechanized for the new age with the body of the actor projected almost as a robot. Instead of seeking sculptural effects, the actor's muscles and tendons were to act like pistons and rods. Consequently, the key to success lay in physical training which consisted of drills conditioning the actor to respond readily to stimuli in a sort of Pavlovian physiological engineering process.

To accompany the algebraic function of the bio-mechanical system, Meyerhold worked out a formula that read $N - A_1 + A_2$ (N, representing the actor; A_1, the playwright; and A_2, the director).[58] Notwithstanding Meyerhold's formula, whereby the actor is the central transformer of the raw material from the text, a process in which he is assisted by the director, in practice the converse was true. As a director, Meyerhold, like Brecht, practiced something quite different from what he preached, or at least, as James Symons points out, "practiced a great deal more than he wrote about."[59]

The good actor—and anybody physically fit could become a good actor—was one with "a minimum reaction time":

> How do we set about moulding the new actor? It is quite simple I think. When we admire a child's movements we are admiring his bio-mechanical skill. If we place him in an environment in which gymnastics and all forms of sport are available and compulsory, we shall achieve the new man who is capable of any form of labour. "Only via the sports arena can we approach the theatrical arena."[60]

"The work of the actor in an industrial society," wrote Meyerhold, "will be regarded as a means of production vital to the proper organization of the labour of every citizen of that country."[61] With his attention to the functional work of the actor, Meyerhold vehemently rejected the inner-directed acting principles of Stanislavsky. Instead, through bio-mechanics, Meyerhold attempted to work out a system of conventionalized movements wherein each gesture would become a sign or "hieroglyph" with its own particular meanings: rage was to be expressed through a somersault, sadistic intent by a leap onto the other actor's chest. Above all, the primacy of physiological gesture over psychological emotion was stressed. Something akin to the highly conventionalized Japanese Kabuki was Meyerhold's intent, wherein only those movements which were "immediately decipherable" were of the essence; everything else was considered to be "superfluous."[62]

To some degree, Meyerhold's writing on the subject of bio-mechanics must be viewed with the same sense of detachment as some of Brecht's more tendentious writing on the theater. Since both Brecht's and Meyerhold's aesthetics were formulated under the guise of proletarian manifestos, they should be taken as attempts on their part to function as creative artists despite their poses. As Edward Braun points out: "There seems little doubt that Meyerhold, spurred on by the polemical mood of the times, exaggerated the scientific aspect of bio-mechanics in order to show that his system was devised in response to the demands of the new age, in contrast to those of Stanislavsky and Tairov, which were unscientific and anachronistic."[63]

The key word in formalist critical language is "structure." This attention to "structure" can be seen in Meyerhold's staging of *The Magnanimous Cuckold* and *The Death of Tarelkin*. The constructions for both sets were solid, removed from the illusion-creating backdrops of canvas; they were something which could be walked upon, passed through, climbed on, swung on, and slid down, resembling the gymnastic equipment of the playground. Much as children, the actors quickly discovered the most effective parts of Popova's construction, such as the revolving door. Later, Stepanova's stage furniture for the *The Death of Tarelkin* also took into account its function as "instruments of play."[64]

Meyerhold's concept of bio-mechanics was important not because of its theoretical significance but because of its results upon the stage. The results were lively, mischievous, and unbridled in their gaiety as only those of clowns or acrobats in the circus can be because of their controlled virtuosity over their bodies and gestures. In themselves, the stage constructions could be transformed only by the actor's using the set as a machine. Thus, the platforms, ramps, and stairs, and the wheels, rolling discs, windmill sails, trapezes, and slides worked only when the actors brought out the kinetic qualities of the set into play. Each time Bruno, the jealous husband, falls into a jealous rage, the wheel of the mill, on which the large Latin letters "CR MM L NCK" were printed, suggesting deconstructed text, would start to turn furiously with a loud clumpety sound.

In Meyerhold's production of *The Death of Tarelkin*, the *commedia dell'arte* typification of characters, already inherent in Sukhovo-Kobylin's text, was sharpened and exaggerated by Stepanova's stage furniture, constructed in such a way that it would collapse, jump, or in some other way respond to the actor's actions according to the principles used by clowns in the circus: "When an actor sat on the constructivist furniture, he would either be tossed into the air by a spring in the seat or a torpedo would go off under him, the chair would somehow turn into a board, a policeman would jump out like a jack-in-the-box."[65] In addition, the actors wore costumes designed by Stepanova that were based on the principles of underscoring the bio-mechanical movements of the actors and of projecting something akin to "prototypes of sports costumes and work uniforms."[66]

Nothing was above ridicule: not the dramatic work, or even the dramatic characters the actors were portraying. One moment an actor would appear to be sincere in his portrayal of a character's feeling, and the next he would step out of character, do something foolish, as if to say, "Aren't these characters an absurd lot." Like Brecht, Meyerhold insisted that the audience must remain conscious of the illusion. "The new spectator," wrote Meyerhold, "is in my opinion quite capable of being freed from the hypnosis of the illusion."[67] Thus, Igor Ilinsky, playing Bruno in *The Magnanimous Cuckold*, exemplified the quality of anti-illusionistic acting by both embodying the idea of suffering and at the same time parodying it, demonstrating it:

> Wearing the sign of a clown in the form of red pom-poms round his neck, he exemplified the grotesqueness of the character's jealous madness by extending and enlarging naturalistic gesture to the scale of bio-mechanical semaphore. His jealous ravings were accompanied by an exaggerated rolling of the eyes, excessive sighing and moaning. In counterpoint to these melodramatic excesses were the wheels on the construction which spun in coordination with, alternately, Bruno's jealousy or his melancholy. In this fashion, states of feeling were kinetically signalled—a stable, external registration of human feelings by an inanimate world, which was the essence of stability and symmetry; the inanimate equivalent of reason in the human world.[68]

In *The Death of Tarelkin*, Meyerhold responded to Sukhovo-Kobylin's notes that "in keeping with the play's humorous nature, it must be played briskly, merrily, loudly—*avec entrain*"[69] by providing elements of slapstick. Much like circus clowns, the actors in their baggy costumes manipulated the stage furniture. Most spectacular was the cage used to simulate a prison cell into which the prisoner was propelled head-first as if through a giant meat grinder. Mikhail Zharov describes the acrobatics required to manipulate the set:

I climbed the ladder to the top of the construction and from there dove head first, landing on the "meat grinder" blade, which was made of rigid plywood. Taking the handle of the "meat grinder," Kachala and Shatala then cranked me as I lay on one of the four blades of this complicated construction. . . . I made a half circle and on reaching the bottom, I crawled into the cage, which also represented the "cooler".[70]

In addition to these feats, intervals in the action were announced by firing a pistol and shouting *"Entre-acte!"*; helter-skelter chases through the aisles and across the stage, with Tarelkin escaping by swinging across the stage on a trapeze, never gave illusion a chance to take possession of the spectator.[71]

Stage constructivism was ultimately only one aspect of Meyerhold's creativity as a director, for in his curriculum for training actors in the Actor's Studio the goals were much more universal: the study of the technique of stage movement, the study of the basic principles of improvisation based on Italian comedy, the study of traditional convention of the seventeenth and eighteenth centuries, attention to musical readings, and the practical study of the material elements of production to include use of space, furnishings, lighting, and makeup.[72] While on the stage everything appeared as light-hearted play, backstage Meyerhold stressed the significance of studying theater from all aspects: "In order to revive the theatre of the past, contemporary directors are finding it necessary to begin with pantomime, because when these silent plays are staged they reveal to directors and actors the power of the primordial elements of the theatre: the power of the mask, gesture, movement, and plot."[73]

The direction toward "gestic" acting and toward using conventionalized codes from other theatrical traditions that would exaggerate theatricality had already become an integral part of Meyerhold's program in his Dr. Dapertutto days, a name taken from the *Tales of Hoffmann*, when Meyerhold, as the director of the Imperial Theater in St. Petersburg, also experimented in intimate cabaret-type theaters. For example, in one episode of Znosko-Borovsky's comedy *The Transformed Prince*, Meyerhold directed the play in such a way that the action occurred simultaneously on stage and in the hall where the audience was seated cabaret-style at tables. As Rudnitsky describes it, "actors were planted among the audience, participated in the action and involved viewers in interactions with other actors" thereby uniting both actors and spectators with "viewers turned into actors and actors into viewers."[74]

In the search for a framework for his style, Meyerhold found in the *commedia dell'arte* several elements. The improvisational is one, since upon improvisation depends a play's immediacy and sense of spontaneity. The audience participates in the elements of obvious "play" by anticipating the events, and despite the anticipation, by being overwhelmed by surprise. Even in such details as whether the husband will appear at the door at an inopportune moment, the skill of the actor lies in making the obvious unexpected, or "defamiliarized."

Thus, in the *commedia dell'arte* he saw the main elements of his emerging style, which comprised a fascination with the fantastic, the grotesque, the marvelous, the popular, and the highly conventionalized. The use of circus conventions by the Futurists—as for example, Mayakovsky's "The Championship of the Universal Class Struggle"—introduced the other element in the development of Meyerhold's style, that of pantomime and acrobatics. Rudnitsky writes:

> There was, evidently, a deeper reason for the director's attraction to pantomime. Meyerhold's basic idea at the time, that of the renaissance of theatricality, caused him to make radical juxtapositions of theatricality and literariness. This concept evidently gave rise to an interest in a theater free from the power of literature, a theater without a play or predetermined text. The *commedia dell'arte* was just such a form.[75]

Another essential element of the *commedia dell'arte* tradition is its use of the masks. Paradoxically the use of masks, as Meyerhold suggests, "may conceal more than just two aspects of a character":

> The two aspects of Arlecchino represent two opposite poles. Between them lies an infinite range of shades and variations. How does one reveal this extreme diversity of character to the spectator? With the aid of the mask. The actor who has mastered the art of gesture and movement (herein lies his power!) manipulates his masks in such a way that the spectator is never in any doubt about the character he is watching: whether he is the foolish buffoon from Bergamo or the Devil.[76]

Thus, behind his mask the actor hides his own personality in order to assume the new one in the spirit of the play. The mask releases his powers as an actor and simultaneously activates the spectator, enabling the latter to see "not only the actual Arlecchino before him but all the Arlecchinos who live in his memory."[77]

Meyerhold found in the repetitious patterns of the *commedia* a mirroring symmetry, since the plots of the typical play were replete with combinations of pairs and doubles, as if in a hall of mirrors. These repetitions are also at the core of Meyerhold's style. For example, in *The Magnanimous Cuckold*, one character bounces off another to illustrate that action did not proceed in a single-directional pattern but emerged rather from the refracted mirror images of characters and their actions. Central to the *commedia* performance was the conscious use of one stereotyped antic after another, an aspect that Meyerhold was to use most effectively, concentrating on tricks that were of the circus kind: the gesture or mimicry of "joy" or "recognition," or the miming of psychological distress by the rolling of the eyes, as in Ilinsky's characterization of Bruno. These theatrical signs used so effectively by Meyerhold in *The Magnanimous Cuckold* had in common with the *commedia dell'arte* that their success was entirely dependent upon the audience's ability to read them.

Meyerhold's intent was to make theater more accessible as theater. Along with the use of techniques from the *commedia,* Meyerhold also explored other theatrical traditions: the theater of the grotesque, the cabotin, the mime, the juggler, the acrobat, and the strolling player. His prerevolutionary essay on "cabotinage" is considered to be seminal to the development of his mature style. The essay emerged as a reaction on the part of Meyerhold to attacks on his work as deception and "cabotinage." "But is theater without cabotinage possible?" replied Meyerhold: "The cabotin is a strolling player; the cabotin is a kinsman to the mime, the histrion, and the juggler; the cabotin can work miracles with his technical mastery; the cabotin keeps alive the tradition of the true art of acting."[78]

According to Meyerhold, the theater was hampered by the public's expectations of seeing literature for reading presented on stage, thus obstructing theatrical "play": "I am convinced that until the writers of neo-mysteries sever their connections with the theatre, until they quit the theatre altogether, the mystery will continue to obstruct the theatre, and the theatre the mystery."[79]

In his attempts at finding an alternative direction to that of the Moscow Art Theater's naturalism, Meyerhold came close to renouncing the very symbolism he had espoused in his work at Komissarzevskaya's theater. "Andrei Bely is right," he wrote. "Reviewing the symbolist theatre of today, he comes to the conclusion: 'Let the theatre remain the theatre, and the mystery—the mystery.' "[80]

As an antidote to the literary play, Meyerhold proposed movement and pantomime as the central actor's instruments. In rejecting the psychological motivation of role building by the actor, Meyerhold insisted instead on a conscious attitude or pose that would present the character, thus anticipating Brecht's later notion of the fundamental "gestus" of each character. In his awareness that theater consists not of a rich stage and stage effects but rather relies entirely on the actor, Meyerhold was also anticipating ideas that later became central to Artaud's theater of ritual and cruelty, and also to Grotowski's Poor Theater:

Movement is the most powerful means of creating theater on stage. . . . Strip the theater of the play, costumes for the actor, the stage, the set and theater building, leaving only the actor and the movements in which he has been trained—and you will still have the theater: the actor will communicate his thoughts and motives to the audience by his movements, gestures, and grimaces. As a theater for the actor any space will serve: without the help of the builder the actor can himself arrange his theater where and how it suits him, and as fast as his skill will permit.[81]

This prerevolutionary essay indicates quite clearly to what extent Meyerhold had already explored the ideas that contributed to his staging of *The Magnanimous Cuckold* and *The Death of Tarelkin.* This attention to stripping the theater of all excesses of naturalism is already manifest in the quintessential production of his prerevolutionary years, that of Alexander Blok's *Balaganchik* (1906). Blok's play employed the traditional figures of Pierrot, Columbine, and Harlequin, whose role was to "smash right through all the dead stuff,"[82] to strip away societal facades and personal masks. The point at issue in this staging was basically that of naturalism versus theatricalism, and the discussion by Meyerhold on the production focuses on the mocking quality of the staging which exposes theater by showing its machinery of illusion. The prompter's box, the wheels and ropes hoisting the curtain were all left exposed:

> The entire stage is hung at the sides and rear with blue drapes; this expanse of blue serves as a background as well as reflecting the colour of the settings in the little booth erected on the stage. This booth has its own stage, curtain, prompter's box, and proscenium opening. Instead of being masked with the conventional border, the flies, together with all the ropes and wires, are visible to the audience. When the entire set in the booth is hauled aloft, the audience in the actual theatre sees the whole process. In front of the booth, the stage area adjacent to the footlights is left free. It is here that the 'Author' appears to serve as an intermediary between the public and the events enacted within the booth. The action begins at a signal on the big drum; the music starts and the audience sees the prompter crawl into his box and light a candle. . . . [83]

When the staging of *Balaganchik* is compared to the later stagings of *The Magnanimous Cuckold* or *The Death of Tarelkin*, elements of theatricality already explored by Meyerhold in Blok's play reappear in the guise of new materials. However, the central "gestus" of the plays is consistent. Each character, much like in the staging of *The Magnanimous Cuckold*, was restricted to his own typical gesture; Pierrot, for example, played by Meyerhold, "always flaps his arms in the same way."[84] The stylized gestures were underlined by a musical leitmotif that was to set off the basic gestic quality of each character. In addition, the gestures accompanied the text, always lagging behind as if to leave the import of the gesture rather than the words hanging in the air.

Meyerhold took the study of gestures several steps further in his training of actors in bio-mechanics, and later, in the staging of Faiko's *Bubus, the Teacher* (1925), foreshortened gestures to precede or to announce the text. The "pre-acting" development emerges from Meyerhold's continued interest in the Japanese theater. Having had an opportunity to invite Japanese actors and jugglers to his studio during his Dr. Dapertutto period, Meyerhold felt that a strong kinship existed between the Japanese theater's use of gestures, masks, and music, and his own studio exercises. He was particularly struck by the way sound and gesture complemented each other in the Kabuki theater, and this reinforced his idea that theater should move away from the dominance of the spoken word and focus instead on new methods of combining visual and aural elements.

From his studies of the Japanese theater, Meyerhold recognized that in the line of development between a theatrical presentation and the dramatic text, the scenic devices did not simply accompany the dramatic text. Instead, the two were totally interchangeable, inseparable elements of a monistic system. The use of music to foreground the gestures of his actors reinforced Meyerhold's belief that in the theater verbal speech is a kind of secondary process, and that the primary, underlying level consists of sensuous and imagistic elements. The techniques of "foreshortening" action through the use of what Meyerhold called "raccourci," which is fundamental to his "pre-acting" techniques, or "instantaneous, expressive moments of pose," relate quite clearly to the poses or *mie* of the Japanese Kabuki theater.

There were other devices drawn from the Japanese theater by means of which Meyerhold attempted to dispel theatrical illusion. In his prerevolutionary production of Molière's *Don Juan* (1910), he flooded the auditorium with full light, abolished the curtain, and introduced little Moorish *kurogos* to handle the objects on stage:

It is no coincidence that I refer to the ancient Japanese theater whilst discussing a production of Molière's *Don Juan*. From descriptions of Japanese theatrical performances of approximately the same period as Molière, we know that special stage-assistants, known as *kurogo* and clad in special black costumes resembling cassocks, used to prompt the actors in full view of the audience. When the costume of an actor playing a woman's part became disarranged at a tense moment in the drama, one of the *kurogo* would quickly restore the graceful folds of the actor's train and attend to his coiffure. . . . If the hero died on stage, the *kurogo* would quickly cover the corpse with a black cloth, and under the cover of the cloth the "dead actor" would run off the stage. . . . [85]

Never a slavish imitator, Meyerhold made no attempt to imitate Japanese symbolic simplicity in his staging of *Don Juan*. Instead, the golden age of Versailles was recreated with ornate costumes, mirrors, chandeliers, and rich tapestries. Nor was this decoration limited to the stage but was continued into the auditorium, with the "liveried Arab boys" running about "like black kittens, doing somersaults on the soft rugs, burning incense, ringing a silver bell and lighting candles."[86] In his postrevolutionary period, the materials changed in that the rich tapestries and rugs were supplanted by stage constructions, but the antics of the theatrical play remained fundamental to Meyerhold's theatrical style.

Impressed by the effects emerging from stylistic rather than naturalistic signs in the Japanese theater, Meyerhold paid much attention to what he defined as the "grotesque," which emerged, according to him, from the conflict between form and content:

The grotesque aims to subordinate psychologism to a decorative task. That is why in every theatre which has been dominated by the grotesque the aspect of design in its widest sense has been so important (for example, the Japanese theatre). Not only the setting, the architecture of the stage, and the theatre itself are decorative, but also the mime, movements, gestures, and poses of the actors. Through being decorative they become expressive. For this reason the technique of the grotesque contains elements of the dance; only with the help of the dance is it possible to subordinate grotesque conceptions to a decorative task. . . . It's no coincidence that the Japanese actor offering a flower to his beloved recalls in his movements the lady in a Japanese quadrille with her torso swaying, her head turning and lightly inclining, and her arms gracefully outstretched first, to a decorative task.[87]

Meyerhold's attention to foregrounded expressive movements comes into focus when one examines Meyerhold's "pre-acting" principle, which theoretically was intended to project a subtext through sudden freezes in order to convey shocked dismay at the discovery of a dilemma. Particularly in the staging of Faiko's *Bubus, the Teacher* (1925), the effect was to be heightened by the use of a "double revolve": "The petrified group would silently retreat; a gap would materialize in the seemingly impassable wall enclosing the stage area; and they would be 'hurled from the stream of life onto the rubbish dump of history.' Once more, props were used sparingly but effectively 'both as an instrument for acting and as a symbolic generalization of a way of life.'"[88]

The intent of pre-acting was to prepare the spectator to decode the dramatic text in such a way that "the scenic situation (was to be) fully resolved in advance." In this manner, the spectator was presented subtextual meanings without having to strain for them. Ultimately, he was also to judge the dramatic character, since the actor's aim was to "present" the character rather than "represent" him:

The actor-tribune needs to convey to the spectator his attitude to the lines he is speaking and the situation he is enacting; he wants to force the spectator to respond in a particular way to the action which he is unfolding before him. . . . The actor-tribune sets himself the task of developing scenic situations not in order to impress the spectator with the beauty of their theatricality, but like a surgeon whose task is to uncover what lies within. The actor-tribune acts not the situation itself, but what is concealed behind it and what it has to reveal for a specifically propagandist purpose.[89]

In *Bubus*, the action was performed against an elegant musical background of Liszt and Chopin, intended not so much as background music as a musical "construction" performed at a concert Bechstein perched high above the stage in a gilded alcove. By revealing the source of music to the spectator, much as the orchestra that sits on stage in the Japanese theater is revealed, Meyerhold hoped to synchronize the music to the text in order to highlight its gestic quality. The text was to be spoken rather than acted, bringing out a recitative quality, wherein music was to serve as a leitmotif to accompany the pre-acted signs. Unfortunately, the pre-acting style tended to drag out the stage sequences, making them ponderous, and the music to a great extent irrelevant to the action.

Notwithstanding the failure of *Bubus*, it is evident that Meyerhold constantly strove to refine the theatrical signs of the *mise-en-scène* to accentuate their theatricality, and thus even his failures contributed significantly to the development of a conscious theatrical style.

To maintain his principles that theater was theatrical was difficult for Meyerhold during the period when discussions on the meaningfulness of art to society dominated the scene. Meyerhold constantly had to walk a fine line between his artistic principles and the demands of Lunacharsky, the People's Commissar of Enlightenment. When, in order to make theater more relevant to the masses, the slogan "back to Ostrovsky" was announced, Meyerhold considered such an attitude reactionary, since it called for the restoration of true-to-life naturalism. His 1924 production of Ostrovsky's *The Forest* strove to make Ostrovsky a contemporary rather than a classic. The presentation was significant in that Meyerhold, who was no novice at reevaluating classics, destroyed both the attitude of the author and the flavor of the period Ostrovsky was attempting to create, thus rebelling against the inviolability of the classical text.

Meyerhold approached the text not as the comedy of Ostrovsky's original, in which the "good" and "bad" characters are depicted quite humanely, but as a spiteful satiric attack on the Russia of the landowners. This was done by breaking up the acts into thirty-three episodes rearranged in such a way that one scene satirized a preceding scene. Often the result was a montage-like progression in which often two or even three episodes went on at the same time. The text was also shuffled into a new order with inserted pantomime interludes to provide effective contrasts of mood and tempo. In addition, each episode was preceded by a brief blackout, during which its title was projected onto a screen above the stage.[90] Later, Meyerhold himself compared the leisurely tempo of the play's progress to the *commedia dell' arte*'s stage tricks, Eisenstein's use of "collision montage" as well as to the episodic structure of Shakespeare's plays.

In his staging of *The Forest,* Meyerhold moved away from the constructivist sparsity of the stage and auditorium by covering the walls of the theater with canvas and filling the stage with furnishings other than stage properties. In fact, an assortment of real objects with no obvious relationship was assembled on stage, to be then turned into stage properties at will by the actors. Furthermore, the stage furniture or objects were not always used in their conventional manner: a table might be used as a bridge, a chair as a hill, and so on, in the manner of the Chinese opera conventions that later came to be adopted by Brecht, particularly in *Puntila and Matti, His Hired Man.*

Not only in terms of stage properties did Meyerhold exaggerate theatrical effects but also in the characterization of the actors who are introduced by means of leitmotifs as puppets or marionettes come to life. Thus, every principal character was costumed to reveal his essential nature in an exaggerated manner, with, in addition, each character wearing a bright wig of red, green, or gold to signal his presence. Typical gestures and actions became the sole property of each dramatic character. A single phrase in Ostrovsky's text saying that Neschaslivtsev had performed tricks was turned by Meyerhold into a demonstration of these tricks on stage. Since Aksiusha recalls that "day and night, since I was six, I have helped my mother work," Meyerhold has her performing tasks constantly when she is on stage. When the merchant declares "I shall give up everything," a flood of furs, shoes, and hats drops upon him from above.

These rapid montage-like episodes were performed against the background of a catwalk hanging in the air and offering the actors a great range of possible uses, and from which they descended by means of a turnstile. Lighting was used to spotlight individual scenes that were being played in quick succession or simultaneously. This manner of staging freed the actor from having to conform to an explicitly predetermined environment and allowed Meyerhold to circumvent the physical limitations of the stage and to arrange the episodes in whatever spatial or temporal sequence he desired.

Above all, montage freed Meyerhold's staging of *The Forest* from the linear and sequential cause-effect progression of naturalistic drama. This attitude was also to prevail in Meyerhold's staging of Gogol's *The Inspector General* (1926), wherein he made bold revisions, so rearranging the scenes and even incorporating a number of variants from Gogol's notebooks as well as from *Dead Souls*, that the whole period was satirized to show "everything bad in Russia." This was done by changing the action from the provincial backwoods of Russia to St. Petersburg. All the characters took on importance, and Anna Andreyevna was transformed from a silly, overripe lady of provincial society into a calculating coquette of the St. Petersburg demimonde.

As in the prerevolutionary staging of *Masquerade*, attention was focused on the luxuriousness of the decadent period. Wood was varnished, the furniture covered in silk and velvet, candelabras glittered, and the costumes were lavish and glittering. The iconic effects of the luxurious furniture, costumes, and lighting played a signifying role in themselves. In addition, Meyerhold introduced a number of characters—civil servants and officers —to exaggerate the numbers of the worldly society of the capital.

In a manner similar to his staging of Ostrovsky's *The Forest*, Meyerhold broke up Gogol's play into fifteen episodes arranged in a rhythmic composition on the Gogolian theme. Meyerhold had worked out the compositional effect of crowd scenes in his staging of *Masquerade*. In *The Inspector General* this effect was choreographed to the degree that even language and gesture were subordinated to the rhythm of the movement of the numerous characters who were on stage at all times as if in symphonic compositions. When a character made a speech the chorus repeated the remarks, focusing in this manner on the all-pervasiveness of the corrupt attitudes of the petty functionaries.

In order to achieve a faster pace and to expand the scope of meaning by making possible the close-up effects that he intended, Meyerhold staged all but four of the scenes of the play on platforms shot off on tracks on which the actors were already prepared in their positions as *tableaux vivants*. Instead of bio-mechanical antics, each actor was restricted to his particular pose or *mie:*

> We have tried in this production to approach realism by new means. We saw that we had to compose the show according to all the rules of orchestral composition, that the "score" of each role would have to have resonance by itself, that we had to fit it into the mass of instrument-roles, weave the instruments into a very complicated orchestration, mark in this complicated structure the path of leitmotifs, and make it all resound together like an orchestra: the actor and the light and movement and even the properties that are shown on stage.[91]

To contrast the varied tempi of the scenes, Meyerhold changed the mode of arranging the scenes by a device he called *perekluchenie* (sudden changeover). At the party for the mayor's daughter, for example, the bright lights and lively movements suddenly yield to crowding and the flickering of candles as the guests put their heads together, transformed into life-sized mannequins frozen in horrified poses. Emmanuel Kaplan describes the effect:

> Then suddenly, as though on a word of command, at a stroke of the conductor's baton, everyone stirs in agitation, pipes jump from lips, fists clench, heads swivel. The last syllable of "revizor" seems to tweak everybody. Now the word is hissed in a whisper: the whole word by some, just the consonants by others, and somewhere even a softly rolled "r." The word "revizor" is divided musically into every conceivable intonation. The ensemble of suddenly startled officials blows up and dies away like a squall. Everyone freezes and falls silent: the guilty conscience rises in alarm, then hides its poisonous head again, like a serpent lying motionless and saving its deadly venom.[92]

The whole production of *The Inspector General* contained something grotesque and Hoffmannesque. James Symons points out that the emerging character of the dramas had little to do with socialist realism, and it is not surprising that critics charged Meyerhold with a deviation from clear purposeful didacticism to the ambiguity of the grotesque, the theater of masks, and Gogol's world of phantoms.[93] His famous staging of the concluding episode seems to bear out the charges of the critics, as Gorchakov describes it, the characters froze in their poses as they came out on the moving platforms:

> They paused for a long time under the spotlights and suddenly began to move and to speak. The actors seemed like mechanical figures, while the motors of the revolving platforms hummed. . . . In the concluding episode they froze in rigid, distorted poses. The lights went out for a few seconds, and when they came on again the audience saw not actors but mannequins in the same ridiculous poses, mannequins whose costumes had been removed.[94]

From these descriptions of the production of *The Inspector General* and from study of Meyerhold's prerevolutionary productions, it becomes clear why Meyerhold's theater fell into disfavor. Instead of stressing a "positive" or "critical" outlook in his productions, Meyerhold developed the theatrical characterizations of his prerevolutionary period, characterizations that relied on the belief that the grotesque and the theater of masks reflect a society more closely than does the "slice of life" realism of the naturalistic theater. As a result, his production of *The Inspector General*, although in terms of theatrical aesthetics acknowledged as most successful, signaled the climax of Meyerhold's career.

After the pointed examination of old regime corruption in *The Forest* and *The Inspector General*, examinations that could also be extended as a mirroring device for certain elements of the population during the NEP period, Meyerhold collaborated with Mayakovsky in the staging of *The Bedbug* (1929) and *The Bathhouse* (1930). In both plays, Mayakovsky exposes the petit-bourgeois vulgarity prevalent in the proletarian paradise during the free enterprise period of NEP, a period during which revolutionaries and utopian idealists were supplanted by businessmen, factory managers, and accountants. Marc Slonim writes:

> The Communist bureaucrat made his appearance next to the Communist idealist—and usurped a constantly increasing sphere. Although the crack-unit morality and military bearing (including Stalin's uniform) remained firmly entrenched in the Party mores as the heritage of the civil war, the Bolshevik leaders were becoming more used to the attitudes of cautious administrators confronted with tremendous practical problems. The Party had to train a ruling class, and it gradually took on the strangely mixed character of a business concern and an educational institution, that also was in charge of working out an infallible credo.[95]

This then is the context for the Meyerhold/Mayakovsky collaboration on *The Bedbud* and *The Bathhouse*. By 1930, Mayakovsky had lost his revolutionary optimism. He no longer had any illusions about the drawbacks of the regime he was serving and in these satirical plays denounced the red tape and triviality that were undermining the heroic dreams of the Revolution. The juxtaposition of the bourgeois and Communist worlds, suggested in an abstract manner in *Mystery-Bouffe*, is made concrete in the staging of *The Bedbug*. Artistic and aesthetic effects are also clearly subordinated to the desire to drive home the satirical point of the play: that the Revolution is in danger of losing its vitality and idealism to the lazy self-indulgence of uninspired citizens, on the one hand, and a sterile, futuristic ideology, on the other.

The play is divided into two parts, with sets for the first part designed by a team of newspaper cartoonists and costumes and properties bought over the counter to demonstrate the tackiness of the prevalent culture. The set for the second part was designed by Alexander Rodchenko, whose 1929 vision of the Communist future was so lifelessly hygienic and sterile "that the spectator was hard put to decide where the parody really stopped."[96] Prisypkin's all-too-human pleas as the house lights go on before the end, revealing the audience to him, project him as a sympathetically human character as he sits confined to his cage in the dreary sanitized world of the future.

The contrast of the heaped piles of trifles on stage and the individualized characterization of dramatic characters in the first part to the white, operating-room sterility of both set and characterization in the second confused the critics, some seeing the future as an inspired vision of advanced technology, others a lifeless abstraction, others still suspecting the characterization as a parody of the achievements of socialism.[97]

The Bedbug was mounted with musical accompaniment (a hallmark of Meyerhold's style), this time with music especially commissioned from Dmitri Shostakovich to underline the cries of the vendors in the first scene as they went down the aisles crying their wares amidst the audience. However, as Marjorie Hoover points out, "such merging with the audience from the start created potential sympathy with Prisypkin's final appeal for human imperfection"[98] and provoked a revulsion towards the stainless proletarian future.

The Bathhouse was an even more strident attack on Stalin's party bureaucracy, for in Mayakovsky's words it was intended to "wash—simply wipe out—the bureaucrats." As in *The Bedbug*, the play is constructed on the contrast of two societies. An inventor devises a machine for launching the present generation ahead of its time into the Soviet future, but his machine is rejected because of "its failure to come within the scope of the plan for next quarter." Ironically, the Future Age of Communism is entirely different from the present depicted in *The Bedbug*. It is a time of perfection; all present difficulties have been overcome. An emissary from the future, the Phosphorescent Woman, invites as passengers with her on her return to the Future Age only those individuals who have contributed to their society. This eliminates the bureaucrat Pobedonosikov and his underlings, with the machine serving as a cleansing bath allowing only the workers and the inventor to accompanying the Phosphorescent Woman as they disappear in a flash of blue light to the accompaniment of "The March of Time."

As in the 1921 production of *Mystery-Bouffe*, the "clean" in *The Bathhouse* are portrayed as caricatured grotesques, the "unclean" as robot-like komsomols in blue overalls whose vigorous and rhythmic movements recall the constructivist stagings of *The Magnanimous Cuckold* and *The Death of Tarelkin*. The set for *The Bathhouse*, created by Sergei Vakhtangov, featured towering scaffolds connected by a series of steps and platforms reminiscent of the early constructivist stage designs of Popova and Stepanova. A huge screen in the form of venetian blind slats used in railway stations and airport terminals, with each slat bearing a political slogan, was lowered from the flies. In the auditorium, slogans by Mayakovsky proclaimed the policies of the theatrical left and poked fun at censors, bureaucrats, critics, and the Moscow Art Theater. These slogans blasted "the drivelling psychology" of the Moscow Art Theater and called the theater to mass action "to shake individuals out of priests' robes." "The thundering slogans," writes Rudnitsky, "were reminiscent of the terminology and emotion of the forever departed days of the Theatrical October."[99] All in all, the production evoked a nostalgic return on the part of Meyerhold and Mayakovsky to the bare stage and the constructivist platforms, with the actors performing as if part of a gymnastic circus.

Theatrical fireworks were not enough to carry the day for the run of *The Bathhouse*. The production was terminated after a week, dubbed subversive by the Party press, and disappeared from the Soviet stage for a period of thirty years, making a comeback only after the death of Stalin. Thhe proletarian writers association (RAPP) judged Mayakovsky to be out of step with the times. His romantic notions about the Revolution were deemed too fantastic and suspect from the point of view of the "good old realism patronized by Lenin." Thus, isolated, unhappy in love, denounced by his fellow writers, Mayakovsky at the age of thirty-six shot himself a few months after the closing of *The Bathhouse*. The collaboration between Meyerhold and Mayakovsky had been so close "that to read Mayakovsky today is to sense the true atmosphere of Meyerhold's theater."[100]

A few months after the closing of *The Bathhouse*, Meyerhold was given permission to take his company on a tour abroad. In the meantime his theater, the old Sohn, was closed for renovation. Originally Meyerhold was allocated money only for essential repairs, however, he insisted on the demolition of the old building, with a new theater to be built in its place according to his specifications. Endless delays left Meyerhold without a theater, compelled to spend the final years of his brilliant career in a temporary theater that seriously inhibited the selection of plays. This factor, combined with the demands from the theatrical arm of RAPP for a repertory that reflected the new social ideals of society, left Meyerhold powerless and was responsible for the general stagnation of his company.

Meyerhold, like Mayakovsky, was a revolutionary, but he did not understand socialism. Proletarian rule, he thought, meant proletarian life, which in the theater was to be entertainment that had the dynamic qualities of the working class, the new technological era, and new expectations. Ironically, showing how out of step Meyerhold was with the times, one of his last presentations at the temporary theater was Dumas's *The Lady of the Camellias* (1934), a production which Meyerhold justified by saying: "I no longer desire ascetic self-denial of my heroes, my settings and my costumes. I wish my spectator joy; I want him to possess the world of beauty which was usurped by the ruling classes."[101]

When the full implications of the First All-Union Congress of Soviet Writers were becoming clear and the Party's campaign against "formalism" took an ominous turn, when other directors took the first available opportunity to confess their past aberrations and affirmed their faith in socialist realism, Meyerhold, in March 1936, spoke out for his rights and the right of all artists to experiment. In the next number of *Soviet Theater*, the organ of the All-Union Committee for Art Affairs, an editorial accused Meyerhold of having "always opposed his method not only to the naturalistic theater but to the realistic theater as well."[102] In addition, he was charged with a continued loyalty to symbolist and aesthetic practices and also for not using Soviet plays in his repertoire. His one attempt at producing a Soviet play, *Natasha*, about the orphan of parents murdered by the Whites who shakes off the oppression of a kulak employer to become a heroine on a collective farm, ended in results that were unworthy and embarrassing.

Continued open discussions on the future of Meyerhold's theater in *Pravda* reflected the official attitude:

> On the occasion of the twentieth anniversary of the Great Socialist Revolution only one out of the seven-hundred professional theatres was without a special production to commemorate the October Revolution and without a Soviet repertoire. That theatre was Meyerhold's Theatre. . . .

> Almost his entire theatrical career before the October Revolution amounted to a struggle against the realistic theatre on behalf of the stylized, mystical, formalist theatre of the aesthetes, that is the theatre which shunned real life. . . .

> It has become absolutely clear that Meyerhold cannot and apparently will not comprehend Soviet reality or depict the problems which concern every Soviet citizen. . . .[103]

Upon this, his theater was officially closed. When the All-Union Conference of Stage-Directors opened in Moscow in June 1939, Meyerhold was listed as the fourth speaker. Official transcripts of the conference, however, do not list him as speaker, nor even as present. Nor do the records show any traces that Meyerhold committed the anticipated act of contrition:

> For my own conscience I consider what is now taking place in our theaters dreadful and pitiful. And I do not know what it is, such as—anti-formalism, or realism, or naturalism or yet any other "ism." But I know that this is without any show of talent and poor and this miserable and pitiful something, that pretends to the title of the theater of socialist realism has nothing in common with art. . . . Here there were the best theaters of the world—here now reigns, by your grace, dismal and orderly arithmetical means, shocking and appalling in its own mediocrity. Is this your aspiration? If yes, oh, then you have done a frightful business. By departing from formalism you have destroyed art.[104]

Immediately after the conference, Meyerhold was arrested and is believed to have been shot in a Moscow prison on 2 February 1940.

In reviewing Meyerhold's theatrical career, it is interesting to note to what extent his theoretical position parallels that of the discussions of the formalists and their theoretical concern with the devices whereby literary works attain their effect of defamiliarization. The work of futurist poets, like Mayakovsky, induced the formalists to go beyond Shklovsky's concept of the "unmotivated" aesthetic device to the position that formal elements of defamiliarization may promote political awareness by undermining habituated modes of perception. This was, perforce, an adjustment on the part of the formalists to the new political climate, as reflected in these observations by Osip Brik:

> Thus art was still "a device"; what had changed from the original Formalist interpretation was the application of the device. The emphasis was shifted from the aesthetic function of the device to its use in the service of a "social demand." All the manifestations of the device, including the extreme case of "the device laid bare". . . were now considered in the light of their potential social utility: "not an aesthetic end in itself," but a laboratory for the best possible expression of the facts of the present day.[105]

As a result of this shift in attitude, the debate on aesthetics focused on the question of aesthetic autonomy versus sociohistorical influences. In spite of art's apparent concreteness, it was recognized, and later developed by the Prague Linguistic Circle, that an aesthetic object is subject to cultural codes which are not things in themselves but processes that are constantly rearticulated in relation to one another. In this debate on the norms and value that inhere in aesthetic objects, a fundamental shift also occurred towards the recognition of the reader or spectator as part of the process. The process of perception was found not to reside exclusively in the text, as the formalists and later New Critics proclaimed, but rather between texts and readers, whose acts of decoding are certainly conditioned by the text itself, but also draw on the whole bundle of ideological relationships which bear upon the production and reproduction of texts. In his stagings of the postrevolutionary period, Meyerhold not only understood this aspect of the process of the aesthetic transformation in the theater but also used it as a basic tenet of his theatricality.

Above all, Meyerhold sought to use the theater as a means of inducing a new perception of reality by revolutionizing the forms through which it is customarily perceived. As such, Meyerhold did not attempt to force a debate that was political in nature with the new order, but rather aimed at producing a shock effect that would reflect the contradictions within that society. The last thing that Meyerhold wanted to do was to conjure reality away by means of an excess of revolutionary optimism reflected in the creation of positive heroes demanded by the ideology of the day. For that reason, Meyerhold's period of intense creativity in the Soviet theater was relatively brief, petering out in adjustments made to conform to the new ideology, culminating ultimately in a trial that questioned Meyerhold's attitude toward the goals of the new society and branding him a traitor for holding the theater more dear than political ideology.

3

Brecht: The Aesthetics of Reception

In order to make an art object the subject of aesthetic pleasure, writes Viktor Shklovsky, "one must pry it loose of the facts of life" the way Ivan the Terrible "used to 'shake up' his henchmen."[1] The aesthetic theory developed by Shklovsky and the Russian formalists, according to which the "automatism of perception" is to be dealt with by a method of "defamiliarization," a "forcing us to notice," had an incalculable effect on the theory of drama as presented by Bertolt Brecht. Rather than promote emotional and aesthetic identification this attitude allows for the recognition of historical processes and makes possible both "the curious role distance of the beholder and the playful identification, with what he ought or would like to be"[2] and provides an exemplary frame of reference in which the spectator has an opportunity to adopt roles not only in "naive imitation but also in freely elected emulation."[3]

To assist the spectator or reader in "shaking up" his perception, it is necessary, according to Shklovsky (and Brecht), to tear the aesthetic object out of the context of habitual perception, to "deautomatize" the seeing of it, "to turn it like a log in a fire."[4] In this manner the object is converted into something "palpable," something "capable of becoming the material of art,"[5] The habitual is "made strange" and presented as if it were being seen for the first time. Artful obstacles between the perceiving subject and the perceived object are interposed to break the perceiver's automatic and habitual associations, in this manner forcing the spectator to "see" things instead of merely "recognizing" them. The spectator is thus "struck by the novelty resulting from placing the object in a new ambiance," of seeing it in "new dress."[6]

The strategy of defamiliarizing perception focuses on the reader or spectator as the center of activity and on making explicit the implicit knowledge that the reader has of the codes that make up texts by focusing attention on a description of the codes and conventions responsible for producing meaning.

Ultimately, both Brecht and the formalists assume that each perceiver inherently has the theoretical and aesthetic understanding to be able to reflect on the artistic devices in the text. Another problem that emerges, particularly in reference to Brecht, has to do with the ideal perceiver, who upon being presented the problem, logically should arrive at a Marxist interpretation. Brecht himself said that for him Marx was the ideal spectator, who, given the ambiguity of the text, could produce the only possible interpretation. Yet, Brecht himself carried defamiliarization to such lengths that ultimately each spectator had to create his own text—in the case of *Mother Courage*, for example, possibly pitying the mother who loses everything in the war rather than condemning her for trying to live off profits from war. It is precisely the ambiguity in Brecht's plays, an ambiguity that made a myriad of interpretations possible due to the deautomatization of the aesthetic device, that created a conflict between Brecht's aesthetics and the needs of promulgating the ideology of Stalinism. Brecht and the formalists believed in the deautomatization of the artistic device, making each text open to new interpretations, a freedom that was contrary to Soviet aesthetics, which demanded the manipulation of the device in order to produce only one possible interpretation.

In the study of Brecht's aesthetics of reception, that which he calls the *Verfremdungseffekt* was not an original observation on the relationship between texts and perceivers. Brecht's ideas penetrated Western theater and literature before the writings of the Russian formalist critics were translated systematically. As a result, Brecht is often credited with creating attitudes and theories that were very much the subject of discussions among the Russian formalists and which were later expanded to include aesthetic function, norm, and values as social facts by the Prague Linguistic Circle.

Because Brecht knew how to borrow wisely and selectively, what seems to be original in Brecht is often an adaptation of someone else's methods. For example, his famous *V-effekt* had already been part of the methods of the Russian revolutionary theater of Meyerhold. Stage constructions, the use of film projections, the cutting up of dramatic texts into short segments similar to those used by Eisenstein in his films, the use of placards, posters, circuslike effects, the attention to gestic acting, the elimination of the psychological motivation of characters, the use of bright lights, and interrupted action had all been part of theatrical practice in the incredibly dynamic period in the Soviet Union at the time of the Revolution.

As avatars in the revolution in the arts in the Soviet Union, the Russian directors worked closely with critics, writers, composers, and artists to produce an aesthetics which would take into account a new way of looking at the world, both aesthetically and socially. Like the circle surrounding Brecht, the Russian formalists and members of the avant-garde socialized together, worked together, and often lived together.

Shklovsky in his essay on Pushkin and Sterne calls attention to the shifts in perception as part of historical processes which "decree that each author is viewed by us not in isolation but against the backdrop of our own traditions."[7] As an example, Shklovsky calls attention to Tairov's Kamerny Theater's production of *Romeo and Juliet* to illustrate the "seeing" of Shakespeare anew:

> What is the scene he [Friar Laurence] acts out by Juliet's corpse if not a harlequinade? And is not the scene with musicians which Shakespeare mounted directly after the scene in which Paris and Juliet's relatives lament her death, also a harlequinade? . . . What then is *Romeo and Juliet* as the modern theater renders it? Let us not mince words. . . . It is a sketch. Yes, a tragi-erotic sketch.[8]

From this, one can see that Tairov's theatrical practice was one of the models for Shklovsky's famous *ostranenie,* or the "making strange" effect. Nor was the work that was done in the Soviet Union at that time totally confined to its borders. Free intellectual interchange was fostered by poetry readings given in Berlin by Mayakovsky in 1925, 1927, and 1928, by the Meyerhold theatrical group's production of Tretyakov's *Roar China* in 1930, by Tretyakov's frequent visits to Berlin, by Asja Lacis's frequent visits to Russia and her reports of the theatrical scene there, and by the German translation of Tairov's *Notes of a Director.* And, much as Meyerhold had been influenced by Georg Fuchs's writings on the theater of the future and the Japanese theater, so too was Brecht. Although Brecht himself did not use the term *ostranenie* or his version of it, the *Verfremdungseffekt,* until after his visit to the Soviet Union in 1935, the attitude of "making strange," of breaking conventional perceptions of the world, hung in the air in the 1920s. This can be seen in the highly unnaturalistic plays of the German expressionists with whom Brecht shared a similar heritage in Frank Wedekind, the first stagings of Georg Büchner's *Woyzeck,* the first German staging of Pirandello's *Six Characters in Search of an Author,* as well as the political concerns of Georg Kaiser and Ernst Toller, the political cartoons of Georg Grosz, Reinhardt's theater for a mass audience, and Piscator's staging of *The Good Soldier Schweik* in his agit-prop theater.[9]

Since there was so much interaction of the Berlin intellectual scene with that of the Soviet Union, and since there was simultaneously a social ferment in the works in Berlin as well, it would be foolish to treat Brecht as a sort of isolated prophet of the theater. Indeed, it is well known that many of his plays were the result of work with collaborators like Elizabeth Hauptmann, Hans Eisler, and Caspar Neher.

This is not to say that in his synthesis of theatrical practice Brecht was not a genius, but it is to say that his ideas were already common knowledge in the Soviet theater prior to his own writings on the epic theater, gestic acting, and his ideas on a theater for pleasure and instruction. What Brecht accomplished was to synthesize the conventionalization of theatrical signs into a theory of aesthetic reception in the theater that took into account the spectator's aesthetic response and intellectual engagement. It is in his attention to the spectator and to the process of aesthetic reception that Brecht goes beyond the Russian formalists. Although Brecht's estrangement devices share the constructivists's scientific approach "to analytically decompose, aggressively rearrange, and then restructure the object world," the discontinuity and interrupted quality in his plays is intended to encourage an attitude of rational intervention by the spectator to reassemble the "real mechanisms of society," rather than to call attention to theatricality for its own sake.[10]

The essence of theater lies in the act of presentation. We have seen in our study of Meyerhold to what extent the concept of "making strange," so central to the Russian formalists' study of literary traditions, also contributed to the development of a new attitude in the theatrical arts during the immediate pre- and postrevolutionary periods. Meyerhold's use of stage constructivism, bio-mechanics, and interrupted action served to defamiliarize the classics he often presented, such as Gogol's *The Inspector General*, Ostrovsky's *The Forest*, or Dumas's *The Lady of the Camellias*, by deforming their naturalistic content through the introduction of stylization which, by calling attention to the form or structure of the presentation, placed the spectator in a new relationship to the work. In this, Meyerhold showed his commitment to Shklovsky's view that "the study of literary tradition, the formal study of art, will be utterly senseless if it does not enable us to see the work anew."[11]

It is doubtful whether the audiences in those early proletarian days were aware of the aesthetic revolution which they were witnessing, but in his productions of *The Magnanimous Cuckold*, *The Death of Tarelkin*, or *The Inspector General*, Meyerhold was laying the foundations for a theater that was as revolutionary in form as in content. Brecht was his natural descendant. Brecht took Meyerhold's ideas on the deautomatization of aesthetic perception, and borrowed from Meyerhold's antinaturalistic conventions to formalize an organum for the theater which focused on involving the spectator both ideologically and aesthetically in his plays. The misunderstanding about the *V-effekt*, which has generally been translated as "alienation," is that it opposes any kind of involvement on the part of the audience. However, in the understanding the Russian formalists have ascribed to *ostranenie* as breaking through the spectator's illusions in order to "shed new light on" the object being viewed, the process paradoxically involves a distancing in order that the spectator may come closer to the object. As John Willett points out, nothing illustrates Brecht's concept of alienation more clearly than some of his everyday examples: "To see one's mother as a man's wife one needs an A-effect; this provided, for instance, when one acquires a stepfather."[12] As Eugene Lunn points out, Brecht's theatrical practices "aimed to assault his audience's passive and fatalistic inertia, its adjustment to the 'course of things,'"[13] in order to encourage an active intervention in the historical process.

The aim of the formalist method was to "shake up" perceptions, to tear them out of the context of habitual association. Ordinary aesthetic perceptions, as evoked in the presentations of the Moscow Art Theater, "glided" over the spectator "like a carpenter's plane over a piece of wood"[14] once it has been planed smooth. Shklovsky, in referring to Stanislavsky's technique of acting, points out that in the Moscow Art Theater actors were able to speak their parts "with feeling," yet were unable to relate them in their own words: "They [their words] have been 'planed smooth.' The habitual words interweave to form habitual sentences, which in turn form habitual paragraphs, and all these roll along inexorably like a bulldozer down the hill."[15]

To prevent habitual perception, Brecht introduced effects in his stagings that had the capacity to "jolt" the spectator, forcing him to "suddenly realize" his own condition,[16] concentrating specifically on the manner in which the spectator's norms and values were to be violated.[17] To accomplish deautomatized perception, identification with characters is pushed aside to allow the spectator to come to his own conclusions. The evidence is presented; the spectator makes certain choices. In Brecht, this evidence is presented from a variety of perspectives in a series of episodes organized to create what Shklovsky calls a "staircaselike" construction, by means of which the object of attention is "bifurcated through the medium of reflections and juxtapositions."[18] As Jurij Lotman puts it in his discussion of Eisenstein: "Narration can result from the joining of a series of shots showing different objects, or a series in which one object alters modalities."[19] According to Brecht, the very same sort of complicated montage with which the film maker creates his text also takes place on stage when scenes are juxtaposed to other scenes. Thus, rather than the linear development found in naturalistic drama, Brecht proposes that each scene stand for itself, the unity emerging from montage rather than from the linear development of plot.

The function of the *V-effekt* is to prevent emotional involvement with the characters on stage. In *Mother Courage*, for example, part of the *V-effekt* is Paul Dessau's music. To prevent the music being subsumed directly as part of the action, Brecht created signs which were lowered whenever a song was to be introduced:

> These consisted of a trumpet, a drum, a flag and an electric globe that lit up: a light and delicate thing, pleasant to look at, even if scene nine found it shot to pieces. Some people thought it a pure frivolity, an unrealistic element. But one ought not to disapprove too much of frivolity in the theater so long as it is kept within bounds. Nor on the other hand was it purely unrealistic, in that it lifted the music above the reality of the action; it served us as a visible sign of the shift to another artistic level—that of music—and gave the right impression of musical insertions instead of leading people to think quite wrongly that the songs sprang from the acting. Those who take exception to this are quite simply against anything intermittent, inorganic, pieced-together, and this is primarily because they are against any breaking of the illusion.[20]

In his theory of the Epic Theater, Brecht foregrounded certain signs to break illusion and to create a frame of reference that was other than that with which the spectator was familiar. To this end, Brecht was well aware of the signifying means used in the classical Chinese theater, which enabled the Chinese actor to portray in a comprehensible manner the most varied actions without having to recreate reality on the stage:

> Above all, the Chinese artist never acts as if there were a fourth wall besides the three surrounding him. He expresses his awareness of being watched. This immediately removes one of the European stage's characteristic illusions. The audience can no longer have the illusion of being the unseen spectator at an event which is really taking place. A whole elaborate European stage technique, which helps to conceal the fact that the scenes are so arranged that the audience can view them in the easiest way, is thereby made unnecessary. The actors openly choose those positions which will best show them off to the audience, just as if they were acrobats.[21]

As demonstrated by his attempts to make theatrical signs visible, Brecht might have agreed with Jiří Veltruský's observation that "the more acting resorts to natural delivery, gestures, etc., the more the distinction between the sign and what it stands for is blurred and can be overlooked by the audience."[22] In his Epic Theater, Brecht attempted to create a limited textual set of signs that could, in presentation, convey a broad range of meanings, and for that reason in his theory of the *Verfremdungseffekt* he absorbed many of the distancing effects of the Chinese theater. The intent of the Brechtian estrangement effect was, as Roland Barthes suggests, to demonstrate that "revolutionary art must admit the arbitrariness of signs, must allow a certain 'formalism' in that it must treat form according to the proper method, which is a semiological method."[23] According to Barthes, it is Brecht himself who is the semiologist who demonstrates a theory of signs in the use of distancing effects in his dramas: "What Brechtian drama as a whole postulates is that today at least drama has not to express the real so much as to signify it. It is therefore necessary that there be a certain distance between the signifier and the signified."[24]

The Brechtian *Verfremdungseffekt* is ideological in nature, and its purpose is, as Brecht insisted over and over, to make the spectator aware that the objects and institutions he thought to be natural were really only historical, and as a result of change, "they themselves henceforth become in their turn changeable."[25] Brecht writes that this technique allows

> the theatre to make use in its representations of the new social scientific method known as dialectical materialism. In order to unearth society's laws of motion this method treats social situations as processes, and traces out all their inconsistencies. It regards nothing as existing except in so far as it changes, in other words is in disharmony with itself. This also goes for those human feelings, opinions, and attitudes through which at any time the form of men's life together finds its expression.[26]

An examination of a play by Brecht, as also of any theatrical form which relies on a strong codified system of signs, takes into account that the spectator is aware of both the text proper of the actual performance as well as of the subtext or of the extratextual information that the perceiver is expected to possess before approaching the text.

According to Brecht, two choices are available to the director and actor in theatrical presentations. One is to play up for all it is worth the charm or "magic" of the theater, to encourage the "willing suspension of disbelief." The other is to present through selected conventionalized signs the visible world of the presentation and to call attention to the forms that are characteristic to theatrical play. While the one attitude presupposes that no audience exists, or that if it exists it is peeping through a keyhole, the other attitude demands the active participation of the audience as a living force in the dynamics of theatrical communication. When theatrical conventions are alienated, or made strange, rather than habituated or automatic, the spectator is encouraged to take note of the conventions or codes emerging from the presentation. This was central to the Russian formalist principle and ultimately became one of the aims of Brecht's *V-effekt*, which in his own definition is a "way of drawing one's own or someone else's attention to a thing" or in "turning the object of which one is to be made aware, to which one's attention is to be drawn, from something ordinary, familiar, immediately accessible into something peculiar, striking and unexpected."[27]

Through the *Verfremdungseffekt*, an image from one semantic plane is suddenly placed in a new semantic plane. The spectator, as a result, is struck by the novelty resulting "from placing the object in a new ambience."[28] As Shklovsky explains, "this is one way of converting an object into something palpable, something capable of becoming the material of art."[29] The montage-like juxtapositioning of images in highly interesting ways motivates the spectator to see the relationships emerging between the images in a new way, since "here everything, as always in art, is motivation of the artifice."[30]

When actors in blue denim in Meyerhold's staging of *The Magnanimous Cuckold* appeared on stage without benefit of footlights or curtain in a theater in which propaganda posters and slogans were plastered on the walls of the auditorium, it was clear that instead of focusing on the traditional duality of content and form Meyerhold was focusing on the opposition of material to artistic devices as a means of heightening what at that time perhaps needed no heightening. In addition, the play was interrupted from time to time by announcements of news about the civil war. As Norris Houghten points out, Meyerhold "took the drama of the hour men were living in and, heated through by the fire of his genius, turned back to the people their own experiences etched in sharper and more vivid strokes. At such moments life and the theater were one; the spectator was the actor—it was his own drama."[31]

The theatrical foregrounding of the events following the Russian Revolution, as "framed" by Meyerhold, served, in Brecht's words, "to mark it off from the rest of the text."[32] This foregrounding in Meyerhold's stagings amounted to an explicit pointing to the presentation as an event in progress in which the actor stands aside in order to comment upon what is happening, through a range of devices such as freezes, slow-motion effects, and unexpected changes in tempo.

In our examination of Meyerhold's staging we saw how the scenic devices of the nonrepresentational stage, with its ladders and scaffolds, its ramps and steps and slides, paralleled attention to the bio-mechanical movements of the actors as a means of depicting a mechanical era in scenic form. By eliminating psychologically motivated action on stage, Meyerhold attempted to portray action which was entirely rational and physiological: "When a person pricks his finger or sits on a tack, he jumps. He does not do this dictated by his emotions. It is a nervous reaction and that only. A tiger springs not in answer to its emotions but because it instinctively knows that its spring will bring it at once to its prey."[33]

The aim of bio-mechanics was the reduction of man to the physiological reflexes studied by Pavlov. Since this style of acting is not aimed at suggesting the individual traits of the character but rather at reinforcing the political lesson of the play, Meyerhold aimed at a socialization of the audience to a new ideology and a new technology of life. He did this by dressing his actors in workers' blue overalls, thereby blurring individual differences. To this end, the gestures of bio-mechanics were calculated with mathematical exactitude to represent human reactions.

Although both Meyerhold and Brecht were subject to similar influences in their study of gestic acting in the Chinese and Japanese theater, Brecht, unlike Meyerhold, wanted to make the actor aware of the "discussible" quality of his gestures, not through physical expression but through intellectual distancing. Building upon Denis Diderot's radical materialism, Brecht asked of the actor "that his tears flow from the brain" thereby linking aesthetic experience with the "intellectually cognitive and politically useful function of art."[34] In this respect he takes Meyerhold's study a step further, beyond the purely theatrical to the politically dialectical, a position that was ultimately to call his methodology into question, since, according to Georg Lukacs, this attitude was "tantamount to viewing the social content apart from its dialectical relationship with its human substratum":[35] "Since these contents [i.e., the contents of the proletarian Revolution], despite a praiseworthy attempt to make them concrete, remain abstract, that is to say immediate surface phenomena, and since they are not the objective motive forces of the Revolution, their revolutionary spirit also remains an abstract sermon, a 'tendency.'"[36]

The debate between Brecht and Lukacs was to continue, with Brecht insisting that it was not the business of the state to restrict realistic writing by imposing limits on its formal expression. He particularly defended the role distance of the actor, which was to surface in a certain manner of saying the text and was inherently part of the gestic quality of the text, a means of provoking a critical attitude of the utterer toward what he is reporting. To assist the dialogic communication between the actor and his part, Brecht used other *V-effekts*, branded as "formalism" by Lukacs and others, as a means of heightening the gestic quality of the text. One of his favorite *V-effekts* was the use of songs, which, according to Brecht, were highly gestic. Their semantic value determined how the message was to be received, not through the emotional pulling in of the spectator but through the presentation of another point of view, a commentary on the action at hand. Above all, the language of the text itself had to contain a gestic quality:

> A language is gestural if it is based on the *Gestus*: if it indicates what precise attitudes are adopted by the man talking toward other men. The sentence: "pluck the eye that offends thee out" is from the gestural point of view less rich than the sentence: "if thine eye offend thee, pluck it out." In the latter, the eye is shown first, then comes the first part of the sentence which contains manifestly the *Gestus* of the conjecture; finally comes the second part, as a surprise-attack, a liberating device.[37]

In his attention to the gestic quality in the presentation of plays, Brecht echoes some of Meyerhold's ideas. Brecht explains that it is essential to establish the social gest of the play, meaning by social an "undertaking between men." Thus, the social gest is "the gest relevant to society, the gest that allows conclusions to be drawn about the circumstances."[38] Meyerhold's approach was rather similar in that he attempted to extract a *jeu de théâtre* from a play, as for example in his production of Chekhov's three one-act plays, collectively titled *33 Swoons*, where the repeated bouts of the neurasthenia of the characters culminating in fainting spells become the central *gestus* of the play.[39]

It is in the difference in vocabulary between Meyerhold's use of *jeu de théâtre* and Brecht's *gestus* that one can see Brecht departing from the purely aesthetic definition that Meyerhold gives to *jeu de théâtre* as an accompanying effect to a new concept of the theater as an arena for learning, an attitude that uses the *mise-en-scène* to place the spectator in the role of interpreter not only of the stage idiolect but also of social and ideological codes. Although Meyerhold shared the avant-garde's sense of tension between art and politics, his vision of the Revolution was primarily artistic rather than political. If Meyerhold's theatrical productions in the 1920s became ostensibly more political, it was because the Revolution gave him the chance to legitimatize the innovations in the theater to which he aspired, and, through the use of Communist terminology, he could make the two seem one. Notwithstanding the use of political posters, workers' choruses dressed in blue denim, and antibourgeois interpretations of the classics, the celebration of a new society on stage was too far removed from proletarian reality. What the masses needed was not a celebration of Soviet life on stage, but a turning to more distant goals in which proletarian ideals would be realized. But first the struggle for those ideals had to be encouraged, a positive attitude had to be fostered. Theater had to become ideological, not theatrical. In this theater Meyerhold had no place; Brecht, on the other hand, took this role upon himself quite willingly, up to a point. Much like Meyerhold, he spouted the appropriate rhetoric, but his plays themselves deny that ideology comes before aesthetics.

The relation between social concerns and the development of aesthetic norms is, as we determined from our previous study of Meyerhold, undeniable. This relationship of a simultaneous effort in aesthetics and social change was initially quite unrestricted. But later in the Russian social transformation, the attempt to discover an aesthetic equivalent to the classless society became a matter of reducing all tastes to the average level. Symptoms were a compromised classicism in architecture and socialist realism in literature in the form of a return to the positive heroes of Dobrolyubov and Chernishevsky. As a result, the attempts of Meyerhold to project aesthetic canons at the highest level were replaced by the promotion of universal acceptance of the average, and only critical realism allowed aesthetics to refer to a universal level "in the sense of the archaization of the aesthetic norm to the lowest plane."[40]

The *Proletkult* ideology encouraged attention to positive heroes and values as they supposedly represented the masses, and Lukacs, who promoted the positive heroes of the nineteenth century, provided historical justification for the new ideology. Brecht, while aspiring to an elaboration of an aesthetics at the highest level, somehow managed to get himself caught up betwixt and between. Not only was this a question of aesthetic norms being lowered, but also represented a change in aesthetic function. Socialist realism in the arts requires, first and foremost, the synthetic depiction and propagation of a new social order. "The common denominator of these varied and sometimes partially inimical tendencies," explains Jan Mukařovský, "is the polemic versus 'artistry' which was so much emphasized in the recent past, i.e., a reaction to the realization of absolute supremacy of the aesthetic function in art—a reaction which is expressed by the current tendency of art to approach the realm of extra-aesthetic phenomena."[41]

The reign of the aesthetic function is not absolute in any of the arts. One can see, even in the productions of Meyerhold or the later Brecht, that drama oscillates between art and ideology, or even propaganda, as part of the communicative function of theater, which by its nature draws on extra-aesthetic codes. In this realm one can see that while Brecht's *Verfremdungseffekt* does indeed draw on the Russian formalists' precept of foregrounding aesthetic functions as a means of evoking a new way of seeing, pure formalism discounts the possibility of viewing ideological content as a legitimate concern of critical analysis.

However, even this conception was modified by the formalists in light of the theoretical demands placed on formalism by the futurists. There is no doubt that the formalists responded to these demands and reexamined the relevance of historical and ideological considerations to the study of literature. In defense of formalism, Jakobson, albeit retrospectively, writes:

> Neither Tynyanov, nor Mukařovský, nor Shklovsky, nor I have preached that art is sufficient unto itself; on the contrary, we show that art is a part of the social edifice, a component correlating with the others, a variable component, since the sphere of art and its relationship with other sectors of the social structure ceaselessly changes dialectically. What we stress is not a separation of art, but the autonomy of the aesthetic function.[42]

Brecht's position on the autonomy of aesthetic function and his defense of his methods culminated in the Brecht-Lukacs debate on "formalism." Brecht's Marxism ultimately was a response to the reified experience of an urban, technological society, and consequently he sought a theatrical practice attuned to a new age. "When certain people see new forms," Brecht writes, "they scream 'formalism', but it is they themselves who are the worst formalists, worshippers of old forms at all costs, people who look only at forms, who pay attention to nothing else, who make them the only object of their scrutiny."[43] Nor is Brecht willing to accept limitations on the aesthetic device in his plays, since according to him creativity is subject to its own laws: "It is wrong to develop a criticism that regards itself as a subject confronting an object, a legislative power for which art provides the executive power," nor is it "the business of the Marxist-Leninist Party to organize poetic production the way it would set up a chicken farm. If it does so, poems will all be as much alike as one egg is like another."[44]

Although he was seemingly unaware of the work of the Prague Linguistic Circle, it is interesting to what extent Brecht took a direction analogous to Mukařovský, Brušák, and Bogatyrev in expanding the framework of formalism to include extra-aesthetic norms while keeping the aesthetic function foregrounded even in his most didactic plays.

To expand the framework of purely aesthetic functions in his plays, and one can see the movement from the early plays like *Baal, Drums in the Night,* or even in *The Jungle of the Cities* to such plays as the *Threepenny Opera* or *A Man's a Man,* Brecht adopted an ideology, in his case Marxism, as a means of bringing his plays closer to the extra-aesthetic realities he felt so strongly. This required an analysis of aesthetic structure as well as social and economic structures. It also required a methodology that was capable of presenting his new position vis-à-vis society. To do this, he simplified his plays, concentrating on the barest minimum of stage effects to bring the contradictions inherent in the social and economic structures, as he saw them, into the foreground. To do this effectively he had to become a semiotician.

"Everything in the work of art," writes Mukařovský, "and its relation to the outside world . . . can be discussed in terms of signs and meaning; in this sense, aesthetics can be regarded as a part of modern science of signs, semasiology."[45] How much of what the Prague structuralists were writing was familiar to Brecht is unknown, yet it is obvious that when pure aesthetic formalism reached an impasse in its exclusive focus on the literary device, the Prague structuralists suggested a viable alternative by placing the problem of art versus society in a more plausible perspective, an attitude which can be found in Brecht, making his Marxism ultimately a part of his aesthetics.

In traditional theatrical presentations the audience is usually given some normative limitations or moral principles in addition to the limitations of place, time, and action. The audience may fundamentally not agree with the orientation that theater imitates life, but it is capable of receiving aesthetic pleasure because it accepts the normative principles as a point of departure for emotional involvement. In his writings on theater, and in his theatrical practice, Brecht repeatedly examined the processes by which the extratheatrical world influences that of the theater and vice versa. The nineteenth-century theater erected an impenetrable barrier between art and life despite its invitation to the spectator to see the theatrical world as merely an extension of reality. This meant that even when enraptured by theatrical characters, the viewer understood that their place was on stage and that he could not imitate them in life without risking seeming ridiculous. Brecht, on the other hand, developed and exaggerated the belief that theatrical and extratheatrical space are separated by so sharp a divergence that, at best, they can only refer to each other. To accentuate this perception, Brecht used out-of-frame devices to separate what he meant as text from what he meant as comment on the text.

Since signs (and at this point we have to return to Bogatyrev's conclusion that on the stage "all is a sign of a sign") are at bottom social facts, the attitude which the individual spectator takes toward a play being presented is not determined by his unique perception, no matter how original, but is determined by the social relationships in which the individual is involved. In this understanding of the aesthetics of reception, Brecht was later to come close to Mukařovský, who writes:

> The result arrived at by the analysis of the sign-like nature of the art work in no way leads to aesthetic subjectivism: we merely concluded that the material ties entered into by the work as sign set in motion the attitude of a viewer toward reality. But the viewer is a social creature, a member of a collective. This affirmation leads us a step closer to our goal; if the material connection introduced by the work affects the manner in which the individual and the collective address themselves to reality, it becomes evident that one important task for us is to treat the question of extra-aesthetic values contained in a work of art.[46]

In his discussion of the epic theater, Brecht emphasizes that "the radical transformation of the theatre can't be the result of some artistic whim."[47] Instead, an "ideological superstructure" must be formed as a means of placing the spectator in a situation in which he "must come to grips with things."[48] By "ideological superstructure" Brecht refers explicitly to Marxism, and goes on to say later that:

> When I read Marx's *Capital* I understood my plays. . . . It wasn't of course that I found I had unconsciously written a whole pile of Marxist plays; but this man Marx was the only spectator for my plays I'd ever come across. For a man with interests like his must of necessity be interested in my plays, not because they are so intelligent but because he is—they are something for him to think about. This happened because I was as hard up for opinions as for money and had the same attitude to both: that they are there not to be hoarded but to be spent.[49]

In adopting Marxism as a relevant ideology, Brecht was also aware that he could not impose the ideology on the spectator but had to engage him in a discussion of the problems presented on stage. Therefore, answers are not offered. "Above all," writes Barthes, "precisely when he was linking this theater of signification to political thought, Brecht affirmed meaning but did not fulfill it."[50] It was up to the spectator, having been presented "objects to be deciphered," to come up with the appropriate conclusion. That message should have been clear, however, for, according to Bakhtin, each field of ideological creativity "forms its specific signs and symbols, which are not applicable to other fields. Here the sign is created by a specific ideological function and is inseparable from it."[51] What makes Brecht's ideological stance unique is that it maintains the dialogic communication of theater foremost, suspending, as Barthes explains, the Marxist meaning by posing it as a question: "This subtle friction between a (fulfilled) meaning and a (suspended) signification is an enterprise which far surpasses, in audacity, in difficulty, in necessity, too, the suspension of meaning which the avant-garde believed it had produced by a pure subversion of ordinary language and of theatrical conformism."[52] The questioning attitude of Brecht's ideological stance illustrates his position that theater has a political responsibility. However, it is in his attention to signifiers, "objects to be deciphered," rather than to the transmittal of positive messages, or signifieds,[53] that Brecht's theater presents signs in formation rather than ossified conventional ideological symbols. For, as Bakhtin explains, "an ideological sign should be immersed in the element of internal subjective signs, resound with subjective tones, so as to remain a living sign and not fall into the venerable status of an incomprehensible museum relic."[54]

The attitude of provoking questioning rather than laying out answers shows to what extent Brecht was aware of the communicative function of the theater. As Peter Handke points out, Brecht is a writer who gives the spectator cause for thought:

The processes by which reality can operate, processes which had hitherto unfolded smoothly before one, were rearranged by Brecht into a system of thinking in terms of contradictions. He thereby made it possible for those processes by which reality operates, which previously one had often seen as operating smoothly, to be conclusively contradicted by means of the Brechtian system of contradictions. And finally the state of the world, which had hitherto been taken as intrinsic and natural, was seen to be manufactured—and precisely therefore manufacturable and alterable. Not natural, not non-historical, but artificial, capable of alteration, possible of alteration, and under certain circumstances needful of alteration.[55]

In his early Marxist period Brecht indulged in what Eric Bentley aptly defines as "undialectical didacticism."[56] In these didactic plays (*Lehrstücke*), Brecht diminishes emotional content and spells out his new Communist convictions, overcoming for the time being his fundamental scepticism and detachment. However, in the plays of his later period—*Galileo, Mother Courage, The Caucasian Chalk Circle*, and *The Good Person of Szechwan*—Brecht develops toward a "much fuller presentation of the dialectics of living." Instead of heightening the emotional charge of his message, Brecht reduced it to a minimum, for "getting worked up for an hour or two," as Eric Bentley writes, "has no value": "'We need to generate enough anger to last a lifetime. Or rather, since we probably have that much already, we need to tap it, to make it available. This, as psychoanalysts know, can only be done by indirection.'"[57]

Through indirection Brecht wanted to involve the spectator in the process of discovering and interpreting the conditions of life. A dialogue is thereby established. To use Bakhtin's terminology, "dialogic communication is the realm of the true life of the world."[58] Brecht's attention to the presentational signs in his plays bespeaks a fundamental understanding that in order to understand what was happening on stage, the spectator had "to orient oneself with respect to it, to find for it the proper place in the appropriate context."[59] Brecht's intent in his theater was to stress that understanding is fundamentally dialogic, first in the stance of the actor vis-à-vis himself as he presents his role, and secondly between the actor and the spectator. This point is put another way by Hans Robert Jauss:

Literature and art only obtain a history that has the character of a process when the succession of works is mediated not only through the producing subject but also through the consuming subject—through the interaction of author and public. And if on the other hand 'human reality is not only a production of the new, but also a (critical and dialectical) reproduction of the past,' the function of art in the process of this perpetual totalizing can only come into view in its independence when the specific achievement of artistic form as well as is no longer just mimetically defined, but rather is viewed dialectically as a medium capable of forming and altering perception, in which the "formation of the senses" chiefly takes place.[60]

It is precisely because the life of theatrical presentations differs from everyday existence that this distance offered the spectator dialectical oppositions, giving him new possibilities for behavior. Brecht assumed that the process of arriving at an appropriate ideological position would evolve out of the careful, dispassionate observation of the character and his socioeconomic determinants, rather than through the spectator's identification with the emotional situation of the character.

Identification is one of those phenomena of aesthetic experience that clearly caused Brecht a problem. He took Aristotelean catharsis as the creation of disinterested interest. However, he discarded the idea that catharsis freed the spectator, so that in the identification with the hero, his emotion could be heightened, and through identification could influence him to perceive what is exemplary in human action. For Brecht this was not sufficient. He developed the idea of a non-Aristotelean theater which was to "counter the alienation of social life through a second alienation,"[61] i.e., through the *Verfremdungseffekt*: the attitude of the actor vis-à-vis his role, the anti-illusionistic staging, and the flooding of the stage and the auditorium with light. The function of these techniques of alienation is to convey events "in their remarkableness and strangeness" so that the spectator will see society presented in such a way "that it becomes subject to control."[62] The issue for Brecht, as writes Lunn, "was not any inevitable psychic depersonalization in the modern, collectivist age . . . but the question of how technology is used and to whose advantage."[63]

Brecht's early excessive expectations that the Epic Theater need only distance or make strange what it presents in order to evoke in the spectator the self-assurance that the seemingly unchangeable world can indeed be changed, required, as Brecht found, more than a mere appeal to reasonable insight on the part of the spectator. The spectator had to be entertained:

> Our representations must take second place to what is represented, men's life together in society; and the pleasure felt in their perfection must be converted into the higher pleasure felt when the rules emerging from this life in society are treated as imperfect and provisional. In this way the theatre leaves its spectators productively disposed even after the spectacle is over. Let us hope that their theatre may allow them to enjoy as entertainment that terrible and never-ending labour which should ensure their maintenance, together with the terror of their unceasing transformation. Let them here produce their own lives in the simplest way; for the simplest way of living is in art.[64]

Despite his revolutionary intent and his anti-Aristotelean stance, Brecht was by nature biased towards a theater that had a strong entertainment value. However, the entertainment value in Brecht's plays was ultimately to emerge from an understanding of the contradictions inherent in society, thus producing intellectual pleasure: "They must be entertained with the wisdom that comes from the solution of problems, with the anger that is a practical expression of sympathy with the underdog, with the respect due to those who respect humanity, or rather whatever is kind to humanity; in short, with whatever delights those who are producing something."[65]

In following the development of Brecht's aesthetic theory, one can see to what extent Shklovsky's "automatism of perception" is to be dealt with by Brecht through methods of "defamiliarization." Were this the only facet of Brecht's aesthetics, it would be a simple matter to designate what his aesthetics of reception represents; ultimately, however, his ideological idiolect cannot be excluded from his aesthetic.

Umberto Eco describes ideological systems as cases of overcoding. Although aesthetic texts may be overcoded in both expression and content through attention to the conventionalized codes of expression, ideological codes can also contain subcodes that express a personal ideological perspective, or ideological bias. "Sometimes," writes Eco, "a text asks for ideological cooperation on the part of the reader; at other times the text seems to refuse any ideological commitment, although its ideological message consists just in this refusal."[66] Although at first glance it may seem that Brecht's plays fall into what Eco designates as demanding cooperation on the part of the spectator, it is also true that at other times his plays—for example, *Mother Courage* and *Galileo*—refuse to present an obvious ideological message, forcing the spectator in such a case to look for "an underlying ideological scaffolding at a more abstract level."[67]

Since the decoding of a message in *Mother Courage*, for example, cannot seemingly be established by its author, but depends on the concrete circumstances of reception, it is often difficult to establish what Brecht means for his readers, particularly in socialist countries.

To illustrate the problem of the reception of Brecht's plays and the problem of influence they may have presented, it is important to consider that, as Jan Mukařovský writes, reception of influence in literature is often considered to be one-sided:

> It may happen that a literature confronts several influences simultaneously and then proceeds to choose among them, graduate them hierarchically, and allows one to prevail over the others; in so doing it gives meaning to this entire set of influences. In other words, influences do not function in the environment which they penetrate without a precondition: They collide with the tradition of the local literature, to conditions and needs of which they are subordinated. The local artistic and ideological tradition can thus create dialectic tensions among the influences.[68]

In analyzing both Brecht's writings on theater and his plays, it is important to bring out the connections between his work and the sociohistorical context. However, as Eco explains, the investigations should "reveal correspondences and not casual relations."[69] This does not mean, Eco goes on to explain, "that casual relations should not be introduced on a historical examination of wider scope," but it is perhaps more revealing to define the sociohistorical context and any other contexts that allow us to perceive "the way in which the work 'reflects' the social context."[70] For that reason, an examination of the parallelisms between the ideological and aesthetic aspects of Brecht's plays is particularly important. This, of course, brings us to the actual reception of Brecht's plays and the relationship between reception and the sociohistoric context.

The problem with integrating ideology into aesthetics had not only to do, writes Jauss, with "how alienation could bring pleasure, but also how the solitary spectator could be motivated to pass from critical reflection to solidary action, and this means how norms of action could be suggested to him without their being overtly or covertly imposed."[71] For that reason, as Jauss emphasizes, the "positive hero" of socialist realism contradicted Brecht's fundamental aesthetic aims. Ultimately, the problem of the reception of Brecht's plays in socialist countries had to do with his refusal to impose ideological norms and values on the spectator, even though he himself may have supported a certain ideology. As Jauss explains, his purpose was to make "discussable"[72] the ambiguity of the conduct of his protagonists.

Brecht's aesthetics not only thematizes role distance as the function of the actor but also creates the possibility for the spectator to experience himself through the doubling process that role enactment presents. In some plays this construct is already built in, as for example the double figures of Shen Te and Shui Ta in *The Good Person of Szechwan* or in the figure of Puntila, who is good when he is drunk and bad when he is sober. In other plays it is the actor's and the spectator's function to provide "otherness" to characters through the process of the double alienation technique. To make this understanding between spectators and actors possible, the structures that lay behind the roles had to be uncovered. To do this effectively, the devices of the theater also had to be laid bare. For as Jauss writes, "concealing the technique of staging from the spectator is the very thing that has not been done since Pirandello and Brecht, and this because the naturalistic illusion concerning social determinants was to be laid bare."[73]

The double alienation effect was to achieve its strongest impact, according to Diderot's famous *Paradoxe sur le comédien,* when the actor retained an inner distance from "the affects whose portrayal moves the audience,"[74] or according to Brecht, "the first condition for the achievement of the *V-effekt* is that the actor must invest what he has to show with a definite gest of showing."[75] Thus, showing, presenting, or demonstrating rather than psychological identification was to be at the center of the typification of social role performance. The next step in the dialectics of the actor between self and role was to stimulate the spectator to adopt this attitude in relation to his own role in society—to become critical, and to step outside his own role as well.

Because Brecht's theatrical aesthetics are concerned not only with signifying but also with a "reflexive discourse about the very process by which it signifies,"[76] actors function in his plays both at the level of theatrical discourse and at that of meta-discourse. To do this effectively, the actors must draw from a multiplicity of codes or semiotic systems in order to foreground both the aesthetic and ideological systems in such a way that they are laid bare or can be seen as if for the first time. The spectator, in a sense, becomes the primary player in the theater, decoding what Eco explains as the relationship between symptoms and causes.[77]

Of primary importance to a performance of Brecht's plays is the attitudinal role of *gestus,* which Brecht defines as "the attitudes people adopt towards one another, wherever they are socio-historically significant."[78] Such "mimetic and gestural expression of the social relationship prevailing between people of a given period"[79] formed the basis of the social criticism effected by Brechtian theater, thus making the spectator aware of the ideological structure of the represented relationship. One of Brecht's models for gestural alienation was the Chinese theater, where the actor "achieves the *V-effekt* by being seen to observe his own movements."[80] He also insisted on flooding the auditorium with light and on making the sources of light visible in order to prevent "an unwanted element of illusion."[81]

Brecht's writings on the aesthetics of reception bring together two of his fundamental interests: his Marxism, and his concern for the way in which signs can, do, and should work in modern society. These writings also form part of a general theory of what theater itself can and should do, and are not only interesting on general aesthetic and political grounds but also provide a good introduction to a more systematic analysis of how communication systems work in modern society. If all signs meant exactly one thing, only one thing and inevitably one thing, then an essential part of human liberty would disappear. That is why the imposition on theater and literature of the positive hero removed from the spectator and reader the fundamental choices given to him by the arbitrariness of language to interpret events in different ways and to constantly see things differently. And if the spectator in the theater were held captive, so to speak, by the signs displayed before him—for example, luxurious costumes or rich scenic devices—then the theater could never become what Brecht wanted to make it: the place where spectators encounter and become conscious of the freedom which they have as individuals to first understand and then to alter history.

As a Marxist, Brecht felt that Marxism too should be seen anew. Like Karl Korsch, with whom Brecht studied, Brecht understood that social consciousness arises from the "social life-process and in turn is a real component of that process."[82] Hence, any social theory must take seriously the critique of ideology inherent in these processes. Walter Benjamin relates an anecdote which illustrates cogently Brecht's understanding of the predicament of Marxism: "Yesterday after playing chess Brecht said: 'You know, when Korsch comes, we really ought to work out a new game in which the moves do not always stay the same; where the function of each piece changes after it has stood in the same square for a while.'"[83]

From this it is evident that Brecht's aesthetics of reception, so closely allied to the Russian formalists' understanding of the mutability of a work of art which through historical processes "after standing in the same square for a while" is forced into another square, also holds for his understanding of political ideology. Brecht's function in his plays is to help the spectator understand "the changing moves" of social processes, but not to give the rules, the strategy, or the probable outcome.[84]

Brecht sees the probable outcome as emerging out of something like a boxing match. At such an event the action is made intelligible because of the openly histrionic nature of the boxer's gestures and attitudes. Like the ideal Brechtian actor, the boxer does not invite or expect the spectator to sympathize with him. Nor are his actions veiled: "No one would expect the lighting to be hidden at a sporting event, a boxing match for instance. Whatever the points of difference between the modern theatre's presentations and those of a sporting promoter, they do not include the same concealment of the sources of light as the old theater found necessary."[85]

Since the action at a boxing match is clearly conventionalized, the spectator can sit back, relax, smoke a cigar with a clear eye on the finish, allowing him a more detached and critical outlook on the way the struggle is being conducted. This detached attitude on the part of the spectator could bring about, according to Brecht, "the downfall of Western art": "He might as well light a bomb as light his cigar. I would be delighted to see our public allowed to smoke during performances. And I'd be delighted mainly for the actors' sake. In my view it is quite impossible for the actor to play unnatural, cramped and old-fashioned theatre to a man smoking in the stalls."[86]

Despite the self-conscious *V-effekts*, Epic Theater, though not naturalistic, belongs, as Bentley writes, to the broad tradition of realism: "If the earlier naturalism came in with the discovery of the 'true meaning of life' in Darwinist science, the later Epic Theater came in with the discovery of the 'true meaning of life' in Marxist 'science.'"[87] The unrealistic stage effects of "slides, charts, film projections" as well as the "interruptive" devices of songs, narrators, and choric commentary are "all devoted to imparting a greater sense of the actual world."[88]

Conflict, as in the great Shakespearean tragedies, is changed by Brecht into an "acting-out" of argument, "a realization of dialectic in word and gesture," as George Steiner writes, "not wholly dissimilar from the drama of a Platonic dialogue."[89] Conflict in Epic Theater is presented as an articulation or exploration, leaving the resolution with the spectator. In socialist realism, however, the aesthetic norm is raised to the level of dogma, leading back much as naturalistic determinism does to sympathetic identification with the hero. Jauss writes:

> The "positive hero" of socialist realism should not be altogether perfect and call forth admiration; nor must he be pitiable, let alone comic. But neither must he negate the prevailing

morality and thus prompt critical reflection, and even less satisfy the need for escape. Fundamentally, he is thus a modern version of the dilemma of Diderot's *père de famille* who could no longer be a perfect hero in the traditional sense nor yet a subjective one in the modern. Because of his blank positivity, he falls into that *genre ennuyeux* which, even before Voltaire's ridicule, frustrated sympathetic identification whenever the reader was not considered mature and therefore given no alternative but to affirm existing norms.[90]

As Bentley writes, "that Brecht should have proved the leading communist writer of the Stalin era is perhaps the most striking of all the Brechtian contradictions."[91] Brecht's protagonists are anything but positive, from the early Kragler in *Drums in the Night* through Azdak in *The Caucasian Chalk Circle* to Puntila in *Puntila and Matti, His Hired Man*. His characters signify anything but "blank positivity." Nor is Courage at all courageous, standing diametrically opposite to courage, and as an "opposite of active virtue, namely passivity."[92]

Brecht disliked the openly propagandist plays written in the naturalistic convention of socialist realism. Martin Esslin writes that in his speech to the Fourth East German Writers' Congress in January 1956, Brecht ridiculed plays in which the new spirit and the new positive man "does in fact get the better of his opponent's point of view" "You must not forget that the representation of militant action on the stage, even from a set point of view, does not by itself automatically produce a militant effect. What we must achieve is the creation of militancy in the audience, the militancy of the new against the old."[93]

This militancy was obviously to be awakened through stimulation of the spectator's critical faculty. There was, however, as Esslin explains, a problem in that Brecht's particular stage conventions "did not necessarily lead the public to a Marxist answer." "The Brechtian theatre is a theatre designed to arouse indignation in the audience, dissatisfaction, a realization of contradictions—it is a theatre supremely fitted for parody, caricature, and denunciation, therefore essentially a 'negative' theatre."[94]

When Brecht does create a hero who comes "within range of the virtue of the Positive Hero in Soviet literature,"[95] he draws the figure in such a way so as not to make him motivated by idealism. Grusha in *The Caucasian Chalk Circle* and Kattrin in *Mother Courage* both act out of instinct rather than positive moral conviction. As Bentley notes, "if one 'sovietized' the play, Kattrin would be the protagonist."[96] But that was not Brecht's intent; instead, as paraphrased by Esslin, Brecht intends to "show the world in a critical spirit—and the audience will automatically see the need for a Marxist solution! It is enough to point out the contradictions in the existing state of society to make people clamor for Communism."[97]

When one studies the reception of Brecht's plays in the socialist countries, it becomes clear that Brecht's stance vis-à-vis the claim of art and politics was at best an unsettled matter and suggests an ongoing conflict of allegiances, a conflict no doubt heightened and complicated by accusations of formalism and the negative portrayal of characters who supposedly should be fighting for social-ist goals. Brecht's reaction to these accusations took several forms. In his non-dramatic writing he seemingly gave credit to the socialist position, while at the same time raking the tenets and implications of socialist realism over coals, ironically mocking its presumptuousness in judging the complexities of artistic creation, and defending the autonomy of art. His ambivalent stand was characteristic. What remains distinct is the impression of an extremely indus-trious artist applying his multiple talents as playwright and director in the crea-tion of stage works that fused specifically theatrical elements in new and striking ways. Equally distinct is the impression of the difficulties that Brecht the artist had in consistently coming to terms in practice with Brecht the ideologically committed fighter for social revolution, regardless of how ideal the union seemed in theory. The best-known previous instance of a similar dilemma in theater is probably that of Meyerhold, whose brutal fate Brecht was spared through his more decided ambivalence.

As Martin Esslin so aptly writes, if Brecht believed that the epic theater "was the truly Marxist theater, the authorities of the Communist world certainly did not."[98] The theatrical practice promulgated in the Soviet Union relied on the methods of Stanislavsky, and these instead of Brecht's epic theater became the official norm for actors, directors, and critics "from Vladivostok to Prague."[99]

To what extent Brecht was forced to buckle under to the charges of formal-ism may be seen in the introduction to his last collection of theoretical writings under the title "Dialectics in the Theatre," which are introduced with the follow-ing cryptical message:

> The works which follow relate to paragraph 45 of the "Short Organum" and suggest that "epic theatre" is too formal a term for the kind of theatre aimed at (and to some extent practiced). Epic theatre is a prerequisite for these contributions, but it does not of itself imply that productivity and mutability of society from which they derive their main element of pleasure. The term must therefore be reckoned inadequate, although no new one can be put forward.[100]

To some degree one could say that Brecht's relationship to the Soviet Union was complicated by his own belief that he was the better Marxist. This can be seen in his early play *The Measures Taken*, wherein he tackles the theme of Communist discipline and the moral problem that emerges for the young com-rade between means and ends. Having broken Party discipline because of too great an empathy for the downtrodden workers, the young comrade pleads for his comrades to kill him. They unwillingly do kill him because the young comrade has betrayed the higher interests of the Party. In the end a control chorus sitting in judgment on the events approves their disciplinary measure and praises them for having been steadfast in spreading the "ABC's of Communism." But it did not follow, as Bentley writes, "that the Party accepted the attentions of its enthusiastic wooer."[101] Instead the Party expressed its horror, since this was the

Stalinist era, and the disappearance of comrades who did not submit to Party discipline was coming into style. Chastisement from the Party press followed:

> One feels that he does not draw his knowledge from practice, that he is merely deducing from theory. . . . The unreal analysis of the premises leads to a false synthesis of their political and artistic consequences. All this mirrors an abstract attitude towards the manifold and complicated store of knowledge derived from experience, which the party possesses.[102]

According to the Party press, Brecht also erred because he postulated an "opposition between reason and emotion, and therefore fell into the sin of idealism."[103] Nor was this position of the Party against Brecht's presentation ameliorated with the passage of time. Ernst Schumacher, a present-day East German critic, goes to great lengths to expose Brecht's errors:

> If Brecht's description in *The Measures Taken* corresponded to an objective revolutionary situation it would not be the young comrade who would be in conflict with party discipline, but it would be a historical situation in which the three party workers would have to be removed from the leadership as reformists and opportunists. . . . Such a removal of the three party officials as they appear in *The Measures Taken* would in any case be necessary as they are obviously beyond him.[104]

Perhaps his overzealous Marxism prevented Brecht from reading the warning signs that Soviet literature had been Stalinized, nor did he protest publicly the disappearance of his friends Tretyakov, Carole Neher, and ultimately Meyerhold. "Because he missed the point of Stalinism," writes David Pike, "the havoc it was bound to wreak on literature and art took him by surprise" and he was "caught off-guard by the impact of Stalinism upon all facets of Soviet art as well as by the natural consequences for the reception of his own work in the USSR."[105] It was almost as if Brecht was reading Lenin too closely:

> And first of all the question arises: how is the discipline of the revolutionary party of the proletariat maintained? How is it tested? How is it reinforced? First, by the class consciousness of the proletarian vanguard and by its devotion to the revolution, by its perseverance, self-sacrifice, and heroism. Secondly, by its ability to link itself, to keep in touch with and to a certain extent, to merge itself with the broadest masses of the toilers. . . . Thirdly, by the correctness of the political leadership strategy and tactics, provided that the broadest masses have been convinced by their own experience that they are correct. Without these conditions all attempts to establish discipline inevitably fail and end in phrasemongering.[106]

At the crux of the discussions on literature in the Soviet Union was the relation of socialist realism's theories to the Russian past and their rejection of all but a handful of men, such as Belinsky, Chernishevsky, and Dobrolyubov, as representative of the historical strivings of the Russian peoples for social change. Even among the most staunch Party members the disagreement about the means, the tempo, and the goals of social change was so profound that it divided them on a score of related issues, including most phases of literature's relationship to life. From the debates of these underlying doctrinal issues emerged the concept of the new hero, who was to be "positive" rather than "superfluous." To some degree this was a continuation of the programmatic demands of the Russian nineteenth-century critics, who attempted to isolate and define the characteristics of the hero they wanted to displace, namely Oblomov, whose predilection for defeat they most vehemently wanted to replace with positive values. In this context it would indeed be difficult to evaluate Courage, Puntila, Galileo, Azdak, or even Gruscha as positive heroes.

Most of the Zhdanovian polemics on literature sound like reworkings of the older texts written by Chernishevsky, Dobrolyubov, or Belinsky. However, Soviet scholars and critics rationalized this awkward similarity by arranging the similarities of ideas into an evolutionary sequence, maintaining that socialist theory was "higher" and more advanced, more profound, and a more useful approach to an understanding of the development of literary processes, since it represented a later and higher stage of economic development. Of course, terminology was then devised to account for these sweeping judgments—for example, classifying the socially conscious writers of the nineteenth century under Lukacs's "critical realism" and giving, since 1932, the designation of socialist realism to "the highest stage in the development of art" and its fulfillment of the historical processes striving toward that goal. Anything in between was viewed as decadent, subjective, superfluous.

Since neither Brecht's plays nor his theories, Marxist though they were, fit the functional needs of literature as espoused by Zhdanov and Stalin, objections to Brecht very soon took on an official tone. And although initially the Russian Association of Proletarian Writers subscribed to a "dialectical materialist creative method,"[107] the association was soon disbanded and its methods supplanted by socialist realism. Thus, Brecht unwittingly found himself on the other side. Gorky announced that "the people need heroes"; Brecht replied in *Galileo,* "Unhappy the land that needs heroes." And so it went. The blending of Communist ideology with national feelings and imperialistic traditions, seemingly unbeknownst to Brecht, replaced the familiar (to him) internationalism of Trotsky and became the determining factor of control of all editorial boards and literary organizations. The official doctrine of 1932 consolidated literary activities, uniting and centralizing all efforts under a single board of censorship.

The result was the incorporation of literature into the fabric of the State, its function to provide a social service. All efforts were evaluated according to their usefulness to the cause of progress. Any writer who put artistic principles above educational and social ones was regarded as a decadent bourgeois formalist, a cosmopolitan, or whatever the current label was. The most significant consequence of these upheavals was the formulation of a literary doctrine that was to represent and reflect reality in such a way that it mattered little what the reality was, but rather how it was to be represented, and this included style, visions, form, and above all, as Gorky insisted, a sense of enthusiasm, sacrifice, and heroism. Gorky urged the writer to carefully choose topics of struggle and conflict, thus imbuing socialist realism with an overzealous revolutionary romanticism.

The main aim placed before Soviet writers was the search for the New Hero, who was supposed both to portray the psychological changes that had occurred in Soviet men as a result of improved social and economic conditions, as well as to portray high principles that kept his eyes on the goal. The New Hero had unwavering faith in Communism, and this faith forged his mentality, ruled his actions, and dictated his attitudes. As a consequence of this attitude, "as soon as the literary character becomes fully purposeful and conscious of his purpose-fulness, he can enter that privileged caste which is universally respected and called positive heroes."[108]

How, then, do Brecht's characters like Macheath, Azdak, Puntila, Galileo, and Courage fit into the larger scheme of socialist purpose? To what extent can Brecht's dialogic theory of reception help to find a place for them in the hall of positive heroes? The answers are complex, but to put things more simply—Brecht survived through endurance, ambivalence toward the events occurring in the Soviet Union, and blindness toward what the greater purpose represented.

But the reception of Brecht's plays was problematic on all fronts, whether reactionary or far left. As Roland Barthes explains, on the reactionary right Brecht's work was discredited because of its Communism; on the right, while his works were accepted, the man was dissociated from them and consigned to Party politics, while his plays were "enlisted under the banners of an eternal theater." Similarly, on the liberal left Brecht was given a humanist reading, which in order to be considered valid had to dissociated from the theoretical part of his writing. And on the far left, as we have seen, reservations were expressed with regard to his opposition to the positive hero and the "formalist" method of his theory.[109] In the end, the extreme right and left merge in their belief that literature must fit an ideology.

Since Brecht's plays and theatrical practice did not fit either the needs or the conditions of socialist realism, it was difficult to accept him as an influence. This was certainly not only true of the Soviet Union but also of East Germany, in reference to which Brecht commented that the theater in the DDR unfortunately belonged to the few theaters in Europe that did not include his plays in its repertories.[110]

Interestingly enough, the attitude toward Brecht in Poland, particularly during the period of sovietization and during the liberalization following Stalin's death, may serve as an appropriate model for studies of Brecht's reception and influence. On the one hand, Poland was the first Soviet Bloc country to openly question the tenets of socialist realism, thereby, by staging Brecht, calling socialist realism into question. On the other hand, Brecht was a questionable model since he was not only a Marxist but also a German as well. As a result, discussions on Brecht polarized both Party dogmatists and nationalist reactionaries in Poland.

Although the aesthetic and ideological *Weltanschauung* of Polish directors and Brecht diverged emphatically, the initial staging of Brecht opened up possibilities for Polish directors to stage the revolutionary plays of the Polish playwrights from the partition period and also the avant-garde plays of Stanislaw Witkiewicz, whose plays, with the exception of a few amateur productions during the interwar period, came into the Polish theatrical repertoire for the first time in the late 1950s. In a sense, Brecht played the part of a "hobby horse" in bringing new values to the impoverished Polish theater during the initial era of sovietization. This would not have been possible, if, as E. H. Gombrich explains, two conditions that are necessary to turn "a stick" into a "hobby horse" had not existed a priori: First, that its form made it just possible to ride on it; secondly, and perhaps decisively, that riding mattered.[111] Since changing circumstances had stretched the definition of socialist realism in Poland to encompass Brecht, the "form" became possible to ride on. And since in the Polish theater, "riding" mattered a great deal, it was natural for the Polish theater to take on Brecht as a means to an end.

That Brecht presented problems for Polish audiences and critics during the interwar years is clear. During this period, only *The Threepenny Opera*—then a phenomenal worldwide success—was staged (1929), which in Poland took on additional significance due to strong anti-German sentiments at that time, and also due to the fact that the producer-director of the play, Leon Schiller, was a known Communist. Thus, the reception of Brecht in Poland was from the beginning closely related to his ideology.

A brief description of the context of the Polish premiere of *The Threepenny Opera* indicates that the production was almost cancelled due to an incident that had occurred a few months prior to the premiere, when actors from the Katowice Opera, appearing in a cultural exchange program in Bytom, which was then within German boundaries, were severely beaten by "local scum" parading under the sign of the swastika.[112] Given all we know of Brecht's work, it is difficult to imagine that his plays might be boycotted because of identification with the Nazi movement. Nevertheless it was so, since national grievances, particularly between Poland and Germany, were not restricted to political ideologies.

In studying the reception of Brecht on the Polish stage, it is important to remember Mukařovský's observation that influences do not operate without the precondition of colliding with the norms and values of local traditions to whose needs they are subordinated. This collision creates a dialectic tension between the influence and those values, and allows for either the acceptance or rejection of that influence. It is also true that had a more ideologically palatable director first staged Brecht in Poland, his *Threepenny Opera* would have probably become as much of a culinary masterpiece there as it had been elsewhere.

In reaction to the political pressure to cancel the rehearsals, Schiller placed greater emphasis on the social significance of the play, making it even more a work of political propaganda than Erich Engel had in the Berlin production. This attitude, of course, negated Brecht's intent by placing the emphasis on the text's social message rather than on its function as an "image-boomerang" or "reversed mirror"[113] of bourgeois values which Brecht foregrounded:

> It is a kind of report on life as any member of the audience would like to see it. Since at that same time, however, he sees a good deal that he has no wish to see; since therefore he sees his wishes not merely fulfilled but also criticized (sees himself not as subject but as object), he is theoretically in a position to appoint a new function for the theater.[114]

Brecht resisted a biting satirical approach by focusing on the "culinary" aspects of opera and comedy, which "further pleasure even where they require, or promote, a certain degree of education, for the education in question is an education of taste."[115] Aesthetics, then, are primary, politics secondary. Since comedy, as Peter Christian Giese explains, views the present as an already historically passing process, it assists the spectator in coming to an understanding of both by the distance it creates between past and present.[116] Bernard Dort writes that what the playgoer discovers in the "very unreality of such an image is himself":

> In the reversed mirror of the stage, which should have given him the vision of another world, his own face appears to him—rising out of the inextricably tangled pieces of a scattered puzzle, Brecht goes theatre magic one better, but only in order to destroy it. The theatre no longer reflects the world of the audience but rather the ideological disguises of that audience. It is then that this mirror suddenly sends us back to our own reality. The play turns against us like a boomerang.[117]

In his notes to the play, Brecht admonished the actors to refrain "from depicting these bandits as a collection of those depressing individuals with red neckerchiefs who frequent places of entertainment and with whom no decent person would drink a glass of beer." Instead, the actors were instructed to present themselves as "naturally sedate persons, some of them portly and all without exception good mixers when off duty."[118]

Unfortunately, Schiller's production was not so light in tone. Reacting to the press's anti-German, anti-Communist, and veiled anti-Semitic polemics, Schiller forgot about Brecht's "cool" attitude and made the production very "hot" indeed. Despite adherence to the Berlin production as a model by using placards, film projections, and banners with messages, Schiller's production had more realistic overtones. For example, the costumes for both the police and public executioner were real English uniforms of that time. In addition, the actors spoke their lines in realistic, sometimes aggressive tones, stressing the social criticism in Brecht's songs. Schiller was determined to draw out the play's antibourgeois "tendentiousness" and to apply it as a direct criticism of the Polish middle class, even at the cost of sacrificing the basic elements of humor and parody within the play.

In a sense, the strident revolutionary tone in Schiller's production brought it much closer to Erwin Piscator's ideas on theater rather than to Brecht's. Writing on the relationship of truth and tendentiousness, Piscator firmly stated that these two elements were not necessarily in contradiction to each other:

> They are completely identical in an era in which truth is revolutionary. The tendentious is a much maligned concept, sometimes becoming synonymous with untruthfulness, or at least with distortion of the truth in a certain manner to a certain end. . . . The most powerful tendentious message possible is inherent in the raw, objective, untouched reality, and it seems to me that nowadays not only the most powerful revolutionary sentiments but also the highest artistic ability are required to present reality on a new level.[119]

The Polish reception of the play was as expected. Fanned by anti-German and anti-Communist sentiment, the critics, as Schiller himself later recounts, "swore that they knew the Gay scenario in the original, that it is a serene presentation in baroque style, out of which the communists—Brecht and Schiller —stripped everything that determined charm, elegance, and humor, replacing them with lies and a Hydra of Bolshevik propaganda accentuated by the use of coarse naturalism."[120]

The refrain from the second finale, particularly the lines—"First comes dinner, morality can wait"—was found to resonate no less clearly than the slogans shouted at First of May demonstrations.[121] Another critic protested that the maxim should not be thrown at a Christian public.[122] Obviously, Brecht's moral did not escape attention, and the provocative nature of its content was manipulated by the critics to emphasize the danger of such pessimistic views.

Not only the text but elements of the staging also came under attack, particularly the use of English uniforms, which were seen by one critic as defamation of the British monarchy and the British Empire. This was soon picked up by the police, who interceded with clear conscience in defense of the threatened social order and as a first step, acting in solidarity with their British brothers, issued an edict that prohibited actors from appearing on stage in police uniforms to prevent the implication that the police were capable of taking bribes.

The production went on for another thirteen nights; however, for the remainder of the run the actors appeared dressed as civilians. Some reviewers then went so far as to jeer at the police for their lack of imagination and "sullen disposition."[123]

> It has come to our attention that the Ministry of Internal Affairs has demanded that English police officers in *The Threepenny Opera* must appear dressed as civilians. . . . While it is true that it is highly improper for uniformed police officers to accept bribes, is it more proper for the police dressed as civilians to do this? Previously, the public could infer from this production that the British police take bribes, now, however, being better informed, it can only judge that all policemen take bribes.[124]

This attitude only served to heighten the antagonism of the police and other public officials. The next restriction imposed on the production was to remove all allusions unfavorable to the religious order, as well as all allusions, refrains, and expressions unfavorable toward the police or anything within the text that implied a connection between the gangsters and the higher orders. As sections of the text were deleted day by day, the actors filled them in with pantomime or improvised telling looks in the direction of the audience, in a way bringing the spectator closer to the sort of collaboration Brecht desired of his audience. In time, however, the elimination of entire verses, and then entire songs, weakened the text. With the text thus reduced, notwithstanding the improvisation of the actors, the context turned to nonsense, and the production closed.[125]

Polemical discussions continued, however, and even the more progressive liberal press spoke out against Brecht and Schiller on the grounds that the play denigrated the nobility of the working class by presenting beggars as profiteers and capitalistic apaches.[126]

We must remember that the context of the reception of Brecht's *Threepenny Opera* in Warsaw in May 1929 was the very same context in which Witkiewicz attempted to present his plays. And the very same critics who threw invectives at Brecht and Schiller also found Witkiewicz's plays and their inherent criticism of bourgeois values, as well as their bleak view of the fascistically inclined repressive Pilsudski regime, equally as disturbing. At bottom, the critics and spectators of the interwar period in Poland were no different from those in the Soviet Union, in that they preferred a theater of illusion to one which demanded that they confront their very image.

From this brief overview on the reactions of the Polish critics, one can infer that the more progressive views of the left were as limiting as those of the right. This similarity in approach to the interpretation of Brecht's plays emerged also during the later era of socialist realism, when the substitution of "Communist" and "anarchist" for invective terms like "formalist" or "decadent" by no means altered the essential attitude of social and political uniformity.

In a sense, this also points to the similarity of Hitler's and Stalin's aesthetics, wherein often the same people were denounced and for the same "reasons." Witkiewicz saw this quite clearly, and, as a result, removed himself to Zakopane in the Tatra Mountains, refusing to espouse any ideology. For Brecht it was a different story. Hitler's particular brand of aesthetics he was able to discern quite clearly; with Stalin, it was another matter. Walter Benjamin's observation on the explicit link between cultural and political concerns cogently unites both ideological extremes: "Fascism aspires necessarily to an aestheticizing of political life: communism answers it with the politicizing of art."[127]

In studying the reception of Brecht's plays in Poland, it is important to remember, as Jan Mukařovský points out, that the objective study of the phenomenon of art "must regard the work as a sign composed of a sensory symbol created by the artist, a 'meaning' . . . lodged in the social consciousness, and a relation that refers to the entire context of social phenomena,"[128] or as Andrzej Wirth proposes, to examine "to whom this theatre directs itself and in what manner does it intend to act on the spectator."[129]

At the end of the Second World War, the Polish theater found itself submitting to a new ideology, that of socialist realism, which had not come about through revolution but had been imposed through Soviet occupation. This made the whole question of socialist realism in Poland somewhat different from socialist realism in the Soviet Union. The problem of introducing socialist realism into the Polish theater was twofold. Since, as Lukacs wrote, "socialist art is, of its nature, national art," and since Poland did not have its own realist tradition, a need to "call in a foreign tradition to redress the balance" became a prerequisite.[130] A question then arose as to which foreign tradition.

The second obstacle in introducing a new aesthetics had to do with the problem of national needs and the fact that the effort "to codify the creative method and the poetics of socialist realism in the Soviet Union during the 1940s, undertaken in the era of isolation, did not take into account the many experiences of socialist realism outside the Soviet Union, nor the various artistic values which, theoretically, it could have assimilated with advantage."[131] Obviously, this was written not so much against socialist realism per se, but against imposition of a foreign brand of socialist realism. Even the staunchest Polish communists were aware of the need for a specifically Polish realist tradition which would not be burdened by a Russian brand of aesthetics. Brecht, ironically, became a means out of the dilemma. He was a Communist, albeit a German, yet not a Russian.

The presentation of appropriate plays in the new spirit was also problematic because there were few Polish directors who were acquainted with Marxist methods of interpretation. In addition, there was always the danger that the interpretation of a seemingly unpolitical play might end up being subject to treatment as political heresy, as formalism, naturalism, or any specific "ism" which did not conform to the purpose of Zhdanovian aesthetics.

The question of introducing Brecht's plays into the Polish theatrical repertoire was initially treated very gingerly. Schiller, however, was able to inspire many younger Polish directors to look towards Brecht for new ideas and new theatrical conventions. Much as in the Soviet Union, official policy toward Brecht was quite ambiguous. Zbigniew Krawczykowski writes:

> Brecht's zeal towards the Party was always acknowledged; however, with respect to theatrical creativity he was always presented as a man lost in the wilderness of formalism. We remember it well, how that term explained and disposed of everything. Branding an artist as formalist permanently severed him from an audience. Everything which stepped beyond factory shops and halls, aside from naturalistic decorations (although the term naturalism was even more severely repudiated) was labelled as formalism. Thus, despite surreptitious readings of his works, which could then be discussed only in the company of close and trusted friends, Brecht's theater was forbidden fruit for our national theater.[132]

For those critics who were able to go to Berlin to see Brecht's own productions, the need for public statements asserting certain flaws in expression became imperative. Brecht's plays were called "expressionistic," and although it was acknowledged that his formalist approach "gives an unprecedented opportunity to display stagecraft," the stagings failed to dispell misgivings concerning Brecht's "incomplete and not always comprehensive ideological expression."[133]

However, at this point (1952), Brecht was invited to visit Poland, and this visit, and a subsequent tour by the Berliner Ensemble later that year, extinguished some of the zeal that had gone into promulgating socialist realism. Since support for Brecht became synonymous with opposition to the vulgar creed of socialist realism, a public revision of Brecht's theories was in order. For example, Wilhelm Szewczyk presented Brecht as a writer in transition from expressionism towards a more concrete representation of reality, due, of course, to the maturation of his political ideology:

> The new form of artistic experiences in Brecht consist not of empty, theoretical formulas, but practical principles. Although these principles were adopted in a definitive form only recently, from the very early years of his creativity, Brecht has espoused ideals which were concurrent with the direction of a new artistic and political program.[134]

The most interesting discussions, however, centered on the reception of *Mother Courage* in its 1952 presentation by the Berliner Ensemble. Discussions ranged from accusations of a lack of "revolutionary discipline," which revealed itself in Brecht's susceptibility to "anarchical dissent," to criticism of the extreme individualization of the characters, and his affinity to the "decline of the West," particularly "to the times of inflation following the First World War." Although it was acknowledged that Brecht condemned the war "with the greatest of passions," the problem was that he did not present it from the perspective of the revolutionary proletariat, nor from the standpoint of class interests. Nor was it expressed in the language of the people. War, as illustrated by Brecht, appeared in terms of "absolute pacifism" and a "total negation" rather than as an evaluation of "its purpose, its character, and its social existence."[135] In addition, and much as in the pre-war discussion of *The Threepenny Opera*, it was constantly noted that Brecht was German, not an easy thing for Poles to stomach:

> For the German bourgeoisie, which has just emerged from two bloodbaths, both rapacious and imperialistic, this immersion into anti-war idealistic historical philosophy may have the after taste of penance. However, this is not an appropriate ideology for the German proletariat, which, from the viewpoint of the Soviet Union and all peace loving nations, must fight to keep peace, differentiating sharply between a war of invasion, a war of national liberation, and a war in defense of the socialist fatherland.[136]

A more personal reaction to the plays of Brecht can be found in a letter written by a spectator to Helene Weigel and published in *Teatr* in 1952, following the visit of the Berliner Ensemble:

> My dear Mrs. Weigel,
>
> With this letter I wish to express my thanks not only for your individual appearance as a great artist and for the artistic thrill that this event aroused, I am also anxious to thank you for explaining the very painful and very Polish matter of emotions that cannot be put into words. You have understood us. I realized this as I listened with bated breath to Brecht's poetry which flowed from the stage of the Warsaw National Theatre, just recently reconstructed from amidst the rubble of the war. Listening to you, I also became aware and confident that nothing that touches human experience is unknown to you, and that you will understand the dread that exists in every Polish heart of hearing the German language, a language which accompanied Polish martyrs, many of whom were close to us, to death. And despite reason and common sense the sound of that language merges with the memory of our blackest national memory. Despite reason! For even when that language sounded triumphantly over our groaning bodies, crushed by booted Nazis, it sounded like the inhuman howling of a hyena, despite our efforts to remember that this was also the language of Goethe, Heine, and Brecht. But there are moments when having suffered to excess, the voice of reason is muffled, and you must know this well, for if this were otherwise your art could not be felt as deeply. A colossal black wall of sick hatred has separated us from German art and culture. When time has started to heal our wounds, when we have started to hear the voices of Germans battling for true democracy, and we have started to learn about the powerful German anti-fascist literature, then it is time to free ourselves from the poisoned atmosphere of the past. We can see for certain that the German Democratic Republic is battling for a free Germany, both peaceful and just and that we today have common goals—socialism and peace. And yet despite reason, there remains in the hearts of quite a few of us an undescribable, invisible scar. From fear of suffering we have kept aloof from the living German word, as if afraid that old wounds might reopen. However, the artistic jolt which the Polish public experienced during the performance of *Mother Courage* gave many of us a feeling of joyful liberation from bondage based on deceitful memory.[137]

Not only was the reception of Brecht in Poland a problem of allowing Brecht to slip in by the back door of supposedly reformed formalism but also a problem due to the intrinsic bitterness and hatred that the Poles felt toward anything German. Despite this dilemma, Brecht was the lesser of two evils. In accepting his dramas but ignoring his ideological stance, the Polish theater escaped the imposition of Soviet drama on its stages. Due to the inherent textual ambiguity of his plays, the Poles could read them as open texts.

From this, one can determine two things: that discussions on naturalistic staging were essentially foreign to the Polish theatrical tradition, which is why socialist realism was so totally unacceptable to the Poles, and secondly, that many of the elements found in Brecht's plays, i.e., action interrupted by songs, dance, and music, as well as nonrepresentational staging, were close to the native Polish theatrical tradition: the epic plays of Mickiewicz, the surrealistic plays of Wyspianski, and the absurd plays of Witkiewicz. That is why Brecht's epic theater theories, his use of alienation techniques, and his attitude toward naturalistic theater provided the necessary effects that Polish drama demanded, and in this manner gave the Polish theater a basis for a new aesthetics.

Following the post-Stalinist thaw, Polish directors, actors, and stage designers, using Brecht as a model, insisted that a true socialist art other than socialist realism was indeed possible. The Polish directors of these early Brechtian productions were primarily concerned with a Polish interpretation of Brecht and often ignored his model stagings in order to emphasize a national tone. Thus, in Polish stagings in 1957 and 1962, *Mother Courage* became the victim of what to the Poles was a recent memory, serving as a reminder of their years of survival. Jan Kott describes one such interpretation:

> From her very first gesture, there is something of the Warsaw smuggler woman under the wartime German occupation. Even in her very first "dearie" one can hear the Warsaw cadence. . . . Irena Eichler is very Polish, Warsowian. She has the bitter wisdom of the years of occupation behind her, and the fierce vitality of the Polish people, and even something of the superb down-to-earth humor typical of the Warsaw streets.[138]

Notwithstanding Brecht's epic distance from his character, the figure of Courage for Polish directors, actors, and spectators was that of a woman determined to survive the war despite the price she had to pay:

> Helene Weigel in the great scene where her son is executed freezes with a silent open-mouthed scream. Eichlerowna looks with the eyes of a dead man. I know that look from the occupation: the silent look and at the end of the act the dead voice with two pauses at the beginning and end: I haggled too long. Eichlerowna's acting is even more restrained and raw than Weigel's. It's as if she was stiffening, as if she was drying up from the inside.[139]

Another memorable production of Brecht in Poland was Erwin Axer's *The Resistable Rise of Arturo Ui*, which was presented in 1962 during the same season as the Berliner Ensemble's second visit with their production of the same play. Many critics felt that although a similarity existed in the interpretation of the text, the difference between the two presentations had primarily to do with the adjustments made by each toward its specific audience. The Polish critics believed the Berliner Ensemble version to be primarily addressed to Germans, particularly Germans living in the West who often visited Berliner Ensemble performances.

As a result, the Ensemble's presentation, according to Polish interpretation, focused on mobilizing the spectator against fascism and the demythification of the heroic image of Hitler. The Warsaw production, on the other hand, subdued the didactic tone and instead presented the play in the manner of a Shakespearean historical drama, using Richard III as a model.

Andrzej Wirth wrote that the Berliner Ensemble's production was much more political than the Polish interpretation. From the Polish perspective, fascism was conceived of as a wartime cataclysm that had been unleashed through a madman. This was the interpretation that Axer chose to present. The Berliner Ensemble, on the other hand, tried to present Ui from the perspective of the sociohistorical conditions that give rise to fascism. Thus, Hitler as such is not significant: the underlying system that created Hitler is the focus of examination.[140]

It is interesting to note that at this time Witkiewicz's plays were also staged, some of them for the very first time. In examining the figure of the mad tyrant in Witkiewicz's plays, one sees, despite differences in style and ideology, how close both Witkiewicz and Brecht are in their understanding of the figure of the mad tyrant as a sociohistorically possible recurring image, rather than, as most of the Polish critics interpreted the Polish production of *Arturo Ui,* as an isolated figure of a particular historical period. In that sense, Witkiewicz's plays were more disturbing to the Poles, since they forced the Polish public to see their own image, and although nationalistically proud of the acclaim Witkiewicz inspired as a precursor of the theater of the absurd in the West, Polish directors often submerged his vision of society in overstylized attention to foregrounding the visually grotesque elements of his plays. Thus, ironically, both Brecht and Witkiewicz were subjected to reinterpretation, a reinterpretation that had to do, as Mukařovský explained, with the collision of one tradition with that of another from which several influences are chosen and gradated hierarchically, allowing one to prevail over the others.

In Brecht's case, the Polish theater was no longer intimidated by either Brecht or the Berliner Ensemble:

We no longer view our theater as a poor sheep given to the wolf. We remember that our theater was nurtured on Brecht; however, given this perspective we can see many things in Brecht's theater that have remained foreign for us. Despite everything, we very much like sharp colors, well constructed sets, polished acting, less incisive commentary, allusions and metaphors, and not placards and allegories. The theater from Schiffbauerdamm has really not changed. We attempt successfully or less successfully to draw suggestions from contemporary drama. They however, attempt to realize their own canons. The Berliner Ensemble is an academy. Brecht is a classic.[141]

As a classic, Brecht is no longer sacrosanct and is subject to reinterpretation. Andrzej Wirth writes that during the Berliner Ensemble's first visit:

Brecht appeared to us as a particularly German personality. Today he is a world figure and his theater is an element within the universal theater. He has also become a part of the Polish theater, particularly during the last years when he has become a classic. The situation has changed considerably. Then the Polish audience and the Polish theater viewed a foreign presentation. Now the German Brecht stands in contrast to the Polish Brecht. The idealized Brecht preserved in the Berliner Ensemble, like the meter standard in the Bureau of Weights and Measures in Sèvres, near Paris, is contrasted with the Brecht assimilated, adapted, and reshaped into the familiar form and likeness of the Wisla Slavs.[142]

Thus, the *Verfremdungseffekt*, so much part of Brecht's aesthetics of reception, ultimately makes it possible for Brecht to be seen anew, the vision of his theater to be "shaken up," "jolted" out of its automatic interpretation as it collides with another cultural system of norms, values, and aesthetic functions and subject to that culture's way of seeing the world. Although not necessarily the only model for study, the reception of Brecht in Poland opens up possibilities not only for the study of Brecht's aesthetics, but also those of other aesthetic codes. Ultimately, Brecht's *Verfremdungseffekt* and the process of distancing the signifier from the signified makes it also possible to view Witkiewicz from a double perspective.

4

Witkiewicz:
The Aesthetics of Pure Form

Since the early 1960s, the plays of Stanislaw Ignacy Witkiewicz (1885–1939) have elicited interest as forerunners of the modern-most currents in the theater. Between 1966 and 1984 there were forty-four presentations of his plays in the United States alone,[1] although his plays and critical writings were not published in Poland until 1957 following the post-Stalinist thaw and the lifting of political restrictions in 1956. Ironically, Brecht served as a precursor of sorts for Witkiewicz in Poland by opening up an aesthetic climate that put Marxist aesthetics into question and made it possible for Witkiewicz to be rediscovered in his native country. When translations of Witkiewicz's works followed, he was hailed as the avant-garde prototype of the theater of the absurd. Thus, although his creative period was concurrent with Meyerhold's constructivist period and Brecht's expressionist and *Lehrstück* period, in terms of reception, he enters both the Polish and international theatrical repertoire long after Brecht had been established as a classic and Meyerhold had been rehabilitated into the Soviet hall of fame.

Conjectures made by various critics suggest that if Witkiewicz's plays had entered the world repertoire during the 1920s, his significant contributions would have placed him in terms of influence among such other modern theater precursors as Büchner, Jarry, and Artaud. Unfortunately this avant-garde Polish artist and thinker of the 1920s is yet to be discovered by the general public. There is a certain irony, as Eugène Ionesco points out with some bemusement, in designating an artist as avant-garde, since obviously the avant-garde can be recognized as such only after the event, "when it no longer exists as such, when it has been joined and even out-stripped by the main army."[2] Such is unfortunately the case with Witkiewicz. Rather more appropriate is Ionesco's conclusion that the avant-garde artist is one who stands in "opposition and rupture" to his society and "runs counter to time."[3] Nor is the avant-garde artist necessarily oriented toward the future but is, rather, by the very nature of the avant-garde, much more oriented toward the past and toward a reappraisal of the forms and basic laws that govern art.[4] Like Meyerhold and Brecht, Witkiewicz sought in his own independent fashion to rid the theater of the naturalistic, psychologically motivated dramas that had dominated the stage since the 1890s.

In reference to Witkiewicz, Jan Kott writes that it would be worthwhile "to devote some attention to this very phenomenon of the precursor who swerves from his time" and also to the problem "of the dialectic of anachronism and innovation." By applying Ionesco's definition of the avant-garde, one could say that Witkiewicz is an artist who came too early in terms of our evaluation of theatrical forms but "seemed to his contemporaries to be a man who came too late."[5]

In light of the observations made by Ionesco and Kott, why study Witkiewicz in the same frame as Meyerhold and Brecht? Meyerhold and Brecht represent in the history of modernism in the theater an attempt to extend art in a politically and socially revolutionary manner through modern technical means such as film projections, newspaper headlines, and moving platforms so as to reveal the constructed and nonlinear quality of the historical process. Witkiewicz represents a more complex and ambivalent case of an artist who, much as Meyerhold and Brecht, was influenced by the aesthetics of cubism, but who extended the fascination of the cubists with objects to a life of dreams. As a result, his plays attempt to depict the simultaneity and mutuality of the confrontation between inner and outer experiences. Ultimately, Witkiewicz's response to the social revolution in Russia gives another point of view to contrast with the optimism of Meyerhold and Brecht.

Projecting disillusionment and a sense of apocalyptic dread, Witkiewicz's plays offer images of hope and fear in dynamic collision with the intent of shocking his audience "from habituated and isolating experiences, especially those of waking and dreaming." What Witkiewicz, Meyerhold, and Brecht do share is a rejection of naturalist mimesis as well as a negation of romantic self-expression. Social reality in Witkiewicz's plays mirrors the experience of a "reified world out of control,"[6] for which, unlike in Meyerhold's and Brecht's aesthetics, there is no solution.

In his concern with the depiction of the world of dreams, Witkiewicz resembles the surrealists. Surrealism, as coined by Apollinaire, is the imposition of a higher reality on reality with the motivation, as writes André Breton, of "embittered rejection of the condition which we were compelled to live at that time."[7] The intellectual influences on the surrealists—Henri Bergson's theory of a mystical and indefinable motivating force in humanity, Freud's theory of dreams, and Einstein's theory of relativity—are also reflected in Witkiewicz's plays and critical theory. In particular, Freud's revelation about the contrast between the dream world in which man reveals himself and waking life as an area of repression is a central concern in Witkiewicz's plays where characters constantly oscillate between the real and illusory, between serious and frivolous, and between sense and nonsense both in their actions and words. Witkiewicz's theory of pure form also reflects this quest for penetrating beyond reality by echoing Breton's resolve: "The Marvellous is always beautiful, everything marvellous is beautiful; Nothing but the Marvellous is beautiful."[8]

Witkiewicz found the framework for his surrealist vision of the "marvellous" or the "mystery of existence" in the cubist aesthetics of polyphony. The cubists challenged old and arbitrarily imposed divisions which isolated art from life. They sought to reclaim the primal polyphony of sensation, perception, and expression through deformation or displacement in the handling of imagery. In particular, the paintings of Picasso gave Witkiewicz the impetus to extend the rendition of the violation of aesthetic norms in the theater. Conventional characters are fragmented and viewed simultaneously from various perspectives, an effect Witkiewicz achieves on stage by presenting characters as several facets of one personality, something akin to the myriad images of the poet in Mayakovsky's play *Vladimir Mayakovsky*. Like Mayakovsky and Marinetti, Witkiewicz applied the device of polyrhythmic construction in dramatic productions by projecting complicated, at times seemingly chaotic imagery by means of very precise orchestration of various levels of dialogue and monologue and of external action and the internal thoughts and moods of his characters.

The representation of chaotic and contradictory states of minds of the characters by Witkiewicz reflected an attitude that addressed issues of relativity, instability, violence, and dehumanization in face of both war and revolution. This disquietude influenced Witkiewicz's artistic exploration of a material reality radically redefined by non-Euclidian geometry and Einsteinian physics. These ideas in turn engendered an exploration of a fourth dimension, a movement toward abstraction which seemingly rejected thematic meanings, logical structures, and anything that might be identified as an ideological position. This then was the direction of Witkiewicz's theater of pure form whose function was to explore the possibility of pure theater according to the same principles as pure music or pure painting.

The lesson of the war and revolution taught Witkiewicz that the individual's right to liberty did not exist anymore, and much like Kragler, the hero of Brecht's early play *Drums in the Night* who evades commitment, Witkiewicz's characters reflect a world of disquietude, disjunction, and distrust from which they seek to escape either through negation or evasion. Witkiewicz's reaction was typical of the general artistic trend in Europe. In France, Jacques Copeau attacked a theater given over exclusively to the awakening of social conscience so evident in many of the plays of the naturalists. The aim of the theater, according to Copeau, was to make the spectator dream by "evoking and suggesting the multiplicity and mystery of life."[9] Gabriel Marcel likewise intimated that the future belonged to a theater of pure fantasy. Benjamin Crémieux talked of a theater which would become pure poetry, without the social content of naturalist drama to weigh down the theater's independent life as pure movement. In

Austria, Hugo Von Hofmannsthal defied the conventions of naturalism in order to focus attention on the inward life of his characters. And in Russia, Meyerhold called for a stylized theater in which external action and the revelation of character was incidental to "penetrating behind the mask, beyond the action into the character as perceived by the mind . . . to the inner mask."[10] Much later, Antonin Artaud, to whom Witkiewicz is frequently compared, proposed a theater of cruelty which would reject psychology and logic for violence, dreams, and the internal world of "man considered metaphysically."[11]

The major recurring themes and obsessions in Witkiewicz's imaginative universe include man's loneliness in the cosmos, death, sexual insatiability, the conflict between creative genius and society, the conflict of the artist and the family, social decay, revolution, the attractions of the tropics for non-Western civilization, and the mechanization of life. While these are overwhelmingly realistic concerns, the dramaturgical devices that prevail in all his plays—the use of exaggerated claustrophobic space, retardation and acceleration of action, the use of a divided stage, the spotlight effect, the viewing of corpses, anachronistic visitors out of historical time, and the use of multiple allusions and quotations from current events and personal life—serve to theatricalize these concerns.

The characters who populate his plays are also highly theatricalized, almost as if emerging from a mad cabaret review. Their presence, suitable to Todorov's descriptions of the fantastic, is a "hesitation" between the real and unreal.[12] Most typical are the demonic-aristocratic woman, the artist in conflict with society, the androgynous figure changing at will to a masculine or feminine persona, the mechanized desexualized servant, the mad tyrant, and the childwitness, forming a "figurative museum of his gallery of portraits of obsolescent and social specimens."[13] In his gallery of madmen, roles are frequently reversed: the tortured become the tormentors, prisoners become jailers, and madmen become sages. As Bernard Dukore aptly states, Witkiewicz's plays might also be described "as a cosmic amusement park, designed by Dali and Magritte, where Strindberg sells peanuts and popcorn, while Spengler performs a cooch dance, Heidigger and Sartre turn somersaults, and Dostoevsky and Nietzsche sling custard pies at each other."[14]

And in all plays, the characters proclaim both social and aesthetic theories. "We live in an age of manifestos," writes Witkiewicz,

Even before an artistic movement spontaneously comes into being, its theory is often already in a state of new perfection. Theories are starting to create movements, and not vice versa. . . . A greater and greater intellectualization of the creative process and the subjugation of the outbursts of genius to principles conceived a priori is the characteristic trait of our times.[15]

In Witkiewicz's plays the whole question of influence seems to be irrelevant, for example, in his play *The Mother* (1924) obvious references to both Strindberg and Ibsen can be found. But so can other references as well: to

Einstein's theory of relativity; to Freud's psychoanalysis; to communism, fascism, and capitalism; to Lenin, Georges Sorel, Leibnitz, Bergson, Chwistek, Malinowski, Picasso, and Schoenberg. These are not only names as such, but representative theories over which the characters in the plays argue passionately and sometimes kill one another.

Nor can personal conflicts be discarded from the realm of his characters and plays. Although the influences at work on his unique *Weltanschauung* appear much later in his plays, deconstructed and deformed to suit his particular needs, Witkiewicz, much like Mayakovsky, played out his life as if it were a drama in its own right, and even in his own time came to be acknowledged as a legendary character. Ultimately, in both Witkiewicz and Mayakovsky, self-awareness became an extension of the creative process, and both expended tremendous energy in the creation of a public persona.

Inevitably the question arises: Do we need to know Witkiewicz's life in order to understand his work? According to the formalists, a concentration on the specific poetic elements in verbal art is the only appropriate task of literary criticism, and the inclusion of any kind of biographical analysis is "unscientific contraband, a 'back-door' approach."[16] However, as writes Boris Tomasevsky, in reference to Mayakovsky: "In the twentieth century there appeared a special type of writer with a demonstrative biography, one which shouted out: 'look at how bad and how impudent I am! Look! And don't turn your head away, because all of you are just as bad, only you are fainthearted and hide yourselves. But I am bold; I strip myself stark naked and walk around in public without feeling ashamed.'"[17]

Obviously, the question of the role of biography in literary history cannot be solved uniformly. We need, however, to mention here only the construction of Mayakovsky's or Witkiewicz's works: they are an open diary in which intimate feelings are recorded. Indeed, in the works themselves the juxtaposition of the texts and the author's biography plays a structural role. Ultimately, as Tomasevsky explains, the biography that is useful to the literary critic is not the author's curriculum vitae but the biographical "legend created by the author himself."[18] This legend then becomes a literary fact integrating the author into his own work.

At the end of World War I, upon his return to Poland after four years in Russia, first as an officer in the Imperial Pavlovsky Regiment and following the Revolution as political commissar of his regiment, the thirty-three-year-old Witkiewicz created his most important character—"Witkacy" (an amalgam of his last and middle names). And so the legend began about the "madman Witkacy"—a sex fiend, drug addict, and unconventional dilettante, permitting Witkiewicz to project to the world his new self, or rather the myriad of selves.

In part, Witkiewicz created "Witkacy" to distinguish himself from his father, a famous Polish artist and critic also named Stanislaw. The father, strongly influenced by Nietzchean notions of the sublime, educated Witkacy entirely at home on the grounds that formal schooling produced only mediocrity and conformity. Witkacy thus became the object of an unusual experiment in education, by means of which his father's ideas about art, culture, and civilization were to form an exceptional, unique individual and an outstanding artist. By the age of five, Witkacy was painting and composing music; at seven he wrote his first plays under the influence of Shakespeare, Gogol, Maeterlinck, and the Polish playwrights Fredro, Mickiewicz, Krasinski, and Slowacki. Among these early gems were *The Cockroaches*, a comedy in one act; *Comic Scenes from Family Life*, a comedy in one act with three variations; and *The Menagerie*, or *The Elephant's Prank*, a comedy in five acts.

These childhood plays reveal an early concern with philosophical issues and exhibit characteristics comparable to the devices of the contemporary theater of the absurd: bizarre names and titles, elements of the grotesque, wildly accelerated action, and irreverence toward established forms and theatrical conventions. The action is episodic, and various possible endings are included. At the same time, these childhood plays also anticipate what would be the major themes in Witkiewicz's mature plays. For instance, *Cockroaches* portrays the reactions of the characters to the impending invasion of the castle by a swarm of grey cockroaches from "Ameri." These predecessors to the grey swarms of mobs gone mad are squashed in a general free-for-all slaughter. In *Menagerie*, the elephant devours the lion's, ape's, and wolf's suppers, adding insult to injury by calling the king of beasts an "old fool." For this he is duly punished and sheds copious tears in remorse. Although in the world of beasts a moral order exists, the lion, an antecedent of the mad tyrants in Witkacy's later plays, takes undue delight in beating up the elephant. And in *Comic Scenes from a Family Life*, the characters talk around each other in non sequitur responses, something akin to the gaps in communication presented in Ionesco's *The Bald Soprano*. These early plays only serve to underline the curious mixture of farce, parody, and metaphysical concerns that were to be so characteristic of Witkacy's later work. Like the similarity between Jarry's childhood farces and his more mature works, Witkacy's principles of dramaturgy did not change appreciably. But in his later plays they are enlarged and stretched to accommodate a tremendous burden of complex social, philosophical, and aesthetic theories and positions.

In his later plays, Witkacy frequently draws on personal experiences from his childhood, particularly his conflict with his father, who demanded that Witkiewicz soar beyond the expectations of the ordinary. Unfortunately, these demands left him in torment and plunged him into morbid self-pity. It was not until he accompanied Bronislaw Malinowski on an anthropological journey through India, Ceylon, Papua, and Australia that Witkacy saw another reality: "I'm unable to describe the wonders I'm seeing here . . . the vegetation madder and madder, and the people more and more gaudily dressed (violet, yellow, and purple, sometimes emerald green), which along with the chocolate and bronze bodies and the strange plants in the background, creates a devilish effect."[19]

Much like the cubists, who also found inspiration for their techniques of displacement in primitive art, Witkiewicz was to draw on visual memories from this expedition when he worked out his theory of Pure Form. He also acquired the distance necessary to examine societal problems in a new light. Above all, like Antonin Artaud, he became aware of the self-destructive qualities of European civilization, which, when confronted with the life of the tropics, result in madness.

"Tropical madness" in Witkiewicz's plays may be regarded as either a sickness imagined by European colonists to justify their cruelties toward the natives, or a genuine form of insanity caused by the heat, the vividness of colors, the spicy food, alcohol, and constant exposure to the sight of naked bodies. In the world of tropical madness, brutality serves as powerful stimulus to sexual desire, a characteristic which pervades all of Witkacy's plays. In his tropical plays, the plague, much like in Artaud's vision, becomes the symbol of the great infection that will precede mankind's extinction. The plague, of course, is civilization. The Europeans have brought with them the very diseases which they hoped to flee. Their flight takes them, not from civilization into a primitive paradise, but to an empty place where they can give free reign to their inherent violence.

In both Witkiewicz and Artaud, violence is seen as a symptom of the psychical distortions breaking out as the repressive behavior patterns imposed by society become unbearable. Alternatively the outbreaks of violence are presented as evidence of the intrinsic violence of our social systems; at other times violence erupts according to a law of nature itself. To re-create this experience for the spectator, Artaud proposes a theater "in which violent physical images crash and hypnotize the sensibility of the spectator." Witkiewicz's most important question for the theater is to ask whether it is possible to re-create the same metaphysical feeling in the spectator that men once experienced when myths and beliefs coincided with a religious impulse. Witkacy demanded that theater must provoke an explosion of metaphysical emotions, a renewal of wildness through the unchaining of "the beast." Artaud proclaimed that "metaphysics can reach our spirits only violently through the skin."[20] This attempt to give theater back its religious significance can be traced back to the symbolists. For example, Andrei Bely believed in theater as a form of worship: "Drama has arisen from mystery. Its fate is to return. When drama approaches mystery, returns to it inevitably it will leave the stage-boards and spread through life."[21]

Both Witkiewicz and Artaud asked similar questions as to whether the "mystery of existence" can be presented theatrically. Jacques Derrida in writing on Artaud suggests that his theater achieves the very "incorporation of life," not "the representation of life" and, thereby, "lays bare the flesh of the world, lays bare the world's sonority, intonation intensity—the shout that the articulation of language and logic have not yet entirely frozen."[22] Likewise, Witkacy's theatrical world is not representational, and much like Artaud, Witkacy rejected a theater of slavish imitation, psychologism, and logic. What happens on the stage of Witkacy's plays is often illogical. In *The Madman and the Nun*, for example, the hero walks out of the insane asylum nonchalantly with the nun, although he has just hanged himself, and his body still hangs on stage. The milieu of the insane asylum makes common, ordinary events seem somewhat unreal. Thus the final coming together of the two lovers, the madman and the nun, represents an estrangement between their metaphysical union and the events of the real world. While this seems devoid of logic, in the context of Witkiewicz's aim to present the world of dreams and illusion, the grotesqueries of his plays appear inherently valid and logical.

While both Witkiewicz and Artaud shared the concern that man as a result of social progress had become more and more absorbed and nullified by the collective, for Artaud the rebirth of theater implied the destruction of the literary theater. This is where, as Jan Kott so aptly suggests, the analogy between Artaud and Witkiewicz ends.[23] While Artaud demands the suppression of speech in the theater in order to bring out the spontaneous magical function of human movement and gesture, one must remember that Witkiewicz was above all a playwright to whom language was to be, along with color and movement, the cause of the "metaphysical shudder" in the spectator. This language was of course deformed and disconnected from its primary function and meaning by estranging signifiers from their signifieds and purposefully changing the relations of adherence and contiguity in such a way that a new unity was to be formed, "connected and disconnected at the same time."[24]

Witkiewicz has often been mistakenly designated as a Polish prototype of German expressionism. Although he shared many of the same influences as the expressionists, such as Maeterlinck, the Strindberg of the chamber and dream plays, Wedekind, and the Polish expressionist Przybyszewski, his attention in plays and in his writings on pure form is placed on making everything in the theater—poetry, scenic art, music, and acting—subordinate to a single transcendent idea of form, while in the plays of the expressionists the distortion of realistic conventions often leads to a theater that is emphatically content-oriented, the plays becoming vehicles for a "message" with characters created to proclaim it.

It is important to remember that Witkiewicz was an artist as well as a dramatist, and that his first attempts to create an aesthetics in which form dominates were directly related to his painting. Pure form for Witkacy is a general theory, rather than a theory particular to theater. In his theatrical practice, as in his art, however, Witkiewicz borrows elements from other dramatists and artists in order to use them for his own aims. These elements are recognizable, but are already functioning in a new way. As in Picasso's paintings, Witkiewicz juxtaposes parts which belong to different modes that may at first appear incompatible. These parts are shown from an unfamiliar angle and the whole appears as something unusual and strange, as in a cubist painting or an atonal composition by Schoenberg.

In his attempts to project meaning through the formal compositional elements of his dramas, Witkiewicz (much like Schoenberg in his setting of *Pierrot Lunaire*) attempted to go beyond words to the tonal elements of language. "Whatever was to be said has been said by the music," writes Schoenberg, "Why then have words as well? If words were necessary they would have been there in the first place. An art says more than words." Schoenberg describes his musical compositions as "sound and mood," "absolutely unsymphonic" with "no architecture, no construction," and with "chord colours" to heighten the impressionistic tone.[25]

Theatricality in Witkiewicz's theory of pure form in the theater stems from an intent to define the theater as an autonomous art. The very idea of an autonomous theatricality invokes a system of specific signs proper only to theater. Thus, the manifestation of the basic theatrical elements results from the formalization of the pluricodal ensemble, a simultaneity of signs in space, and a temporality that is not a linear temporality.

For Witkiewicz, liberating the *mise-en-scène* from the confines of the realistic style had to do with the elimination of intrigue and action based on cause-effect sequences. Clearly, the point of departure had to do with the negation of the conventions of naturalism. This rejection of established conventions constitutes the basic tenet of Witkacy's program for the renewal of the theater and determines the character and scope of his proposed changes. The destruction of the story—and here our analysis makes use of the distinction between plot and story proposed by the Russian formalists, that the story is the objective reality reflected in the work, while plot is the means of reflecting and organizing this reality through language, gestures, costumes, scenery, and so on—ought to lead to the extinction of those meanings which arise from causal relationships and on which the didactic, political, and social functions of the theater are grounded. Thus, Witkacy's plays present a shift of the boundary between story and plot, and, in fact, the story in the above sense is clearly absent. Instead, the plot, in particular the construction of dialogue, takes the place of the story. Plot, which in naturalist drama is an element of form rather than content, here becomes the content.[26]

In Witkacy's plays, pure theatricality depends on the formalist conception of "making strange" as a means of changing the materiality of expression. The projection of reality is violated, forcing the spectator to take note of signs and their operation. In short, Witkacy's theory of pure form in the theater, with its attention to the materiality of expression, ultimately brings about changes in the semantic systems of content. Since the normative principles of place, time and action are disrupted, pure form is conceived of as "a way of breaking down automatism in perception, and the aim of the image is held to be, not making a meaning more accessible for our comprehension, but bringing about a special perception of a thing, bringing about the 'seeing' and not just the 'recognizing' of it."[27]

In a highly aesthetic use of language and scenic composition signifiers manifest a high degree of "plurality" of ambiguity. "Semiotically speaking," Eco writes, "ambiguity must be defined as a mode of violating the rules of the code."[28] Instead of the social criticism inherent in the naturalistic theater, Witkacy attempts through the process of reduction, condensation, and concentration to present the torment which results from man's denial or inability to accept the paradox of his isolation. Theatricalism in Witkacy is a self-conscious awareness of the play as a play, permitting the characters and the playwright to comment on the absurdity of the usual discoveries emerging from naturalistic dramas. In that sense, Witkacy's pure form, to use Jacobson's expression, represents "organized violence" committed on the conventions of the naturalist theater,[29] which, having discarded its metaphysical function, had as its principle aim the imitation of the banal relationships and situations of everyday life, thereby blurring the line which divides art from life. Like Artaud in his often-quoted question "whether in this slippery world which is committing suicide without noticing it, there can be found a nucleus of men capable of restoring to all of us the natural and magical equivalent of the dogmas in which we no longer believe,"[30] Witkacy likewise urges the theater to abandon psychological tricks and human interest stories. "We've had psychology up to our ears," he writes. "Instead the theater should usher us into a dimension of experience totally different from life into the sphere of metaphysical feelings where the mystery of existence can be apprehended emotionally."[31]

To illustrate his theater based on pure form, Witkacy presents this example:

Three characters dressed in red come on stage and bow to no one in particular. One of them recites a poem (it should create a feeling of urgent necessity at this very moment). A kindly old man enters leading a cat on a string. So far everything has taken place against a background of a black screen. The screen draws apart, and an Italian landscape becomes visible. Organ music is heard. The old man talks with the other characters, and what they say should be in keeping with what has gone before. A glass falls off the table. All of them fall on their knees and weep. The old man changes from a kindly man into a ferocious "butcher" and murders a little girl who has just crawled in from the left. At this very moment a handsome young man runs in and thanks the old man for murdering the girl, at which point the characters in red sing and dance. Then the young man weeps over the body of the little girl and says very amusing things, whereupon the old man becomes once again kindly and good-natured and laughs to himself in a corner uttering sublime and limpid phrases. The choice of costumes is completely open: period or fantastic—there may be music during some parts of the performance. In other words, an insane asylum? Or rather a madman's brain on the stage? Perhaps so, but we maintain that, if the play is seriously written and appropriately produced, this method can create works of previously unsuspected beauty; whether it be drama, tragedy, farce, or the grotesque, all in a uniform style and unlike anything which had previously existed.[32]

That Witkiewicz in his theory of pure form in the theater was highly conscious of breaking existing codes and creating ambiguity is certainly evident from the preceding example. In this example the rule-breaking roles of ambiguity and self-reference are fostered and organized. The effect is to generate an "aesthetic idiolect," a special language peculiar to that text, inducing in the spectator a sense of what Eco calls "cosmicity."[33] In Witkiewicz, the function of the aesthetic idiolect is to create an impression on the spectator as if "of waking up from a strange dream in which the most trite things have an elusive deep charm, characteristic of dreams, not comparable to anything."[34]

Witkacy postulated that if a painting should be no more than a set of "oriented tensions" of line and color and if modern painting tended toward a refusal to represent anything, could not drama be conceived of as "pure action"? However, deformation for its own sake, Witkacy notes, is only a means and not an end, and such plays cannot be devised in cold blood, artificially, to satisfy the cravings of the bourgeoisie for innovation. "Our aim is not programmatic nonsense, we are trying rather to enlarge the possibilities of composition by abandoning in art any life-like logic, by introducing a fantastic psychology and fantastic action in order to win a complete freedom of formal elements."[35] Any attempts at a mimetic approach are rejected, echoing the expressionists: "Die Welt ist da. Es wäre sinnlos sie zu wiederholen."

What Witkiewicz seeks to render are metaphysical states and violent emotions welling up from the innermost recesses of the subconscious. Extreme moods, such as despair or ecstatic joy, are externalized by projecting them through distorted manifestations of color, shape, syntax, vocabulary, and tonal relationships. Dissonance is closely related to the grotesque, which reveals the rift between the nominal and the phenomenal world and shows man to be ill at ease in the presence of events and situations eluding his grasp. Witkiewicz fuses extremely subjective elements with starkly objective ones by doubling up the role of the characters. His characters step outside the complicated intrigues in which they are hopelessly entangled and view their own dilemmas ironically and from a great distance. Awareness of the play as play allows for a shifting perspective. The origin and aim of art is treated by Witkiewicz in metaphysical terms; he puts particular stress on the expressive functions of art, but at the same time he describes the structure of the work in a highly formalistic manner as a logical pattern of "simple and complex elements" chosen consciously and purposefully.

The theory of pure form is based on the principle premise of Witkiewicz's philosophy—that of "unity of plurality." During the performance of a play the formal elements should form an integral entity, irrespective of what preceded a particular moment or what is going to follow it. In this manner, the subject of the work loses its significance and the text is freed from the demands of the chronological ordering of events, consistency of plot, continuity of time, and all laws governing the psychological development of characters.

A "fantastic" psychology of characters, according to Witkacy's theory, must correspond to the alogical action. Traditional means of characterization—the individualization of physical appearance, manner of speaking, and gesturing—are forsaken and, what is most significant, the characters are liberated from all laws of psychology, ethics, even physics and biology. Death—like time and space—becomes relative: the dead are likely to be resurrected in the next scene.

To accommodate the training of the actor, Witkacy proposed a method based on the application of cubism to drama, its function to break up reality into many components. "The actor, in his own right should not exist," he writes, "he should be the same kind of part within a whole as the color red in a particular painting or the note C sharp in a particular musical composition." "Forget completely about life" he goes on to urge the actor, "and pay no attention to what is happening on stage at any given moment as it relates to what is about to happen at the next moment."[36] Witkacy's actors exist on two planes simultaneously: on the plane of action and on the plane of commentary, by means of which they criticize and digress on the events occurring. Precisely because of their doubleness, the actors direct the spectator's attention not to the message but rather to the expression. In this manner any possibility of establishing motivation is disrupted, and the spectator is made aware of the theatricality inherent in Witkacy's plays by the constant interjections by the actors concerning stage directions on how they are to say their lines and react to events: For example, the stage directions in *The Shoemakers* (1934) indicate:

(Scurvy sets down to work feverishly, whining from nervousness and haste. He whines more and more, and growing sexual excitement is "written all over" every moment he makes; nothing goes right for him, and everything simply falls out of his hands, because of his excessive state of erognosological excitement.)

Scurvy: Growing sexual excitement is "written all over" every movement I make, scatological pseudobourgeois that I am. Erognosologically speaking I'm almost a saint—a Turkish saint, I might add to make it respectable, since I reek of cowardice and am a coward from way back. I have to whine, or otherwise I'd burst like a child's balloon. . . .[37]

From this example we can determine that through the use of digression, polemics, philosophical discourse, personal invective, literary criticism, invented obscenities, and ironic parodies Witkacy foregrounds theatricality and completely shatters illusion.

Although it is not known whether Witkacy saw any of the Russian theatrical experiments of Meyerhold, Vakhtangov, or Tairov, or for that matter whether he attended the plays presented at the Moscow Art Theater during his sojourn in Russia while in service with the Imperial Army, one thing is clear: Witkiewicz vehemently rejected the tenets of the Stanislavsky method. According to Witkacy, "wallowing in stale emotional entrail-twisting" was precisely what the

Stanislavsky school of acting encouraged actors to regard as their highest calling. According to Witkacy, the actor must stop all attempts to experience emotions and must likewise stop trying "to send audiences into convulsive emotional twitchings, spasm, and fits." "In our opinion," he writes, "Shakespeare staged with Stanislavsky's realism stops being Shakespeare, Beethoven played sentimentally stops being Beethoven."[38]

To interpret the characters from Witkacy's grotesque museum of characters, the actor must switch the spectator from the plane he has just reached to one that is totally unforeseen. This requires, according to Witkiewicz, a special acting technique in which the actor must neither live his part nor embody it, because his aim is opposed to creating and suggesting particular feelings as such but rather to calling attention to and exploiting the dramatic framework in which the actors themselves exist. In "significative acting," as this method is called, the actor is not to convey the truth of life, but the truth of form. Witkacy suggests that the actor should forget his body and should speak rather than act his role. This is to be done with perfect elocution, but without emotional stresses. The function of the actor is to confine himself solely to bringing out either "the sound or the content (in the artistic sense) value of words." This principle, however, does not compel the actor to stick to only one convention of acting. Rather, the actor may apply what Witkacy calls the technique of "dissonance," which encourages the actor to make cheerful statements with an air of gloom and tragic ones with laughter.[39] This disjunctive dialogue—used thirty years before Beckett—should be viewed not as a potential conversation between the dramatic characters but rather as arias in an opera, in which each character projects his own inner voice.[40] The inner voice must not be distorted by gesture, facial expression, or movements that attempt to project psychologically motivated feelings: "all tremolandos coming from the heart and the stomach, all dewy tears, spasms of the diaphragm and other organs have to go."[41]

Arrangements of actors on the stage was not to be accidental, but rather with regard to the stage design so as to produce, possibly at all times, "the impression of a definite pictorial composition." Witkiewicz was, however, careful not to relegate the text to a position subordinate to the purely visual elements of the play. Concerning the function of the dramatic text, Witkacy states that "the spoken word in the theater is a thing of major importance and other elements must be subordinated to it." The predominance of decor, costumes, and even movement over spoken words might lead, Witkacy cautioned, to "tableaux vivants and pantomimes."[42]

The purpose of Witkacy's theater of pure form is to produce a play which will excite the spectator's deadened nerves to the point of vibration. "Everything must be transformed in a way no one has ever seen before,"[43] proclaims his prototype artist character in *The Beelzebub Sonata* (1925). Concerned with the increasing mechanization of life, Witkacy hoped that his theater would shock the spectator's nervous system and act as a stimulating shower after long hours of stupefying mechanical work.

The leading idea behind Witkiewicz's theoretical system is the same idea that determines the fate of the characters in his dramas and novels. Almost all his characters are busy looking for situations and ways to experience metaphysical sensations and thus gain an understanding of the strangeness of existence. Unfortunately, as in his prototype chamber play *The Pragmatists* (1919), they are characters who are never able to accomplish this aim, so they must depend on substitute forms, like sex, drugs, politics, and art: "The infernal banality of existence." Plasfodor, the nonartist protagonist in *The Pragmatists*, declares: "It's four o'clock in the afternoon. Then there'll be supper, then an orgy, then a seance, then the nightly bad dreams, then the usual dose of pills to give us strength to go. Oh, it's unbearable." In *The Pragmatists* Witkacy emphasizes repetition to symbolize lack of essential change. "Now, once again, I'm the same young boy I used to be years ago," says Plasfodor, who near the end of Act I "sits down with the same gesture of despair as at the beginning of this act."[44] Thus, an essential characteristic of Witkacy's plays is not that a play ends happily or unhappily, or that it ends precisely as it began, but rather—apart from revealing an essential absence of change despite some change—that the ending denies the exclusiveness of either tragic or comic endings. Witkacy's comedies with corpses depict the death of individuals who may return, but not necessarily. Death is not necessarily irrevocable, nor is it necessarily revocable. Everything is contingent on arbitrariness.

Although it can be assumed that the characters in *The Pragmatists* have a common memory and that references to that memory become the subject of their dialogue, the basic axioms of dialogue are violated. All the characters express themselves in the same voice—the voice of the playwright. As a result, the dialogue has a continuous tonality and each character has his particular set refrain or aria. It is curious how the characters, in violating communication's axioms, continually pay attention to the signicative value of words. "Isn't conversation the most significant way of experiencing life?" Plasfodor asks Mammalia, his mute mistress. "Let's talk about anything at all. . . . Actually, just the fact of talking itself . . . with words the wealth of possibilities is far greater than with events. If only it were possible to grasp what flows as the flowing itself in its own terms, and not as something standing for something else."[45]

Nobody in Witkiewicz's play seems to forward the action, such as it is. On the contrary, each character spends his time in egoistical self-absorption or hopeless yearning. Characteristically the dialogue is not about something to be done or faced, but consists rather of a series of self-revelatory monologues cut up in alternate speeches. These characters do not listen; they merely think aloud. As their thoughts flitter from one thing to the other, they change the subject without warning. In a sense, Witkacy pushes the impasse of communication found in

Chekhov's plays to an ultimate degree. It's as if the characters from *The Cherry Orchard* have found themselves in exile on Witkiewicz's stage once the cherry orchard has been chopped down. Unable to stop the course of life, they wait to be taken out of their cosmic loneliness.

The Pragmatists serves as a good example of pure form in action. As the characters in the play are introduced, they are characterized with a set of recurring expressions, gestures, and phrases which provide them with a sharp pictorial and musical definition. Unlike the authors of naturalist drama, Witkacy organizes his plays on contrasting pairs of *commedia dell'arte*, circus, or cabaret characters, closely corresponding to the pairings later found in Beckett's *Waiting for Godot* or *Endgame*. Conceived of as a constellation of physical, spiritual, and philosophical qualities, the characters are presented as projections of interrelated and opposed qualities, fixed as polar qualities of male and female, life and death, action and contemplation, business and art, and East and West. The struggle between these polarities produces a stalemate. Clearly, Witkacy superimposed a new form on the model provided by Strindberg in *The Ghost Sonata*, in which the struggle for domination, the battle of the sexes, as well as the interplay between human and other-worldly powers is also at play. Thus, in Witkacy, as in Strindberg, a continuum exists in which every trait can be viewed as both itself and its opposite. And like the stock characters in *commedia dell'arte*, all roles are cast in advance.

The opening scene and the mysterious and presumably sexual implications of Plasfodor's and von Telek's speeches are a fair indication of the conflict within the play, namely, a kind of primeval, demonic Strindbergian battle of the sexes fought with enormous ferocity. The essential reality of *The Pragmatists* is created out of the polaric nature of things and the centripetal struggle of opposites. Thus, the struggle between Plasfodor and Mammalia is not just the struggle of a man and woman. It is between *the* man and *the* woman, the only man and the only woman, something akin to the savage treatment of relations between a man and a woman shown by Oskar Kokoschka in *Murderer, Hope of Women*. Furthermore, this man and woman must struggle as though all the hate or all the love of chaos is present in them. Unable to confront their real nature with all its implications of terror and beauty, the characters pragmatically find consolation in the "poisons" that give them relief. As a result of this inability to confront metaphysical wonder, the characters in *The Pragmatists* remain hopelessly unsated by life. Like cruelty for Artaud, insatiability characterizes the climate of Witkiewicz's theater. This insatiability propels his characters to murder, torture, and rape without scruples, not for selfish reasons but to produce metaphysical shock, a shock much akin to the effect Witkacy desires to produce in the spectators.

This shock must, however, emerge from consideration of the formal elements of the play. In *The Pragmatists*, for example, Witkiewicz attempts to put together the plot as though it were a musical composition or painting, using the human voice primarily for its sound value and gesture as an aspect of pictorial arrangements. Color, sound, and gesture are the chief scenic elements, and dialogue becomes but one controlled aspect of the entire orchestration. The colors and shapes are projected not only from the setting but from the makeup of the actors and their costumes as well. The color progression in the play is from predominately red tonalities at the beginning, to an addition of yellow in the middle section, to prevailing blacks and ultimately grey at the end. Each color has its significative value. The white of boredom of Plasfodor's pajamas is in contrast to the red robe of emotion and passion worn by Mammalia. White also signals the draining of color to show reduced dimensions of the psyche. In the middle section the mummy appears wearing a yellow robe, the color yellow representing decay. In each succeeding scene darker colors overpower the brightness of the first scene, particularly when von Telek enters wearing black pajamas as a contrast to Plasfodor's white ones. When the characters depart through the black door in the middle of the stage, grey as the dominant color of existence and pragmatism pervades the stage.

Although Witkacy's silence in the area of influences makes it difficult to relate his ideas to other theatrical explorations, the following observations made by Georg Fuchs on the nature of the Japanese theater bear a strong resemblance to the effects Witkacy sought:

> For example, we have a scene in which a man and a woman are conversing quietly. Suddenly, the conversation takes an ominous turn. In an instant, the color harmony is changed. If at first the scene was pale green with a decoration of cherry blossom, at the significant moment the garments of the characters suddenly fall back from their shoulders revealing undergarments of crimson and simultaneously several scarlet clad supernumeraries appear in the background bringing some necessary appurtenance—an altar, a rug—and the color harmony is suddenly blood red and black. The effect is more weird, more horrifying, than all the mechanical thunder and lightning which in our theater . . . make their appearance with such suspicious promptness.[46]

A resemblance in orchestration of color is also evident between Witkacy and Kokoschka. Since both Witkiewicz and Kokoschka were artists who reacted against realism and impressionism, the characteristic elements in their pictures were dynamic rhythms and the use of symbolic colors. A key term to both was "internal necessity," and for that reason both in *The Pragmatists* and *Murderer, Hope of Women* patterns of visual images and colors are used to articulate their intensely personal vision of archetypal sexual patterns of domination and destruction. In a way similar to the use of color in *The Pragmatists*, Kokoschka uses color as a motif repeated in costumes, scenery, and lighting. While action in Witkiewicz's play is often static, erupting suddenly into violent action, Kokoschka uses violent physical action in a sequence of choreographed rhythms.

Both, however, shared the aim of creating a drama in which the stimulation of the audience through formal means would replace traditional emotional transference through character development.

Witkiewicz's emphasis on the nonliterary formal construction of his plays can be related to the general movement in Russia to extend the possibilities of each form. Vasily Kandinsky described synthesis in the arts as an attempt of each art "to become immersed in itself" while simultaneously desiring the breaking down the boundaries dividing the arts. "Naturally, as each individual art becomes immersed in itself, it looks with involuntary interest into adjacent areas to observe how another art will apply itself to the same problems. Never have musicians followed with such interest the development of painting, painters of architecture, architects of poetry, etc."[47] The poetry of Blok and Khlebnikov was straining to burst into music, explains James Billington, the music of Scriabin was seeking to encompass color, and the colors of Kandinsky the language of music. Kandinsky, the pioneer of abstract art, sought to extend art into a kind of "abstract musical arabesque . . . purified like music of all but its direct appeals to the spirit," as for example in his scenario *The Yellow Sound*. This attempt to extend language and sound "beyond reason" led to the most abstract and purified expression—that of silence, or the "white on white" of Malevich's paintings. "Whiteness," writes Billington, "space, and infinity had replaced the sea as the symbol of this fulfillment-in-obliteration."[48]

Due to Witkiewicz's silence in the area of influences, we don't know to what extent he was familiar with Kandinsky's ideas on art, but even from a brief overview it is evident that Witkacy's ideas on pure form resemble those of Kandinsky. Like Witkacy, Kandinsky believed colors and shapes had specific emotion-signifying powers that could be codified and combined scientifically into a harmonious whole, reflecting the harmony of the cosmos. This idea was an even more literal interpretation of composition in music, in which notes and rhythmic patterns can indeed be assigned fixed values. Whereas, in the composition of a painting, abstract lines, shapes, and colors assume similar values.

We have seen to what extent Witkacy attempted to apply pure form in his *Pragmatists*, where he not only assigns each character a color but also a particular gestic or movement. Mammalia, who is mute, undulates about the stage, "her whole figure expressing unbearable tension." Plasfodor reclines looking straight ahead "with an expression of frightful insatiability." Masculete has an expression on her face that is always mischievous. The Mummy has "bulging movements" as she slowly moves across the stage. Von Telek walks like a man "strong as a bull." The particular aria of each character provides the sound value, with the Mummy's song as counterpoint in the background, uniting all characters in their common memory of the secret from the past.

However, a danger lies in viewing Witkiewicz's solely from a pictorial standpoint. Witkacy's world is a kinetic one. Tensions are constantly shifting, receding, and building up, with occasional explosions along the way. This kineticism is the result of the tensions between the hero and the forces around him, emerging from his desire to define himself and his horror at accepting that definition, which by its nature would categorize him. As a result, in *The Pragmatists* there is no frozen moment in time, no stasis, only constant flux; explosions and implosions are continually occurring. These explosions happen in a hermetically sealed claustrophobic space from which there is but one outlet—through the black door at the middle of the stage.

Faced with the impossibility of communicating their quintessential experience, the characters can only rave or splutter. Throughout the three short acts of *The Pragmatists*, they abuse and attack one another with a ferocity that is physical as well as verbal. Mammalia tries to stab von Telek with a Japanese knife, she repeatedly shoots the already dead Mummy, knocks von Telek to the floor and tries to throttle him, while von Telek jabs a tie pin into Plasfodor's hand and bashes in Masculete's head with an unholstery hammer. Maiming and killing are deliberately made surprising without adequate preparation or follow-through. The dead will not stay dead. Masculette, who had been demolished by von Telek in the first scene of Act III, sits as a corpse with a bandage around her head in the next scene, then, upon the Mummy's command, crawls out the door on her elbows and knees.

Everytime that a relationship has been established, Witkacy arbitrarily decides to disturb it by working in the element of surprise—his special province—based on a technique of omitting foreshadowing, explanation, and all psychological or narrative interconnections. Since we are dealing with characters who constantly expose their feelings and desires, there is no problem of a "subtext." Although it would be possible to unearth several stories buried beneath the surface, Witkacy refuses to develop the lines of action clearly or coherently. For example, in a grotesque travesty of the grim revelations found in naturalist drama, it is revealed that von Telek is Mammalia's brother and that he seduced her when she was eight years old. We also learn that Plasfodor stole Princess Tsui, now the Mummy, from her ancestral home. After he drank all her blood "through a straw made of dried Wu grass" she turned into a Mummy, and Mammalia was struck dumb forever in horror at the crime. But these frightful revelations do not bring us closer to the characters.

Witkacy frequently stressed that pure form should be regarded as a theory for an ideal work of art, the execution of which is practically impossible, admitting that only some of his pieces could be considered as being closer to Pure Form. *The Pragmatists* can be seen as a drama that is concerned not with depicting reality but in constructing its hypothetical model. Thus, presentational form is achieved through an arbitary model of reality and not through a representational analogy. Witkiewicz's play acts as a kind of author's commentary which confirms the general outlines of the system he invented.

The task that Witkacy set himself was an impossible one—to attack and transform a theater in which he had no part. Unlike Brecht and Meyerhold, who had both official and public affirmation for their theatrical experiments, Witkacy found little support and had no stage. As a result the majority of his plays were not staged until the 1960s. However, Witkiewicz's theory of Pure Form, taken too seriously by most directors who attempted to stage his plays in the 1960s, should be seen as a polemical exaggeration, in much the same way as we now view Brecht's theory of epic theater. Pure form in the theater only indicates Witkiewicz's intention to intensify the use of presentational elements. Thus, his theory more closely resembles Meyerhold's theatrical practices and should be understood as pure theatricality rather than pure form. Presentational form is achieved through the presentation of an arbitrary model of reality. This has an important consequence in that Witkiewicz's plays are not quotable in the sense that there is no one statement in them which contains the message; the structure ultimately is the message.

Viewed in this light, the theory of pure form should not be seen as a purification of the drama of its content of reality. It is not the rejection of reality, but rather its transformation into new dimensions opened up by the new realities of that time by psychoanalysis, anthropology, technology, and the Russian revolution. Pure form is thus a way of trying to increase the possibilities for the drama by getting rid of the old laws of psychology and historiography which had dominated theater and to some extent dictated its laws.

The misunderstanding concerning Witkacy's theater is to view it solely as a "revolution in theatrical technique." And although Witkiewicz's theory of pure form in the theater seems to suggest a purely formal attitude, fortunately, Witkiewicz, like Brecht, as a theoretician and as a practitioner are two not quite identical persons. This misunderstanding has unfortunately often led to stagings of Witkacy's plays as "happenings" or pure nonsense, or perversions of the absurd, "the stranger the better."

Part of the problem lies, of course, in the paradox that Witkacy, in creating the theory of Pure Form, did not treat his plays as an area of experience for testing its soundness. Instead, he subordinated his plays to his historical, political, and social theses, illustrating through the example of the fates of his heroes his forecast for the future of culture and the future of society. Thus, to reduce Witkacy to the absurd or to an artistic spectacle is to lose almost entirely the problems embodied in his work.

And because Witkacy's plays lack "internal congruity, pragmatical motivations, and life-like probability,"[49] they have unexpectedly, much like Jarry's *Ubu*, become also quite realistic. His characters, through their roars and their mad thrashings around, resemble the abominable Father Ubu with his exclamation "Merrdrre" and his machine for blowing up brains. Witkiewicz delighted in coining names for his characters appropriate to their behavior. Much like the prankster Jarry, Witkacy also invented many names that are untranslatable puns, nicknames for friends, and embodiments of philosophical, political, and psychological ideologies. Instead of middle-class husbands and wives and mistresses, bizarre mathematicians, artist-misfits, unashamedly lurid women, and members of the international set populate his plays, forming a cabaret of raving madmen, or caricatures of opera-buffa, in which, instead of murders out of jealousy or suicides, sham murders and sham suicides abound. Most often, though, the murders and suicides are negated as the corpses are resurrected and rejoin the play.

Like Jarry, Witkiewicz always retained a large dose of the childlike in his dramaturgy. Both playwrights carry over into their mature works the child's delight in sudden surprises and spectacular effects, as well as naive enjoyment of killings, accidents, and disasters. This very childlikeness outraged contemporary audiences, who demanded social and psychological realism. Ultimately, the bypassing of naturalistic conventions is a major source of what is fresh, spontaneous, and theatrical in Jarry and Witkiewicz, and clearly underlines their emulation of Shakespeare. As a precursor, Jarry destroyed the illusion of simple reality and made the audience conscious of the artistic process that was taking place on the stage by allowing the viewer to see the skeleton under the gilt and color of the stage, never permitting the spectator to forget that what he was seeing was "an unpleasant comedy, so necessary in our times."[50]

And like Jarry's protosurrealistic farce *Ubu*, Witkacy's non-Euclidian drama *Gyubul Wahazar* (1921) explores the unconscious urges lying deep in its buffoon protagonist. However, in *Ubu* all those impulses are reduced to the lowest physiological level and then magnified out of proportion. Ubu is all Id, ruled by his guts and motivated by physical survival at all costs; in Jarry's words Ubu is *un être ignoble* who in the openhanded employment of childishly ingenuous deceit foreshadows the irrationality of power, thereby evoking W. B. Yeat's response, "After us the Savage God." Witkacy's Gyubul, on the other hand, is a saintly martyr, the very prototype of the paranoid ascetic revolutionary crazed by a fanatical belief in a cause which he alone embodies and for which he is ready to lay down his life. Both *Ubu* and *Gyubul Wahazar* show the frightening and yet absurd consequences that follow when absolute power is dominated by absolute caprice.

An astonishing characterization, Gyubul Wahazar is presented so accurately that even the combination of madness and delusions of personal grandeur is presented within the context of "scientific claptrap," such as the purity of race later proclaimed by Hitler and the purposeful scientific Marxist jargon of Stalin. "I'm sacrificing myself for all of you," proclaims Wahazar:

None of you appreciate that and I don't expect you to. I know you say monstrous things about me. I don't want to know anything about that. I don't have secret informers and I'm not going to, just as I don't have any ministers. I am alone, like God, I alone rule everything, and I'm responsible for everything, and answer only to myself alone. I can condemn myself to death, if I feel like it—if I become absolutely convinced that I'm wrong. I don't have any ministers—therein lies my greatness. I am a lone solitary spirit—like the steam in the engine, like the electrical energy in the battery. But then I really do have a machine under me, and not some living pulpy mush. My officials are automats, like the ones you see in train stations. I put a penny in and out comes a chocolate, and not a peppermint. . . . Understand that? Huh?[51]

The mad Wahazar purports to be creating a utopia in which "Everyone will be set in his own little box filled with cotton like a priceless gem—solitary, single, unique in the superhuman dignity of his deepest being: exactly the way I am now." In the meantime, he has created an absolute dictatorship with automated diplomats, automated mothers, mechanized women, and unlimited terror: "I am the first martyr of my six-dimensional continuum,"[52] he rages.

Real power as differentiated from apparent power is at the root of the social and dramatic conflict in *Gyubul Wahazar*. On the surface there is the apparent power of Gyubul himself. To the time of his fall, Wahazar's power seems absolute and complete, and ultimately does not seem to lie with any of the other characters: the mad scientist Doctor Rypmann, Morbidetto, Father Unguenty, nor with Piggykins, the angelic little girl who orders Wahazar around. Hidden in the interplay, however, is the miller Clodgrain. Since he is the true technocrat, concerned with production, the concealed intimate of power who goes on regardless of shifts in its apparent seat, Clodgrain alone understands the manipulation of power: "They'll change, adapt, adjust, then there'll be some new injections for them."[53]

In *Gyubul Wahazar* death hovers over all, sudden and certain, explicable and inexplicable. But the ultimate death is the eventual impossibility of dying, the terrible state of being only a "mishmash of transformational possibilities." Wahazar dies, but his glands live on in Unguenty-Wahazar. The revolutionary Wahazar and the mystic Unguenty become united in one body. The individual as a concept, a unit that used to be sacrosanct, is destroyed. Note for example the treatment of some of the women: some are mad Masculettes, their sex and their role changed to suit the whim of Wahazar or the needs of the state. Social levelling is now the all, except for the meta-individual at the top of the heap.

Witkacy subtitled *Gyubal Wahazar* "Along the Cliffs of the Absurd" and also designates it "A Non-Euclidian Drama," perhaps because the universe Witkacy presents is not rational and predictable, as classical geometry is: "Real space has no structure," states Father Unguenty, and Morbidetto claims, "I know what the essence of Existence is: metaphysical swinishness." Unpredictable, unstructured, and arbitrary to the individual's well-being, Wahazar's power is indifferent, even to his own death. Although Wahazar wants a society of cattle with himself on top, wielding whip and prod, this fascist superman, like the unindividualized herd, loses his own identity in the mishmash of "transformational possibilities, adjustments and adaptations."[54]

The characters seem to be suspended between action and waiting, and as the play opens one of them comments: "hell is one gigantic waiting room." From the very first moment of their appearance, the characters are externally established by a precise definition of costumes, colors, shapes, features, and manner of speaking. Frequent repetition, with variation, of each small segment of the initial composition calls the spectator's attention to the familiar yet enigmatic words and gestures that bind them together in a complex unity. The social and political spheres of the play are dissected, and then the parts are reassembled. There results from the dissection-assemblage method a perspective which the spectator did not expect and an insight into the working of totalitarianism.

In the foreground Wahazar's habitual actions, foaming at the mouth (for which Witkiewicz recommends that the actor stuff "his mouth full of soda tablets or Piperazina flakes from Klawy's drugstore"),[55] swearing, kicking, falling into abject states of stupor, set up the primary rhythm. In the background, recurring motifs composed of the surging movement of the crowd, court processions, arrivals and departures of guards, Perpendicularists and the Barefoot Pneumatics with their antiphonal chants, curses, screams echo back and forth as a continuous vocal accompaniment. The surging effect is used by Witkacy to underline the powerful but unseen forces emanating from Wahazar as the crowd surges forward and back in response to his ravings.[56]

The high level of physical aggression in *Gyubul Wahazar*, with the characters constantly slapping, hitting, and throttling one another, is one of the most characteristic Witkacian theatrical feats and underlines that even above the topmost kicker another ready to kick him in turn can be felt in a kind of indeterminancy structured according to Albert Einstein's theory of relativity. In other words, as Daniel Gerould points out, "Witkacy imagines future totalitarianism as a world of indeterminacy and endless transformation, based on the postulates of modern science."[57]

Behind the figure of *Gyubul Wahazar*, "They" are concealed. "They" are a bizarre collection of fanatics, lunatics, adventurers, and idlers who ultimately are more sinister than Wahazar, since they destroy not one's body but one's mind, tickling the victim and making him laugh as he agrees to his own annihilation. Witkacy's play *They* may be viewed as a political commentary which deals with the "visibility" of government. A *farce dell'arte* about secret governments and the police state, it presents Balandash, the protagonist threatened by the forces of a "secret government committee" whose nature and even existence are not clearly defined. In *They*, Witkacy addresses the creative process and its relation to automated society. In this play Witkiewicz explores the crux of mechanization, thought control, "the destruction of art, confession to crimes not committed, social regimentation and indoctrination, government by secret organizations and secret police, and also presents the view of revolution as theater improvised out of boredom and perpetually continued out of despair."[58]

Although the play was written in 1920, it could very well be taken as a prophetic vision of the Soviet Union in the 1930s and 1940s. "They" destroy Balandash's art gallery and murder his mistress. The world of the play is a special Witkacian world full of gnawing fear, where people and events do not abide by either natural laws or social expectations. However, despite the threatening nature, Witkacy's world is also a zany burlesque of the real world in which, on both sides, the characters are split and empty, reduced to mere watching, "no longer capable of experiencing anything" for themselves.

The only way out is to live vicariously and theatrically. For Balandash, theater is the enjoyment of living through art and collecting artistic sensations. For his alter ego and opponent Tefuan, theater is an arena for suppression and destruction. Both Balandash and Tefuan act out their respective dramas through their unhappy love for the same woman, an actress, who, ironically, feels truly herself only on stage, playing someone else. Although they live theatrically, both men are particularly suspicious of the theater and the art of acting. In order to undermine the theater, Tefuan writes avant-garde plays so extreme that they will bring the theater into a decline and lead to its total collapse. Balandash, on the other hand, invents a theory of pure form that excludes theater. The theory itself will be useless once modern art is destroyed. The avant-garde playwright intent on improving mankind and the theorist of modern art desiring to increase man's aesthetic pleasure reach the same sterile impasse and ridiculous negation. *Coup de théâtre.* Witkacy destroys himself.

In part, Witkacy addresses himself to the conflict of the *fin de siècle* confronting modern revolution. However the enemy is not only without but within. The dilettante aesthete Balandash is as divided as the world around him, and all his convictions are riddled with self-contradictions. The treatment of the Revolution in Witkacy's plays is purified of any historical authenticity, despite Witkacy's firsthand experience in the events of the Russian Revolution on both sides, first as an infantry officer in the Tsarist regiment of the Imperial Guard, and then, after the fall of the old regime, as a political commissar.

Unlike the bleak optimism in the plays of a number of his contemporaries, such as Kaiser, Toller, Meyerhold, and Mayakovsky, Witkiewicz does not see a phoenix rising from the ashes of Imperial Russia. Instead, he shows in a number of his plays a newly entrenched regime which is far more oppressive to the individual and his aspirations than the one it overthrew. Just as the French Revolution of 1789 illustrated for Georg Büchner the futility of revolutionary ideals and provided despairing insight into the nature of man, the Russian Revolution was for Witkacy a model that was transhistorical and symptomatic of forces and circumstances that lie beyond individual control. This response to the revolution emerges in the tendency toward the grotesque, the metaphysically absurd and the displacement of reality, endowing the Revolution with mythosymbolic existential significance.

To Witkacy, the revolution represents the increasing mechanization of man. In his novel *Insatiability*, a pill is offered by Murti Bing, a shadowy and enigmatic Malay from the island of Balampang, which softens the brain of the already deranged, exhausted Europeans so that they can painlessly swallow the political regimentation which will liberate them from their own madness and despair. Through the bizarre narcotic Davamesque B2, society becomes entirely mechanized, since all desires and creativity have been suppressed.

Unlike Kaiser and Capek, to whom mechanization means the enslavement of the human to the machine, ultimately producing machine-like robots, Witkiewicz fears a mechanization that is social in nature and in which mechanization is something occurring in men's minds. Witkacy sees the human mass as the crux of mechanization and the suppression of individual possibilities. In his vision of the future of mankind Witkiewicz comes very close to Eugene Zamiatin's prophetic novel *We* (1920) and Rozanov's apocalyptic indictment of society. In *We*, Zamiatin portrayed the coming totalitarianism with such penetrating acuteness that the novel has yet to be published in the Soviet Union. The narrator hero of the novel (D-503) combines Prometheanism and sensualism, a major preoccupation of the late imperial period in Russia, making explicit his opposition to the "measured tread of the mammoth" that was taking over Russia: "Revolution is everywhere, in everything; it is endless, there is no last revolution, no last number. Social revolution is only one of innumerable numbers: the law of revolution is not social, but infinitely greater—a cosmic and universal law."[59]

Much like Witkiewicz, Zamiatin was gloomily convinced that Russia's "only future was in its past." Ultimately, that vision proved to be prophetic, and like Witkiewicz in *The Shoemakers* and *Gyubul Wahazar*, Zamiatin foresees revolutionary aspirations and ideals "giving way to Stalin's world of fixed quotas and five-year plans; crescendo, to silence; electrification, to liquidation."[60]

Unlike the constructivists's romantic fascination with the possibilities of the machine, for Witkacy the machine represents suppression. He sees the revolution as a machine gone mad. In his play *The Crazy Locomotive* (1923), the machinery of civilization has gone berserk. In the destructive journey of a locomotive, Witkacy finds a powerful metaphor for the violent destiny of man and the fatal course of Western civilization. Along with Zamiatin, Witkacy saw nothing ahead but the collapse of old, exhausted values, and the coming of totalitarian regimentation: This unleashing of antisocial forces is projected on stage in *The Crazy Locomotive* through the use of film, and as the camera projects a machine-made background, these images move with increased rapidity with the acceleration of the locomotive. The action of the play itself takes on the attributes of film, its speed and jerky, abrupt movements. Thus, two machines—the steam engine and the film projector—give the play its driving rhythm. In the hands of madmen, the locomotive becomes an obsolescent technological plaything running wild at high speed. As the play progresses, the rhythm of the train gains possession of the movement of human thought and action to the extent that the engine by its very motion shapes and defines them. In the end, Trefaldi, the protagonist, exclaims: "I've become the engine."

In his vision of the mechanization of life, Witkacy demonstrates that modern drama can no longer be written according to the precepts for a well-made play but rather must be written in keeping with the postulates of Freud, Marx, and Lenin, Einstein, Schoenberg, and Picasso. Much like Zamiatin, Witkacy views naturalism in the theater as suitable only for the outmoded "flat coordinates of a Euclidian world." True realism, writes Zamiatin, is better projected by the absurd: "Yes. The meeting of parallel lines is also absurd. But it is absurd only in the canonical, flat geometry of Euclid: in non-Euclidian geometry it is an axiom. . . . For today's literature the flat surface of life is what the earth is for an airplane: a take-off path for the climb from ordinary life to true being to philosophy to the fantastic."[61]

Since the world as Witkacy sees it can be better explained by the axioms of non-Euclidian geometry, he uses techniques in his plays that do not follow predictable conventions. Accordingly, to jar the spectator out of this mechanized state, Witkacy experiments with techniques of irritating and assaulting the audience, making use of delay, non-action, and waiting followed by sudden explosion and violent *coup de théâtre,* often filling the stage with disintegrating shapes and forms suggesting the ultimate triumph of nothingness come to pass. As in a Picasso painting, pieces of dramatic structure are misplaced, deformed, and recombined in new arrangements. Such displacement and restructuring of the traditional movement of drama liberates it from the constraints of motivation, purpose, and explanation. As in Meyerhold's use of constructivist settings and objects, once characters and objects are separated from contextual significance, they become theatrically pure things in themselves, in much the way that practical objects, when defunctionalized and displayed by the cubists, achieve a different significance and freedom.

Although the years that Witkiewicz spent in Russia (1914–1918) are still enveloped by mystery and mythification to which he himself contributed, it is quite clear that the social and political philosophy of Witkiewicz was to a large extent formed by the Russian Revolution. That revolution later became and would remain for him the prototype of revolution per se—in contrast to Mayakovsky or Brecht, for example. For them the October Revolution always remained "the" revolution,[62] and their attitudes would later undergo significant changes, as in Mayakovsky's later plays on the subversion of revolutionary ideals by a grey bureaucracy, strangely reminiscent of Witkacy's *They,* or Brecht's transition from the committed figure of the mother in Brecht's adaptation of Gorky to his treatment of the extinction of individuality as neither positive nor negative but necessary as *The Measures Taken.*

Witkacy's treatment of the theme of revolution is in direct antithesis to the Russian handling of the theme, particularly during the early postrevolutionary period when the October Revolution gave rise to a whole body of epic theater celebrating the revolutionary ethos and its larger-than-life heroes. Witkiewicz's *The Anonymous Work* (1921) and the second version of Mayakovsky's *Mystery-Bouffe* (subtitled "A Heroic, Epic, and Satiric Representation of Our Era") were both written in the same year by the two major figures of their respective national avant-garde, and yet it would be hard to imagine two more dissimilar treatments of the same theme. For Witkacy the theme of revolution is not a moral or social problem but a situation bearing down on the imponderables of human destiny.

In the background of many of his plays are fascist and communist revolutions, which sometimes enter the foreground. To Witkacy, liberal democracy was fraudulent and bankrupt, communism a terrifying prospect that would level civilization. Fascism was the ultimate horror that would destroy civilization completely. Notwithstanding the choice between communism and fascism, the state of the future would become repressive, conformist, and mechanized, in a grey dehumanized world.

Since Witkacy's characters often find themselves adrift, it is appropriate that the setting reflects this ambiguity. Thus, in many of Witkacy's plays the old order is seen nearing its ultimate end, bringing about an atmosphere of fear, insecurity, and conflict enhanced by arbitrary rules of terror and unending *coups d'état*.

The options presented to the characters are few and limited. In *The Anonymous Work*, the artist Plasmonick refuses to make a choice between two political ideologies that both call for a revolution. Instead he announces: "In our time there are only two places for metaphysical individuals, prison and the insane asylum."[63] How prophetic this rings when we examine the treatment of writers-dissidents in the Soviet Union today. Plasmonick intends to continue to paint and create, assuming that whatever the new order may be, it will (like the old) continue to allow him to do so in confinement. However, he can no longer find safety in prison; as in Witkacy's *The Madman and the Nun*, modern psychiatry has invaded the prison, negating even that potential for salvation of the artist-individual.

Revolution figures in Witkacy's plays multifariously. It may be depicted symbolically, evoked offstage, or it may receive an onstage dramatic treatment. In those plays where social upheavals and *coups d'état* are evoked behind the scenes, Witkiewicz deliberately uses the stage as a grand guignol to dramatize the effects of a world in violent transition. In *The Water Hen* (1921), for example, everything in the play conspires to establish a precarious parallel between the mayhem of interhuman relationships on stage and the historical mayhem beyond, which reaches its apotheosis in the play's final act when history actually does intrude upon the action in the form of an ominous red glare and the clatter of machine-gun fire, an experience "like swimming the black sea of a mob gone mad."[64]

Witkacy's tragicomedies or "spherical tragedies" or "comedies with corpses" stand in defiance of the Aristotelean canon concerning a complete action. While Witkacy's plays incorporate some type of dramatic movement, it is marked by an essential absence of change or of meaningful progress. At the end of Witkacy's "spherical tragedies" a revolution inevitably erupts, the social order collapses, an explosion occurs, and complete chaos dominates. But this movement contains a twist, for despite traditional forward motion, there is an absence of meaningful change. If anything changes, it is not the essence but the form of power. In the spherical movement, it does not matter where on the sphere one begins: the route is still circular.[65] For the individual and for society, change for the worst occurs, but the essentials remain the same. Sajetan, the protagonist of Witkiewicz's last play, *The Shoemakers* (1934), sums up his version of Witkiewicz's nightmare in a dying lecture: "We're all cancers on the body of society in its transitional phase, caught between the greatness that has crumbled and been pulverized, and the true social continuum to come in which the separate ulcers of individuals will flow together into one great 'plaque muqueuse' of absolute perfection in one universal organism."[66]

And so the spherical tragedies continue with no solution in sight. In no play is this more clearly presented than in Witkacy's *The Shoemakers*, in which Witkiewicz presents a societal cataclysm in three stages. In Act I there is a revolution from above, as Scurvy and his Vigilant Youth introduce a fascist state on dying capitalism. In Act II a counterrevolution from below is instigated by the shoemakers' uprising in the name of a peasant-populist brand of communism. In Act III the final revolution brings an end to all ideologies and renders all previous classes and the class struggle obsolete, ushering in technocracy with its new ruling elite, the technicians of power who will solve all problems pragmatically and run the machinery of state in a way that reserves the best material comforts and commodities for themselves. But then, that is the history of progress: "Why is it everything in history has to blow up and can't move smoothly into the future along the well-greased tracks of reason: the law of discontinuity,"[67] exclaims Sajetan, the chief shoemaker.

Witkacy refers to *The Shoemakers* as a "theoretical play with 'songs' in three acts." The first act can be seen as a grotesque depiction of the Polish reality in the 1930s. This reality was the result of prior social and political conflicts hinted at in Wyspianski's *The Wedding* (1905). In *The Wedding* one sees the paralysis of the aristocratic order, which hopes to rejuvenate itself by marrying into the "noble" peasantry, thus preventing its own demise. *The Wedding* ends with the guests of the wedding party frozen into an eternal ghostly dance, with Mulch, the straw figure, in the lead. Under the Mulch's sinister spell, various historical, legendary, and symbolic figures from Polish history arrive as ghostly visitors, and as the Mulch fiddles a ghostly tune, the guests, like mechanical puppets, join him in a frozen dance.

In *The Shoemakers*, the figure of Mulch is not only alluded to as "Mr. Wyspianski's Mulch" but also appears as a character within the play. He is ultimately exposed as a fraud and the "Dream of Poland," suggested in *The Wedding*, in the events of pre-World War II Poland loses all meaning. The utopian solution of wedding the peasants to Polish ideals through a union with the intelligentsia and aristocracy is destroyed, as the three peasants who accompany the Mulch are beaten up and tossed out, with the comment "That's the way we settle the peasant problem."[68] In the world of power politics, it is not a wedding, but rape, that will unite the social classes. Thus, Wyspianski's ideals and symbols are exposed as ludicrously anachronistic in light of the brutal realities of a later era. In Witkiewicz's vision, a synthetic mass-produced culture replaces the folklore, peasants, and fiddles which Wyspianski and Witkiewicz's father saw as the symbols of the Poland that was to emerge in a new age. Although Witkacy admired Wyspianski's efforts to create an antirealistic theater that fused sight and sound in a total spectacle and considered the painter-playwright an important precursor of his ideas on pure form in the theater, he challenges Wyspianski in *The Shoemakers* by looking underneath the outer trappings of national symbols.

One could say that *The Shoemakers* serves both as prologue and epilogue to Mayakovsky's *The Bedbug*, in which the Russian poet-dramatist prophesied the perversion of revolutionary ideals. "To destroy a class is to create a class," reads the message from *The Shoemakers* as an echo and answer to Mayakovsky: "A class will remain a class until its last bedbug is destroyed."

Intercourse among the classes is overwhelmingly sexual. Each class lusts for the other. Unable to achieve their aims, the social classes can only hope to rape one another. Rape becomes an image for social violence. The Duchess, for example, arouses the shoemakers in order to excite Scurvy to violence. Scurvy plots the ravishment of the Duchess, and Sajetan and his apprentices seek to defile and deflower everything and everyone above them. "It all comes down to the different classes eating one another up,"[69] says the Duchess. Ultimately, raping and eating activities shape the action of the play. By bringing the shoemakers flowers of culture, as well as giving lectures on the revolution, the Duchess hopes to incite the workers to a creative rape on the body politic. Sexual fantasies and longings represent the expression of social frustrations. The play is based on an amorous triangle, a ménage à trois, consisting of the working class, the bourgeoisie, and the aristocracy. In the total warfare that rages, mutual fascination among the classes and their desire for self-degradation erode all ideological lines.

Nothing is sacred in Witkacy's vision of interwar Poland. Above all, national symbols are demythified and exposed. Even the peasants, so ennobled by his father, are ridiculed by Witkacy as pompous fools, and their role in the arena of world politics is totally discredited. In order to give their revolutionary cause a sense of history, the peasants bring along Wyspianski's Mulch. The Mulch, however, turns out to be a fraud. When his straw falls off he turns out to be a Mulch-about-town, ready to dance his life away in the tango, "the real culture of the mulches of that period."[70] By pushing Wyspianski's symbols ahead into the brutal realities of the day and bringing them rudely up to date, Witkacy exposes them as ultimately anachronistic and meaningless.

When the revolt of the shoemakers fails, the crushing order of banality can no longer be overcome. Work and play become equally meaningless, and exhaustion, sterility, and breakdown result. Boredom and endless discussion dominate, with boredom becoming aggressive to the point that the shoemakers, starved by compulsive idleness, throw themselves on their tools and commit a rape on work. Instead of "art for art's sake," the slogan in *The Shoemakers* could very well be "work for work's sake." Ironically, what Sajetan and his apprentices discover to be their inheritance from the former ruling classes are not the limitless privileges which they had imagined, but "Dread, boredom, hangover, and terrible apprehension about what's coming next."[71]

Compulsory boredom is the torture imposed by the fascist in "the hall of compulsory unemployment." The revolutionary shoemakers are imprisoned in emptiness, but in full view of a "magnificently equipped shoemaker's workshop." They cry out for work. Compulsory idleness is driving them mad. Wretched from boredom, the first apprentice cries, "I've never wanted a good piece the way I want to get my hands on workbenches and tools."[72] Scurvy returns to gloat, but his victory is short-lived, as Sajetan leads the shoemakers in a last desperate revolt towards an orgy in creation.

The focus falls squarely on internal relationships within society and the problems of distributing among the different classes the goods and benefits produced by man's labor. The simple opposition of artist versus masses in *The Anonymous Work* or *The Madman and the Nun* gives way to broader issues. The question of human creativity, what the Shoemaker Sajetan calls "this pure desire to produce something," is no longer seen exclusively as a matter of art, but rather of culture in general.

Much like the unexpected forces lurking in the background of *Gyubul Wahazar*, the seat of power in *The Shoemakers* is also concealed. After three acts of revolution and counterrevolution, and endless social, political, and metaphysical battles, comes the announcement, "THEY HAVE ABSOLUTE POWER NOW!" Two men enter "dressed in English suits," followed by the Hyperworkoid, the personification of the automated human being. "They" ignore everyone, stepping over crawling humans and corpses, effortlessly taking absolute control. Although they address one another as "comrade," evoking the imagery of a revolution from below, they are technocratic pragmatists, making far-reaching economic decisions with "only as much compromise as is absolutely necessary" to consolidate power. Everything is reduced to functionality. The Duchess, previously a symbol of the unattainable to the burgeois Scurvy and the Shoemakers, is reduced to a "piece of tail," whom they will use for a "little rest and relaxation." This is the extent of their human desires: "It's too bad we can't be automatons ourselves."[73]

The Shoemakers is a frightening play, a black prophecy of the world in the time of Hitler. In its allegorical pronouncements, *The Shoemakers* becomes a record of historical experiences that transcend the setting of Poland in Wyspianski's *The Wedding*. The despair Witkiewicz presents is the despair of mankind. His vision of a mechanized society with its resulting boredom, alienation, and anxiety foreshadows the concerns of writers such as Beckett, Ionesco, and Camus.

A sign with the word BOREDOM appears several times in the last act, particularly following ideological discussions of an idealistic tone. As the newly resurrected Sajetan ceaselessly expounds on the meaning of life and death, a placard, "Boredom getting worse and worse," appears in the place of the previous one which thereupon disappears. Thus, on another level, Witkacy negates all hope for a humanistic solution and ultimately destroys his own play. The void cannot be breached, and even creative effort is useless in the face of coming events.

No longer concerned with the possibility of performance, Witkiewicz deliberately overloads and stretches to the bursting point the nature of the dramatic genre. His most trenchant comments on theatrical illusion and its inherent limitations frequently appear in the stage directions, and the characters themselves often speak the playwright's directions on how they are to say their lines and react to events. The distinction between the dialogue and the author's commentary is thus blurred by digressions, polemics, philosophical disquisitions, personal invective, gags, literary criticism, invented obscenities and ironic parodies, and attacks on his contemporaries and predecessors.

If Witkiewicz introduces semantic choices into the text, it is precisely because he wants his plays to be read in a certain sense. But this sense in Witkacy's plays has all the richness of the cosmos. Nor should the spectator deduce that this tendency toward openness of the text operates "only at the level of indefinite suggestion and stimulation of emotional response,"[74] as Eco explains. What is at stake is a convergence of new canons and requirements which the forms of art reflect by way of "structural homologies." Thus, the concepts of "openness" and dynamism that are characteristic of Witkacy's plays and his theory of pure form may be also seen in terms of Einsteinian physics, in indeterminacy and discontinuity, as Eco writes:

> The thing which distinguishes the Einsteinian concept of the universe from quantum epistemology is precisely the faith in the totality of the universe, a universe in which discontinuity and indeterminacy can admittedly upset us with their surprise apparition, but in fact, to use

Einstein's words, do not presuppose a God playing random games with dice but the Divinity of Spinoza, who rules the world according to perfectly regulated laws. In this kind of universe, relativity means the infinite variability of experience as well as the infinite multiplication of possible ways of measuring things and viewing their position.[75]

The possibilities which Witkacy's plays make available through their openness are always at work within a given field of relations, offering the performer and the spectator a work to be completed. Much like Brecht's plays, which offer the spectator a series of facts to be observed and which in the end do not present solutions at all, Witkacy's plays demand collaboration from the spectator to organize and structure the composition presented by the *mise-en-scène*, a structure which once organized still remains open, "a work in movement," suggesting the universe as it is conceived by modern, non-Euclidean geometries.

If the structural arrangement of scenes in a play no longer necessarily determines the immediately following ones, if there is no one element which allows the spectator to infer the next step from what has preceded, a general breakdown of causation occurs, leaving the work stripped of necessary and foreseeable conclusions. The common factor, as Eco writes, is the mutability of the material offered for the performer's manipulation. Brecht's plays appear to elicit free and arbitrary responses, and yet are rhetorically constructed in such a way as to elicit a reaction toward Marxist dialectic logic. A solution is seen as desirable and is actually anticipated, in Brecht's case converting "openness" into "an instrument of revolutionary pedagogics."[76] Witkacy takes "defamiliarization" one step further by suggesting possible structures, only to bring about a *coup de théâtre* whose ultimate aim is to project a work in movement, a work in continual progress. Despite their seeming lack of structure, Witkacy's plays have unifying characteristics which guarantee that they will always be seen as "texts" and not just as conglomerations of random components.

As Czeslaw Milosz explains, Witkiewicz presented a dilemma in postwar Poland. He did not oppose Marxism on political grounds. "On the contrary, few Marxist writers or sympathizers could compete with him in his disdainful appraisals of the 'free world.'"[77] And he grasped perhaps even better than Brecht the working of fascism. For Witkiewicz, the 1917 Revolution was not a transitional period during which a new freedom of the individual would be established, as Brecht believed, but a final and catastrophic stage in the history of civilization. The prophetic quality of Witkiewicz is in marked contrast with the diagnostic attitude of Brecht. For Brecht the contemporary world can be represented only as a subject to be changed, while Witkiewicz discards all solutions. Witkiewicz's world of the future is one of the enslavement of the individual to an arbitrary totalitarianism, while for Brecht the future is one of communist utopia. With regard to his vision, it seems that Witkiewicz was more realistic and more prophetic. Ironically, it is Witkiewicz with his notions of the absurd who was more capable than either Meyerhold or Brecht of describing the apparatus of fascism and totalitarianism.

Much like Mayakovsky, Witkacy clearly saw the conflict between ideals and reality. And although ultimately this knowledge proved to be intolerable, he drove himself to create so as not to face despair. It is perhaps fitting in this attempt to determine both the cultural and aesthetic signs in Witkacy's plays to note that the title of one of his plays, lost during the razing of Warsaw, was *The End of the World.*

Conclusion

The study of signs in theatrical productions and their ensuing polysemy can be more easily interpreted when inscribed within the historical and social continuum of concretization and reception. Structural aesthetics as practiced by the Prague School stresses that the aesthetic value of art is a function of its signs, which allow aesthetic function to be foregrounded while subordinating other functions. The focus of theatrical presentations is to be specifically aesthetic. However, other nonaesthetic and arbitrary aspects of signs may acquire value according to their collective, social, and historical dimensions, and are thereby integrated into the aesthetic signs. So that, as Mukařovský writes, a recognition of the presence of the aesthetic function of signs "is a social phenomenon, and it involves a public which somehow becomes aware of the aesthetic function and makes a decision that it is or is not present, whether it is in a dominant or a subordinate role."[1]

The aesthetic function of signs is subject to mediation by aesthetic norms. Validation of the dominance of aesthetic function implies that the social collective knows "both what constitutes any given norm and whether such a norm has been realized in a work of art."[2] Mukařovský notes that the spectator comes to anticipate certain structural and formal qualities from art, and this anticipation exerts normative influences on both presentation and reception. However, these expectations on the part of the spectator must be deautomatized, or else theatrical presentations will become automatic, boring, and ultimately, cliches. It is at this point that the significance of the "making strange" of the artistic device, as described by the Russian formalists, or the *Verfremdungseffekt*, as practiced by Brecht, or deformation, as understood by Witkiewicz, merge as means of violating norms in order to engage the interest of the spectator.

The process of violation, or the "making strange," of the aesthetic device is continuous. As a result, the aesthetic norm too is subject to constant violation. To stage "classics" without paying attention to this process turns the productions into museum pieces, lifeless and dry. To stage Brecht and Witkiewicz, or to revive Meyerhold's constructivist stagings, precisely in the form of the original productions would be to ignore the process of change in aesthetic norms and also to ignore that this process is tied to a social collective which constantly produces new norms and then violates them.

Mukařovský explains that the process of violating aesthetic norms is not one-sided, but one which acknowledges the power of art and its effects on those who perceive it. Thus, the spectator's confrontation with a work of art also influences his aesthetic concretization, leading us to recognize that the interrelationship of art and society is highly complex. Since both aesthetic and extra-aesthetic signs occur simultaneously, the spectator transforms the extra-aesthetic values to aesthetic functions. This leads us to the general conclusion that theatrical presentations are social facts as much as other social events. The distinction between art as a social fact and other social facts is based on the assumption that aesthetic function, norm, and value are valid only in relation to the spectator, and then only to the spectator as a social product.

Study of the Russian formalists and the Prague School proved particularly valuable in analyzing Meyerhold's aesthetics of presentation, Brecht's aesthetics of reception, and Witkiewicz's aesthetics of pure form. The focus on sign structures in their plays and productions deemphasizes the notion of viewing theatrical presentations as self-contained art objects, isolated from a social context and system of values. On the contrary, focusing on sign structure added complexity and depth to my understanding of theatrical presentations by calling attention to conventions and norms that are relevant to the process of making an aesthetic value judgement. Since the theater is a social phenomenon, this value judgement must by its very nature include consideration of society and its organization. The Prague structuralists saw a work of art as a component of a broader structure of aesthetic history, and saw the latter as a process arising out of the dynamic tension between production and norm, between the historical context of theatrical presentations and the context of changing norms and public attitudes. Mukařovský writes: "The entire dynamics of social development, the ongoing regrouping and conflict of each of its strata and its environment, the struggle of classed, nations and ideologies—all that is intensely reflected in the relation between art and society and even in the development of art itself, despite the fact that the changes in the structure of art appear as continuously sequential and ordered."[3]

The pioneer work of Tynjanov, Mukařovský, and Vodička in developing a theory of aesthetics based on reception sees the main task of literary history as describing the context of the polarity between the work of art and reality, "which is to be materialized and historically described according to the manner of its perception, i.e., the dynamic connections between the work and the literary public."[4]

In my study of Meyerhold, Brecht, and Witkiewicz, I have found that their perception of the social changes occurring in the wake of the First World War and the Russian Revolution endows their work with semiotic multifunctionality, taking into account both aesthetic and social processes. But these shattering events were not necessarily the subject of their creativity, as they were for other playwrights and writers, particularly the socialist realists, in whose works the revolution was the dominant subject of attention. Instead, social change made it possible for Meyerhold, Brecht, and Witkiewicz to shake off the constraints of the bourgeois theater and gave them the opportunity to present reality in a new way. Fundamental to all three was the aim of "shaking up" the spectator's perception, to make him "see" things and not simply "recognize" them. Although the corresponding ideological, psychological, and sociological aspects of society in the wake of the First World War and the Russian Revolution are not necessarily the spectator's primary target of observation, their relevance is not ruled out.

The structuralist attitude views the individualizing process of the spectator to be equally as important as the individualizing creative process of the artist. The creative factor, as Mukařovský explains, "need not be a single individual, but may be a group . . . a generation, or even a collective, such as a nation."[5] The Russian formalists exerted a strong influence on the poets of their day, and these poets in turn exerted influence on the conclusions that the Russian formalists drew about the function of the artistic device. In the theater the active participation of the audience as a "collective individual" is felt more intensely than in the other arts. Meyerhold, Brecht, and Witkiewicz, each in his own way, revolutionized the relationship between what was happening on stage and what the spectator perceived. By foregrounding theatrical signs in a new way they forced the spectator to become involved in a new process of decoding theatrical presentations. In reaction against "slice of life" representations, Meyerhold, Brecht, and Witkiewicz, each in his own way, focused on the theatricality of signs, thereby flaunting them, and shattering illusion. Thus, the spectator's attention was drawn to the sign vehicle and its theatricality, rather than to the signified and its textual equivalent.

We have seen how Meyerhold accomplished this by openly borrowing from the circus and cabaret as well as from the highly conventionalized traditions of *commedia dell'arte* and the Japanese theater. In addition, he consciously foregrounded signs related to the machine age and the new social ideology by reducing the actor to bio-mechanical functions played out on constructions that acquired significance only through the actor's movements.

In his critique of the bourgeois theater, Brecht drew on the intertexuality of theatrical conventions which had also influenced Meyerhold. He also synthesized an aesthetics of reception that relied on the Russian formalists' concept of "making strange." But Brecht's purpose was to bring about aesthetic pleasure not only through the foregrounding of highly theatrical conventions, such as interrupted action by songs, film projection, or theatrical asides, but also to bring about intellectual pleasure, a pleasure based on conclusions drawn from a dialectical presentation of social problems.

Witkiewicz, drawing on the tradition of antipsychological development of plot and characters as practiced by Jarry and Strindberg, deformed not only the psychological construct of his characters by projecting the dissonance between life and art but also violated communications axioms by omitting foreshadowing, explanation, and all narrative interconnections, thereby almost eliminating subtexts. Presentational form in Witkiewicz's plays is achieved through an arbitrary model of reality, not through a representational analogy. Pure form serves to purify theater of the old laws of psychological and historiographic development. An essential characteristic of his plays is not that they end happily or unhappily, but rather that the ending denies the possibility of change.

Brecht's presentations differ significantly in style from Witkiewicz's. In *Mother Courage*, for example, the wanderings of Courage on the revolving stage suggest that change is not possible unless Courage understands that the war is the result of private ownership of the goods of society, thus Brecht offers the possibility of change.

As we have seen, the perceptions of Meyerhold, Brecht, and Witkiewicz of social changes occurring in the wake of industrialization, the First World War, and the Russian Revolution were highly individualized. Nonetheless, all three toppled the taboos of the ruling aesthetics and offered spectators new possibilities for viewing the world. Obviously, this is not entirely unique to the revolutionary theatrical figures considered in this study, but if we go back to the Russian formalists and the Prague structuralists we can understand that the violation of aesthetic norms was necessary to the process of foregrounding the aesthetic function of signs. The "making strange" of the devices of art by Meyerhold, Brecht, and Witkiewicz reversed the relationship of question and answer characteristic of the aesthetic function of signs used by the bourgeois theater and instead confronted the spectator "with a new 'opaque' reality that no longer itself to be understood from a pregiven horizon or expectation."[6]

The problem we now confront as students of the aesthetics of Meyerhold, Brecht, and Witkiewicz is to assume that their aesthetics are to be viewed as rigid and unchangeable canons. Instead, their aesthetics must be subjected to the process of continuous mediation of past and present art, an attitude which requires the abandonment of convenient paradigms established by tradition. A play by Brecht staged in the 1980s according to the canons of the Berliner Ensemble does not allow the *Verfremdungseffekt* to function anew in his plays. Nor does the staging of Witkiewicz's plays as "happenings," rather than as the highly realistic plays they have come to be, make them more accessible to us. Nor would it serve any useful function to stage, for example, Crommelynck's *The*

Maganimous Cuckold using Meyerhold's stage constructions and bio-mechanical movements. What Meyerhold, Brecht, and Witkiewicz accomplished was to show us the power of deconstructing, deforming, and defamiliarizing aesthetic norms. This process, as I have tried to show, is ultimately continuous. The past, as Hans Robert Jauss writes, "needs the productive work of understanding in order to be taken out of the imaginary museum and appropriated by the interpretative eye of the present."[7]

Notes

Introduction

1. Patrice Pavis, "The Classical Heritage of Modern Drama: The Case of the Postmodern Theatre," *Modern Drama* 29 (March 1986): 1–22.

2. Roland Barthes, "From Work to Text," in *Textual Strategies*, ed. Josué V. Harari (Ithaca: Cornell University Press, 1979), pp. 73–77.

3. Ibid., p. 80.

4. Jochen Schulte-Sasse, "Foreword" to Peter Bürger's *Theory of the Avant Garde*, trans. Michael Shaw (Minneapolis: University of Minnesota Press, 1984), p. xv.

5. Bürger, p. 18.

6. Jiří Veltruský, "Man and Object in the Theater," in *A Prague School Reader on Esthetics, Literary Structure and Style*, ed. P. Garvin (Washington, D.C.: Georgetown University Press, 1964), pp. 83–84.

7. Roman Jakobson, "Closing Statement: Linguistics and Poetics," in *Style in Language*, ed. Thomas Sebeok (Cambridge: MIT Press, 1960), pp. 350–77.

8. Jiří Veltruský, "Dramatic Text as a Component of Theatre," in *Semiotics of Art: Prague School Contributions*, eds. Ladislaw Matejka and I. Titunik (Cambridge: MIT Press, 1976), pp. 94–118.

9. Umberto Eco, *A Theory of Semiotics* (Bloomington: Indiana University Press, 1976), p. 161.

10. Julia Kristeva, *Desire in Language*, ed. Leon S. Roudiez (New York: Columbia University Press, 1980), p. 36.

11. Maria Ley-Piscator, *The Piscator Experiment: The Political Theater* (Carbondale: Southern Illinois University Press, 1967), p. 277.

12. Keir Elam, *The Semiotics of Theatre and Drama* (London: Methuen, 1980), p. 93.

13. Ibid.

14. Wolfgang Iser, *The Act of Reading: A Theory of Aesthetic Response* (Baltimore: The Johns Hopkins University Press, 1978), p. x.

15. Felix Vodička, "The Concretization of the Literary Work," in *The Prague School: Selected Writings, 1929–1940*, ed. Peter Steiner (Austin: University of Texas Press, 1982), pp. 103–4.

16. Roman Ingarden, *The Literary Work of Art,* trans. George Grabowicz (Evanston: Northwestern University Press, 1973), pp. 343–55.

17. Jan Mukařovský, quoted by Peter Steiner in preface to Vodička's essay, "The Concretization of the Literary Work," op. cit., p. 103.

18. Viktor Shklovsky, quoted by Boris M. Ejxenbaum, "The Theory of the Formal Method," in *Readings in Russian Poetics,* ed. Ladislaw Matejka and Krystyna Pomorska (Ann Arbor: Michigan Slavic Contributions, 1978), p. 13.

19. Jurij Tynjanov, "On Literary Evolution," in *Readings in Russian Poetics,* pp. 72–73.

20. Shklovsky, op. cit., p. 13.

21. Ejxenbaum, op. cit., p. 14.

22. Jiří Veltruský, *Drama as Literature* (Lisse: The Peter de Ridder Press, 1977).

23. Ibid.

24. Veltruský, "Dramatic Text as a Component of Theatre," op. cit., p. 96.

25. Leo Bersani, "Artaud," *Partisan Review* 3 (1976), p. 440.

26. Peter Brook, *The Empty Space* (London: Macgibbon & Kee, 1968), p. 12.

27. Roland Barthes, *Critical Essays,* trans. Richard Howard (Evanston: Northwestern University Press, 1972), pp. 261–64.

28. Bernard Beckerman, *Dynamics of Drama: Theory and Method of Analysis* (New York), p. 13.

29. Petr Bogatyrev, "Semiotics in Folk Theater," in *Semiotics of Art: Prague School Contributions,* op. cit., p. 33.

30. Barthes, *Critical Essays,* op. cit., p. 61.

31. Antonin Artaud, *The Theater and Its Double* (New York: Grove Press, Inc., 1958), p. 110.

32. Eugène Ionesco, *Notes and Counternotes* (New York: Grove Press, Inc., 1964), p. 16.

33. Ibid., p. 26.

34. Veltruský, "Man and Object in the Theater," op. cit., p. 84.

35. Peter Handke, "Nauseated by Language," *The Drama Review* (Fall 1970), p. 57.

36. Bogatyrev, "Semiotics in Folk Theater," op. cit., p. 33.

37. Ibid., pp. 33–42.

38. Irena Slawinska, *La Sémiologie du théâtre in status nascendi: Prague: 1931–1941* (Warsaw: Roczniki Humanistyczne, 1977), p. 64.

39. Bogatyrev, "Semiotics in Folk Theater," op. cit., p. 48.

40. V. N. Volosinov, *Marxism and the Philosphy of Language,* trans. Ladislaw Matejka and I. R. Titunik (New York: Seminar Press, 1973), p. 11.

41. Petr Bogatyrev, "Forms and Functions of Folk Theater," in *Semiotics of Art: Prague School Contributions,* op. cit., p. 52.

42. Max Frisch, *Sketch Book, 1966–1971* (New York: Harcourt, Brace, Jovanovich, Inc., 1971), pp. 66–67.

43. Philip Thody, *Roland Barthes* (London: The Macmillan Press, 1977), p. 10.

44. Mordecai Gorelik, *New Theatres for Old* (New York: E. P. Dutton & Co., Inc., 1962), p. 142.

45. Ibid.

46. Mukařovský, *Structure, Sign, and Function*, op. cit., p. 218.

47. Jindřich Honzl, "Dynamics of the Sign in the Theater," in *Semiotics of Art: Prague School Contributions*, op. cit., p. 75.

48. E. Gordon Craig, *The Art of the Theatre* (London: T. N. Foulis, 1905), p. 54.

49. Jiří Veltruský, "Theatre in the Corridor: E. F. Burians's Production of *Alladine and Palomides,*" *The Drama Review* 23 (December 1979): 67–80.

50. Richard Wagner, *Wagner on Music and Drama,* ed. Albert Goodman and Evert Spinchorn, trans. H. Ashton Ellis (London: Victor Gollancz Ltd., 1970), pp. 19–29.

51. Ibid., pp. 188–89.

52. Honzl, op. cit., p. 87.

53. Ibid., p. 86.

54. Jan Mukařovský, *The World and Verbal Art,* ed. and trans. Peter Steiner (New Haven: Yale University Press, 1977), p. 112.

55. Jurij Tynjanov, "Rhythms as the Constructive Factor of Verse," in *Readings in Russian Poetics,* op. cit., p. 128.

56. Jan Mukařovský, *Aesthetic Function, Norm and Value as Social Facts,* trans. Mark E. Suino (Ann Arbor: Michigan Slavic Contributions, 1979), pp. 54–96.

57. Ibid., pp. 85–86.

58. Leon Trotsky, *Literature and Revolution,* quoted by Rufus W. Mathenson, *The Positive Hero in Russian Literature* (Stanford: Stanford University Press, 1975), p. 123.

59. Eugene Lunn, *Marxism & Modernism: An Historical Study of Lukács, Brecht, Benjamin and Adorno* (Berkeley: University of California Press, 1982), p. 86.

60. Ibid., p. 57.

Chapter 1

1. General studies in English on the Prague School include: René Wellek, *The Literary Theory and Aesthetics of the Prague School* (Ann Arbor: Michigan Slavic Contributions); Jan M. Broekman, *Structuralism: Moscow, Prague, Paris* (Dodrecht: D. Reidel Publishing Co., 1974); a foreword by René Wellek to the *Word and Verbal Art: Selected Essays by Jan Mukařovský,* ed. and trans. John Burbank and Peter Steiner (New Haven: Yale University Press, 1977); the postscript by Ladislaw Matejka to *Semiotics of Art: Prague School Contributions,* ed. Ladislaw Matejka and Irwin R. Titunik (Cambridge: MIT Press, 1976); and *The Prague School Selected Writings, 1929–1946,* ed. Peter Steiner (Austin: University of Texas Press, 1982).

2. Victor Erlich, *Russian Formalism: History-Doctrine* (The Hague, 1955) has a chapter on Czech Structuralism, treating it as an outgrowth of Russian Formalism.

3. Ladislaw Matejka, "Postscript: Prague School Semiotics," in *Semiotics of Art: Prague School Contributions*, op. cit., p. 270.

4. Peter Steiner, "The Roots of Structuralist Esthetics" in *Prague School*, op. cit., p. 174.

5. Mukařovský, "Art as a Semiotic Fact," in *Semiotics of Art*, op. cit., p. 349.

6. Ibid.

7. Mukařovský quoted by Steiner from "Standard Literary Language and Poetic Language," in *Structure, Sign, and Function*, op. cit., p. xiv.

8. Steiner, "The Roots of Structuralist Esthetics," op. cit., p. 203.

9. Mukařovský, *Structure, Sign, and Function*, p. 88.

10. Ibid., p. 86.

11. Mukařovský, *Aesthetic Function, Norm, and Value as Social Facts*, op. cit., pp. 94–96.

12. František Deák, "Structuralism in Theatre," *The Drama Review* 20 (December 1976): 88.

13. Shklovsky, quoted by Ejxenbaum, "The Theory of the Formal Method," op. cit., p. 17.

14. Essays by Petr Bogatyrev on the semiotic properties of folk art, "Costume as a Sign," "Folk Song from a Functional Point of View," "Semiotics in the Folk Theatre," and "Forms and Functions of Folk Theater"; as well as Karel Brušák's essay, "Signs in the Chinese Theater"; Jindřich Honzl's two essays, "Dynamics of the Sign in the Theater" and "The Hierarchy of Dramatic Devices"; and Jiří Veltruský's three essays, "Dramatic Text as a Component of Theater," "Basic Features of Dramatic Dialogue," and "Construction of Semantic Contexts," appear translated and edited by Ladislaw Matejka and Irwin R. Titunik in *Semiotics of Art: Prague School Contributions*, op. cit. In addition, Jiří Veltruský's *Drama as Literature* is useful (Lisse: The Peter de Ridder Press, 1977). Unfortunately, the work of Otokar Zich, *Estetika dramatického umeni* (*Aesthetics of Dramatic Art*) (Prague: 1921) has not been translated.

15. Bogatyrev, "Semiotics in the Folk Theater," op. cit., p. 45.

16. Mukařovský, *Structure, Sign, and Function*, p. 210.

17. Patrice Pavis, "Notes toward a Semiotic Analysis," trans. Marguerite Oerlemans Bunn, *The Drama Review* 23 (December 1979): 103.

18. These four components of theatrical art were established by Otokar Zich in his *Estetika dramatického umeni*.

19. Mukařovský, *Structure, Sign, and Function*, p. 205.

20. Ibid., p. 203

21. Roman Ingarden, *Das Literarische Kunstwerk* (Halle: Max Niemeyer Verlag, 1931).

22. Ladislaw Matejka, "Postscript: Prague School Semiotics," *Semiotics of Art: Prague School Contributions*, p. 280.

23. Karel Brušák, "Signs in the Chinese Theater," *Semiotics of Art: Prague School Contributions*, p. 68.

24. Ibid., pp. 67–68.

25. Bogatyrev, "Costume as Sign," in *Semiotics of Art: Prague School Contributions*, p. 14.

26. Bogatyrev, "Semiotics in the Folk Theater," op. cit., p. 34.

27. Ibid.

28. Brušák, op. cit., p. 62.

29. Jiří Veltruský, "Construction of Semantic Contexts," in *Semiotics of Art: Prague School Contributions*, p. 138.

30. Veltruský, "Dramatic Text as a Component of the Theater," op. cit., p. 95.

31. Ibid., pp. 115–16.

32. Roberta Reeder, "An Encounter of Codes," *The Drama Review* 23 (December 1979): 89.

33. Veltruský, "Man and Object in the Theater," op. cit. pp. 83–85.

34. Ibid., p. 85.

35. Mukařovský, *Structure, Sign, and Function*, pp. 215–16.

36. Veltruský, "Man and Object in the Theater," p. 86.

37. Ibid.

38. Bogatyrev, "Semiotics in the Folk Theater," p. 33

39. Constantin Stanislavsky, *My Life in Art*, p. 358 ff., quoted by Veltruský, "Dramatic Text as a Component of Theater," p. 106.

40. Mukařovský, "A Structural Analysis of a Dramatic Figure," in *Structure, Sign, and Function*, p. 175.

41. *Brecht on Theatre*, ed. and trans. John Willett (New York: Hill and Wang, 1964), p. 110.

42. Bogatyrev, "Semiotics in the Folk Theater," p. 34, and Mukařovský, *Structure, Sign, and Function*, pp. 172–73.

43. Brušák, "Signs in the Chinese Theater," p. 63.

44. Veltruský, "Dramatic Text as a Component of Theater," p. 102.

45. Ibid.

46. Ibid., pp. 102–3.

47. Ibid., p. 103.

48. Mukařovský, *Structure, Sign, and Function*, p. 207.

49. Veltruský, "Dramatic Text as a Component of Theater," p. 104.

50. Eisenstein quoted by Pavis, "Notes toward a Semiotic Analysis," op. cit., p. 95.

51. Honzl, "Dynamics of the Signs in the Theater," op. cit., p. 79.

52. Ibid., p. 75.

53. Ibid., p. 76.

54. *Brecht on Theatre*, ed. and trans. John Willett (New York: Hill and Wang, 1964), p. 87.

55. Mukařovský, *Structure, Sign, and Function*, p. 213.

56. Otokar Zich, quoted by Mukařovský, *Structure, Sign, and Function*, p. 214, from *Estetika dramatického umenì*, p. 246.

57. Ibid.

58. Ibid., p. 217.

59. Georges Mounin, *Introduction à la sémiologie* (Paris: Les Editions de Minuit, 1970), p. 80.

60. Elam, *The Semiotics of Theatre and Drama*, op. cit., pp. 33–35.

61. Bogatyrev, "Semiotics of Folk Theater," op. cit., pp. 51–56.

62. Mukařovský, *Structure, Sign and Function*, op. cit., p. 218.

63. Ervin Goffman, *Frame Analysis: An Essay on the Organization of Experience* (Cambridge: Harvard University Press, 1974), p. 237.

64. Ibid., p. 507.

65. Jerzy Grotowski, *Towards a Poor Theater* (New York: Simon and Schuster, 1968), pp. 56–57.

66. Ibid., p. 162.

67. Mukařovský, *Structure, Sign, and Function*, p. 209.

Chapter 2

1. Umberto Eco, *A Theory of Semiotics*, p. 261.

2. Bürger, p. 49.

3. Nikolai A. Gorchakov, *The Theater in Soviet Russia* (New York: Columbia University Press, 1957), p. 109.

4. Ellendea Proffer and Carl R. Proffer, eds., *The Ardis Anthology of Russian Futurism* (Ann Arbor: Ardis Publishers, 1980), p. 181.

5. Ibid., pp. 182–83.

6. František Deák, "Blue Blouse," *The Drama Review* (March 1973): 40.

7. B. Souvarine, quoted by James Billington, *The Icon and the Axe* (New York: Vintage Books, 1970), p. 530.

8. Ibid., p. 535.

9. Gail Harrison Roman, "The Ins and Outs of Russian Avant-Garde Books: A History," in *The Avant-Garde in Russia, 1910–1930*, eds. Stephanie Barron and Maurice Tuchman (Cambridge: MIT Press, 1980), p. 104.

10. Eco, *A Theory of Semiotics*, p. 274.

11. Vikor Shklovsky, quoted by Boris Ejxenbaum, "A Theory of the Formal Method," in *Readings in Russian Poetics: Formalist and Structuralist Views*, ed. Ladislaw Matejka and Krystyna Pomorska (Ann Arbor: Michigan Slavic Contributions, 1978), p. 32.

12. Ibid., quoting Jurij Tynjanov, p. 31.

13. Alexander Tairov, *Notes of a Director*, trans. William Kuhlke (Coral Gables: University of Miami Press, 1969).

14. Alma H. Law, "The Revolution in the Russian Theater," in *The Avante-Garde in Russia, 1910–1930* (Cambridge: MIT Press, 1980), p. 67.

15. Georg Fuchs, *Die Schaubühne der Zukunft* (Berlin, 1906), p. 34.

16. Ibid., pp. 34–36.

17. Huntley Carter, *The New Spirit in the Russian Theater, 1917–25* (London: Brentano's Ltd., 1929), p. 105.

18. Eco, *A Theory of Semiotics*, p. 274.

19. Vsevolod Meyerhold, *Meyerhold on Theatre*, ed. and trans. Edward Braun (New York: Hill and Wang, 1969), p. 256.

20. Ibid., p. 254.

21. Vsevolod Meyerhold, "Der Schauspieler der Zukunft," in *Wsewolod Meyerhold, Alexander Tairov, Jewgeni B. Wachtangow*, ed. Ludwig Hoffman and Dieter Wardetzky (Frankfurt: Roderberg), p. 354.

22. Ibid., p. 101.

23. Konstantin Rudnitsky, *Meyerhold, The Director*, trans. George Petrov (Ann Arbor: Ardis Publishers, 1981), p. 236.

24. Meyerhold, quoted by Edward Braun, *The Theatre of Meyerhold* (New York: Drama Book Specialists, 1979), p. 140.

25. Rudnitsky, p. 232.

26. Znosko-Borovsky, *Ruskii teatr nachal xx veka*, quoted by Gorchakov, p. 75.

27. Rudnitsky, p. 239.

28. Cited by Braun, *The Theater of Meyerhold*, pp. 143–44.

29. Gorchakov, p. 134.

30. Vladimir Mayakovsky, *The Complete Plays*, trans. Guy Daniels (New York: Simon & Schuster, Inc., 1968), pp. 45–46.

31. Rudnitsky, p. 259.

32. Mayakovsky, *The Complete Plays*, p. 45.

33. Ibid., p. 46.

34. Ibid., p. 39.

35. Malevich, quoted by Braun, *The Theatre of Meyerhold*, p. 150.

36. James M. Symons, *Meyerhold's Theatre of the Grotesque* (Coral Gables: University of Miami Press, 1971), p. 56.

37. Gorchakov, p. 136.

38. František Deák, "The Agit-Prop and Circus Plays of Vladimir Mayakovsky, *The Drama Review* (March 1973): 48.

39. B. Alpers quoted by Gorchakov, p. 137.

40. *Meyerhold on Theatre*, p. 174.

41. Ibid., p. 170.

42. Robert C. Williams, *Artists in Revolution: Portraits of the Russian Avant-Garde 1905–1925* (Bloomington: Indiana University Press, 1977), p. 13.

43. Ibid., p. 34.

44. Nick Worral, "Meyerhold's *The Magnificent Cuckold*," *The Drama Review*, 57 (March 1973): 15.

45. Ibid.

46. *Meyerhold on Theatre*, pp. 190–92.

47. Sergei Eisenstein, quoted by Lon Barna, *Eisenstein* (Bloomington: Indiana University Press, 1973), p. 35.

48. Sergei Eisenstein, *Film Form*, trans. Jay Leyda (New York: Harcourt, Brace, Jovanovich, 1949), p. 38.

49. Yutkevich, quoted by Luda Schnitzer, Jean Jeund, and Marcel Martin, eds. *Cinema in Revolution* (New York: Hill and Wang, 1973), p. 18.

50. Marie Seton, *Sergei M. Eisenstein* (New York: A. A. Wyn, Inc., 1952), p. 61.

51. *Meyerhold on Theatre*, op. cit., p. 205.

52. Law, op. cit., p. 65.

53. Gorchakov, p. 113.

54. Liubov Popova, "On Exact Criteria, Ballet Numbers, Deck Equipment on Battleships, Picasso's Latest Portraits, and the Observation Tower of the School of Military Camouflage in Kantsevo," *The Avant-Garde in Russia*, op. cit., p. 222.

55. John E. Bowlt, ed. and trans., *Russian Art of the Avant-Garde Theory and Criticism 1902–1934* (New York: The Viking Press, 1976), p. xxxvii.

56. Ibid.

57. Rodchenko, quoted by Bowlt, p. 259.

58. *Meyerhold on Theatre*, p. 200.

59. Symons, op. cit., pp. 71–72.

60. *Meyerhold on Theatre*, p. 197.

61. Ibid., p. 201.

62. Ibid., p. 198.

63. Braun, *The Theatre of Meyerhold*, op. cit., p. 168.

64. Law, op. cit., p. 69.

65. Gorchakov, pp. 204–5.

66. Law, p. 69.

67. *Meyerhold on Theatre*, p. 173.

68. Worral, op. cit., p. 24.

69. Braun, *The Theatre of Meyerhold*, p. 176.

70. Law, p. 69.

71. Braun, *The Theatre of Meyerhold*, pp. 177–78.

72. *Meyerhold on Theatre*, p. 152.

73. Ibid., p. 125.

74. Rudnitsky, p. 158.

75. Ibid., p. 167.

76. *Meyerhold on Theatre*, p. 131.

77. Ibid.

78. Ibid., p. 122.

79. Ibid., p. 121.

80. Ibid.

81. Ibid., p. 147.

82. Braun, *The Theatre of Meyerhold*, pp. 70–71.

83. Ibid., p. 71.

84. Ibid.

85. *Meyerhold on Theatre*, pp. 99–100.

86. Marjorie Hoover, *Meyerhold: Art of Conscious Theater* (Amherst: University of Massachusetts Press, 1974), p. 53.

87. *Meyerhold on Theatre*, p. 141.

88. Ibid., p. 196.

89. Ibid., p. 206.

90. Braun, *The Theatre of Meyerhold*, pp. 196–97.

91. Meyerhold, quoted by Hoover, op. cit., p. 160.

92. Kaplan, quoted by Braun, *Meyerhold on Theatre*, p. 218.

93. Symons, op. cit., pp. 163–64.

94. Gorchakov, p. 214.

95. Marc Slonim, *Soviet Russian Literature, Writers and Problems: 1917–1967* (New York: Oxford University Press, 1967), p. 42.

96. Braun, *Meyerhold on Theatre*, p. 236.

97. Braun, *The Theatre of Meyerhold*, p. 232.

98. Hoover, op. cit., p. 195.

99. Rudnitsky, p. 450.

100. Braun, *The Theatre of Meyerhold*, p. 242.

101. Ibid., p. 251.

102. Ibid., p. 262.

103. Ibid., pp. 264–65.

104. Gorchakov, p. 366.

105. Osip Brik, quoted by Tony Bennett, *Formalism and Marxism* (New York: Methuen, 1979), p. 32.

Chapter 3

1. Viktor Shklovsky, "Parallels in Tolstoy," in *Twentieth-Century Russian Literary Criticism,* ed. Viktor Erlich (New Haven: Yale University Press, 1975), p. 81.

2. Hans Robert Jauss, *Towards Aesthetic Experience and Literary Hermeneutics,* ed. and trans. Wlad Godzich (Minneapolis: University of Minnesota Press, 1982), p. 10.

3. Ibid.

4. Shklovsky, op. cit.

5. Ibid.

6. Ibid.

7. Viktor Shklovsky, "Pushkin and Sterne: *Eugene Onegin,*" in *Twentieth-Century Russian Literary Criticism,* op. cit., p. 65.

8. Tairov, quoted by Shklovsky in "Pushkin and Sterne: *Eugene Onegin,*" op. cit., p. 65.

9. John Fuegi, *The Essential Brecht* (Los Angeles: University of Southern California Studies in Comparative Literature, 1972), pp. 12–13, 123–26.

10. Lunn, pp. 122–23.

11. Shklovsky, "Pushkin and Sterne: *Eugene Onegin,*" op. cit., p. 68.

12. John Willett, *Brecht in Context* (London: Methuen Inc., 1984), pp. 220–21. Also see Eric Bentley, *The Brecht Commentaries* (New York: Grove Press, Inc., 1981), pp. 255–61.

13. Lunn, p. 143.

14. Shklovsky, "Pushkin and Sterne: *Eugene Onegin,*" op. cit., p. 68.

15. Ibid.

16. Ibid., p. 67.

17. Eric Bentley, *The Brecht Commentaries,* op. cit., p. 256.

18. Shklovsky, "Parallels in Tolstoy," op. cit., p. 81.

19. Jurij Lotman, *Semiotics of Cinema,* trans. Mark Suino (Ann Arbor: Michigan Slavic Contributions, 1976), p. 59.

20. *Brecht on Theatre,* op. cit., p. 217.

21. Ibid., pp. 91–92.

22. Jiří Veltruský, "Construction of Semantic Contexts," in *Semiotics of Art: Prague School Contributions,* eds. Ladislaw Matejka and Irwin R. Titunik (Cambridge: MIT Press, 1976), p. 138.

23. Roland Barthes, quoted by Frederic Jameson, *The Prison House of Language: A Critical Account of Structuralism and Russian Formalism* (Princeton: Princeton University Press, 1972), p. 58.

24. Ibid.

25. Ibid.

26. "A Short Organum for the Theatre," *Brecht on Theatre,* op. cit., p. 193.

27. Ibid., p. 81.

28. Shklovsky, "Parallels in Tolstoy," op. cit., p. 81.

29. Ibid.

30. Ibid., p. 85.

31. Norris Houghton, *Moscow Rehearsals: The Golden Age of the Soviet Theatre* (New York: Grove Press, Inc., 1962), p. 90.

32. *Brecht on Theatre,* op. cit., p. 203.

33. Houghton, op. cit., p. 94.

34. Lunn, p. 112.

35. Henri Arvon, *Marxist Esthetics* (Ithaca: Cornell University Press, 1973), pp. 104–5.

36. Lukacs, quoted by Arvon, p. 105.

37. *Brecht on Theatre,* p. 104.

38. Ibid., pp. 104–5.

39. *Meyerhold on Theatre,* ed. and trans. Edward Braun (New York: Hill and Wang, 1969), p. 248.

40. Jan Mukařovský, *Aesthetic Function, Norm and Value as Social Facts* (Ann Arbor: Michigan Slavic Contributions, 1979), pp. 48–50.

41. Ibid., p. 10.

42. Jakobson, quoted by Tony Bennett, *Formalism and Marxism* (New York: Methuen & Co., 1979), p. 33.

43. Arvon, op. cit., pp. 107–8.

44. Ibid., p. 109.

45. Ibid.

46. Jan Mukařovský, quoted by Victor Erlich, *Russian Formalism: History-Doctrine,* 3d. ed. (New Haven: Yale University Press, 1981), p. 159.

47. Jan Mukařovský, *Aesthetic Function, Norm and Value as Social Facts,* op. cit., p. 83.

48. *Brecht on Theatre,* p. 23.

49. Ibid.

50. Roland Barthes, *Critical Essays,* trans. Richard Howard (Evanston: Northwestern University Press, 1972), p. 263.

51. M. M. Bakhtin, quoted by V. V. Ivanov, "The Significance of M. M. Bakhtin's Ideas on Sign, Utterance, and Dialogue for Modern Semiotics," in *Semiotics and Structuralism: Readings from the Soviet Union,* ed. Henryk Baran (White Plains, NY: International Arts and Sciences Press, Inc.), p. 313.

52. Barthes, *Critical Essays*, op. cit., p. 264.

53. Ibid., p. 263.

54. Bakhtin, op. cit., p. 320.

55. Peter Handke, "Brecht, Play, Theatre, Agitation," *Theatre Quarterly* (October–December 1971), p. 89.

56. Bentley, op. cit., p. 259.

57. Ibid., p. 260.

58. Bakhtin, op. cit., p. 321.

59. Ibid.

60. Hans Robert Jauss, *Towards Aesthetic Experience and Literary Hermeneutics*, op. cit., p. 105.

61. Ibid.

62. Ibid.

63. Lunn, p. 117.

64. *Brecht on Theatre*, p. 205.

65. Ibid., p. 186.

66. Umberto Eco, *The Role of the Reader* (Bloomington: Indiana University Press), p. 22.

67. Ibid.

68. Jan Mukařovský, *Structure, Sign, and Function* (New Haven: Yale University Press, 1978), p. xxi.

69. Eco, *Role of the Reader*, op. cit., p. 126.

70. Ibid.

71. Jauss, *Towards Aesthetic Experience and Literary Hermeneutics*, op. cit., p. 107.

72. Ibid., p. 108.

73. Ibid., p. 139.

74. Ibid., p. 138.

75. *Brecht on Theatre*, p. 136.

76. Shoshana Avigal and Shlomith Rimon-Kenan, "What Do Brooks' Bricks Mean?" *Poetics Today* (Spring 1981): 11.

77. Umberto Eco, *A Theory of Semiotics* (Bloomington: Indiana University Press, 1979), pp. 16–17.

78. *Brecht on Theatre*, p. 86.

79. Ibid., p. 139.

80. Ibid.

81. Ibid., p. 141.

82. Karl Korsch, *Revolutionary Theory,* ed. Douglas Kellner (Austin: University of Texas Press, 1977), p. 37.

83. Ibid., p. 102, quoting Benjamin.

84. Ibid.

85. *Brecht on Theatre,* p. 141.

86. Brecht, quoted by Willett from *Schriften zum Theater,* vol. I, p. 165, in *Brecht on Theatre,* pp. 8–9.

87. Bentley, *The Brecht Commentaries,* op. cit., p. 45.

88. Ibid.

89. George Steiner, *Language and Silence* (New York: Atheneum, 1977), p. 139.

90. Jauss, *Towards Aesthetic Experience and Literary Hermeneutics,* op. cit., p. 177.

91. Bentley, *The Brecht Commentaries,* p. 99.

92. Ibid., p. 100.

93. Martin Esslin, *Brecht: The Man and His Work* (Garden City, NY: Doubleday & Company, Inc., 1961), p. 143.

94. Ibid.

95. Bentley, *The Brecht Commentaries,* op. cit. p. 98.

96. Ibid., p. 99.

97. Esslin, op. cit., p. 143.

98. Ibid., p. 144.

99. Ibid.

100. Brecht, quoted by Willett, *Brecht on Theatre,* p. 287.

101. Bentley, *The Brecht Commentaries,* p. 251.

102. Esslin, op. cit., p. 155, quoting from *Die Linkskurve* (Berlin, January 1931).

103. Ibid., p. 156, quoting Kurella, *Literatur der Weltrevolution.*

104. Ibid., p. 156, quoting Schumacher, *Die dramatischen Versuche Bertolt Brecht's 1918–1933,* p. 365.

105. David Pike, "Brecht and Stalin's Russia: The Victim as Apologist (1931–1945)," in *Beyond Brecht: The Brecht Yearbook,* vol. 11, 1982 (Detroit: Wayne State University Press, 1983), p. 143.

106. Lenin, quoted by Rufus W. Mathenson, *The Positive Hero in Russian Literature* (Stanford: Stanford University Press, 1975), p. 112.

107. Pike, op. cit., p. 144.

108. Abram Tertz (pseud.), *Towards Positive Realism* (New York: Pantheon Books, 1960), p. 172.

109. Barthes, *Critical Essays,* op. cit., p. 72.

110. Karl Hartmann, *Das polnische Theater nach dem Zweiten Weltkrieg* (Marburg: N. G. Elwert Verlag, 1964), pp. 49–50.

111. E. H. Gombrich, "Mediations on a Hobby Horse or the Roots of Artistic Form," in *Aspects of Form* (New York, 1951), p. 217.

112. Accounts of the incident in Bytom appear in Konrad Gajek's *Bertolt Brecht na scenach polskich* (Wroclaw: Wroclawskie Towarzystwo Naukowe, 1974), pp. 13–15, and in Leon Schiller's account reprinted in *Pamietnik Teatralny* (1955), pp. 33–34.

113. Bernard Dort, "Epic Form in Brecht's Theatre," *Yale Theater* (Summer 1969): 26.

114. Brecht, "The Reading of Plays: *The Threepenny Opera* Notes," in *Brecht Collected Plays*, vol. 2, eds. Manheim and Willett (New York: Vintage, 1975), p. 277.

115. *Brecht on Theatre*, p. 35.

116. Peter Christian Giese, *Das Gesellschaftlich Komische: Zu Komik und Komödie am Beispiel der Stücke and Bearbeitungen Brechts* (Stuttgart: J. B. Metzlersche Verlagsbuchhandlung, 1974), p. 11.

117. Dort, op. cit., p. 27.

118. Brecht, "Notes to *The Threepenny Opera*," *Brecht on Theatre*, p. 317.

119. Erwin Piscator, *The Political Theater*, ed. and trans. Hugh Robinson (New York: Avon Books, 1978), pp. 109–10.

120. Schiller, *Pamietnik Teatralny*, op. cit., p. 34.

121. Adam Grzymala Siedlecki, quoted by Gajek, op. cit., p. 21, from *Kurier Warszawski* (7 May 1929).

122. Wasilewski, quoted by Gajek, p. 22, from "Propaganda za trzy grosze," *Mysl Naradowa* (12 May 1929).

123. Nowaczynski, quoted by Gajek, pp. 22–23.

124. Antoni Slonimski, "Teatr Polski: Opera za trzy grosze," *Wiadomosci Literacki* (19 May 1929), quoted by Gajek, pp. 24–25.

125. Gajek, op. cit., pp. 25–29.

126. Ibid., pp. 31–32.

127. Walter Benjamin, *Lesezeichen: Schriften zur deutschsprachiger Literatur* (Leipzig, 1970), pp. 403 ff.

128. Mukařovský, *Structure, Sign, and Function*, op. cit., p. 85.

129. Andrzej Wirth, *Teatr jaki moglby byc* (Warszawa: Wydawnictwo Artystyczne i Filmowe, 1963), pp. 5–6.

130. Georg Lukacs, *Realism in Our Time: Literature and the Class Struggle* (New York: Harper & Row, 1964), p. 105.

131. Stefan Zolkiewski, "Is Socialist Literature Enough?" in *The Modern Polish Mind*, ed. Maria Kuncewicz (New York: Gossett & Dunlop, 1962), p. 377.

132. Zbigniew Krawczykowski, "Spojrzenia Wstecz," *Teatr* (22 1956): 6.

133. Ryszard Matuszewski, "Berlinski Listopad," *Kuznica* (January 1950): 3.

134. Wilhelm Szewczyk, "Bertolt Brecht i jego teatr," *Teatr* (April 1950): 50.

135. Jan Szczepanski, "Jeszcze o teatrze Bertolta Brechts," *Teatr* (April 1952): 6.

136. Ibid.

137. Izabela Czermakowa, *Teatr* (February 1953): 23.

138. Jan Kott, "Eichlerowna i inni," *Przeglad Kulturalny* (August 1962).

139. Bohdan Tomaszewski, "Matka Courage," *Przegald Kulturalny* (August 1962).

140. Wirth, *Teatr jaki moglby byc*, op. cit., pp. 280–82.

141. Jan Klossowicz, "Szkola Brechta," *Przeglad Kulturalny* (August 1962).

142. Wirth, op. cit., p. 279.

Chapter 4

1. Peter von Becker, "Herz Zwei. Die Welt Geht in Trümmer-Passe!" *Theater Heute* 2 (1986): 5.

2. Eugène Ionesco, *Notes and Counternotes* (New York: Grove Press, 1964), p. 40.

3. Ibid., pp. 40–41.

4. Ibid., pp. 54–55.

5. Jan Kott, "Foreword," in The Madman and the Nun *and Other Plays*, ed. and trans. Daniel Gerould and C. S. Durer (Seattle: University of Washington Press, 1968), pp. vii–viii.

6. Lunn, p. 57.

7. George Wellworth, *Modern Drama and the Death of God* (Madison: University of Wisconsin Press, 1986), p. 57.

8. André Breton, "First Surrealist Manifesto," in *Avant-Garde Drama*, ed. Bernard F. Dukore and Daniel C. Gerould (New York: Thomas Y. Crowell Company, 1976), p. 567.

9. Jan Kott, "Witkiewicz and Artaud: Where the Analogy Ends," *Theatre Quarterly* 5: 18 (1975): 68.

10. *Meyerhold on Theatre*, ed. Edward Braun (New York: Hill and Wang, 1969), p. 60.

11. Antonin Artaud, *The Theater and Its Double* (New York: Grove Press, Inc., 1958), p. 44.

12. Tzvetan Todorov, *The Fantastic: A Structural Approach to a Literary Genre*, trans. Richard Howard (Ithaca: Cornell University Press, 1975), p. 25.

13. Daniel Gerould, *Witkacy* (Seattle: University of Washington Press, 1981), p. 341.

14. Bernard Dukore, "Who Was Witkacy? Witkiewicz East and West," *Theatre Quarterly* 18 (1975): 62.

15. Witkiewicz, *Czysta Forma w teatrze* (Warsaw: Wydawnictwa Artystyczne i Filmowe, 1977), p. 57.

16. Boris Tomasevskij, "Literature and Biography," in *Readings in Russian Poetics: Formalist and Structuralist Views*, ed. Ladislaw Matejka and Krystyna Pomorska (Cambridge: MIT Press, 1978), p. 47.

17. Ibid., p. 53.

18. Ibid., p. 55.

19. Daniel Gerould, "Witkacy," in *Tropical Madness* (New York: Winter House Ltd., 1972), pp. 245–46.

20. Antonin Artaud, *The Theatre and its Double* (New York: Grove Press, 1958), pp. 82, 86.

21. Andrei Bely, quoted by Rudnitsky, *Meyerhold the Director*, p. 84.

22. Jacques Derrida, *Writing and Difference*, trans. Alan Bass (Chicago: Chicago University Press, 1978), p. 240.

23. Kott, "Witkiewicz and Artaud," op. cit., p. 69.

24. Ibid.

25. H. H. Stuckenschmidt, *Schoenberg, His Life, World and Work*, trans. Humphrey Searle (London: John Calder, 1977), p. 177.

26. Boris M. Ejxenbaum, "The Theory of the Formal Method," in *Readings in Russian Poetics*, op. cit., pp. 16–17.

27. Ibid., quoting Shklovsky, p. 14.

28. Eco, *Theory of Semiotics*, op. cit., p. 268.

29. Roman Jakobson, quoted by Ejxenbaum, op. cit., p. 26.

30. Artaud, *The Theatre and Its Double*, op. cit., p. 32.

31. *Czysta Forma w teatrze*, op. cit., pp. 57–58.

32. Ibid., pp. 77–78.

33. Eco, *The Theory of Semiotics*, p. 270.

34. *Czvsta forma w teatrze*, p. 78.

35. Ibid., p. 105.

36. Ibid., pp. 156, 145.

37. Witkiewicz, *The Shoemakers* from the collection of plays *The Madman and the Nun*, ed. and trans. Daniel Gerould (New York: Winter House Ltd., 1972), p. 283.

38. *Czysta Forma w teatrze*, pp. 109, 111.

39. Ibid., p. 169.

40. Andrzej Wirth, "Avant-Gardist as a Classical Author of the Period," *The Polish Review* 18 (1973): 17.

41. *Czysta Forma w teatrze*, p. 171.

42. Ibid., pp. 169–70.

43. Witkiewicz, quoted by Bernard Dukore, "Witkiewicz's *Beelzebub Sonata* in Hawaii," *Theatre Quarterly*, 18 (1975): 80.

44. Witkiewicz, *The Pragmatists* from collected plays *Tropical Madness*, ed. Daniel Gerould, pp. 12, 14.

45. Ibid., p. 26.

46. Georg Fuchs, *Revolution in the Theatre* (Ithaca: Cornell University Press, 1969), p. 90.

47. Cited by Juliette R. Stepanian, *Mayakovsky's Cubo-Futurist Vision* (Houston: Rice University Press, 1986), p. 1.

48. James H. Billington. *The Icon and the Axe* (New York: Vintage Books, 1966), p. 517.

49. Kott, "Witkiewicz and Artaud," p. 70.

50. *Czysta Forma w teatrze*, p. ii1.

51. Witkiewicz, *Gyubul Wahazar* from *Tropical Madness*, p. 110.

52. Ibid., pp. 111, 118.

53. Ibid., p. 171.

54. Ibid., pp. 142–44.

55. Ibid., p. 101.

56. Gerould, *Witkacy*, p. 156.

57. Ibid., p. 151.

58. Ibid., p. 115.

59. Cited in Billington, p. 512.

60. Ibid., p. 513.

61. Ibid., p. 512.

62. Andrzej Wirth, "Brecht and Witkiewicz: Two Concepts of Revolution in the Drama of the Twenties," *Comparative Drama* (Fall 1969): 198–99.

63. Witkiewicz, *The Anonymous Work* from *Twentieth-Century Polish Avant-Garde Drama,* ed. Daniel Gerould, p. 115.

64. Witkiewicz, *The Water Hen* from collection *The Madman and the Nun*, p. 77.

65. Bernard Dukore, "Spherical Tragedies and Comedies with Corpses; Witkacian Tragicomedy," *Modern Drama*, 8 (September 1975): 295–96.

66. Witkiewicz, *The Shoemakers* from *The Madman and the Nun*, pp. 283–84.

67. Ibid., p. 275.

68. Ibid., p. 285.

69. Ibid., p. 281.

70. Gerould and Durer, Introduction to *The Shoemakers, The Madman and the Nun*, p. 218.

71. Ibid., p. 281.

72. Ibid., p. 245.

73. Ibid., pp. 287–88.

74. Umberto Eco, *The Role of the Reader* (Bloomington: Indiana University Press, 1979), p. 55.

75. Ibid., p. 61.

76. Ibid., pp. 55–62.

77. Czeslaw Milosz, "Stanislaw Ignacy Witkiewicz, a Polish Writer for Today, " *Tri-Quarterly* 9 (Spring 1967): 153.

Conclusion

1. Mukařovský, *Aesthetic Function, Norm and Value as Social Facts*, op. cit., p. 98.

2. Ibid., p. 100.

3. Mukařovský, quoted by Ladislaw Matejka, "Postscript: Prague School Semiotics," in *Semiotics of Art: Prague School Contributions*, op. cit., p. 274.

4. Jauss, *Toward an Aesthetic of Reception*, op. cit., p. 72.

5. Mukařovský, *Aesthetic Function, Norm and Value as Social Facts*, p. 96.

6. Jauss, *Toward an Aesthetic of Reception*, p. 44.

7. Ibid., p. 75.

Selected Bibliography

Formalism, Structuralism, Semiotics

Bailey, R. W., L. Matejka, and P. Steiner, eds. *The Sign: Semiotics around the World*. Ann Arbor: Michigan Slavic Contributions, 1978.

Barthes, Roland. *A Barthes Reader*. Susan Sontag. New York: Hill and Wang, 1982.

———. *Critical Essays*. Trans. Richard Howard. Evanston: Northwestern University Press, 1972.

———. *Elements of Semiology*. Trans. Annette Lavers and Colin Smith. New York: Hill and Wang, 1967.

———. *Mythologies*. Trans. Annette Lavers. New York: Hill and Wang, 1972.

———. *The Pleasure of the Text*. Trans. Richard Miller. New York: Hill and Wang, 1973.

———. *S/Z*. Trans. Richard Miller. New York: Hill and Wang, 1974.

Beckerman, Bernard. *Dynamics of Drama: Theory and Method of Analysis*. New York: Knopf, 1970.

Bennett, Tony. *Formalism and Marxism*. New York: Methuen, 1979.

Bouissac, Paul. *La Mésure des gestes prolégomènes à la sémiotique gestuelle*. The Hague: Mouton, 1973.

Broekman, Jan M. *Structuralism: Moscow, Prague, Paris*. Dordrecht: D. Reidel Publishing Co., 1974.

Brook, Peter. *The Empty Space*. London: Macgibbon & Kee, 1968.

Bürger, Peter. *Theory of the Avant-Garde*. Minneapolis: University of Minnesota Press, 1984.

Craig, E. Gordon. *The Art of Theatre*. London: T. N. Foulis, 1905.

Culler, Jonathan. *On Deconstruction*. Ithaca: Cornell University Press, 1982.

———. *The Pursuit of Signs*. Ithaca: Cornell University Press, 1981.

———. *Structuralist Poetics*. Ithaca: Cornell University Press, 1975.

Dahlhays, Carl. *Wagner's Aesthetics*. Bayreuth: Editions Musica, 1972.

Deák, František. "Structuralism in Theatre." *The Drama Review* 20 (December 1976): 83–94.

De George, Richard and Fernande. *The Structuralists from Marx to Levi-Strauss*. Garden City, NY: Doubleday & Co., Inc., Anchor Books, 1972.

Derrida, Jacques. *Of Grammatology*. Trans. G. C. Spivak. Baltimore: The Johns Hopkins University Press, 1976.

Eco, Umberto. *The Role of the Reader*. Bloomington: Indiana University Press, 1979.

———. *A Theory of Semiotics*. Bloomington: Indiana University Press, 1976.

Ehrmann, Jacques, ed. *Structuralism*. Garden City, NY.: Doubleday & Co., Inc., Anchor Books, 1970.

Erlich, Victor. *Russian Formalism*. New Haven: Yale University Press, 1965.

———. *Twentieth-Century Russian Literary Criticism*. New Haven: Yale University Press, 1976.

Eschbach, Achim. *Pragmasemiotik und theater. Ein Beitrag zur Theorie und Praxis einer pragmatischen orientierten Zeichenanalyse*. Tübingen: Gunter Verlag, 1979.

Goffman, Ervin. *Frame Analysis on the Organization of Experience*. Cambridge: Harvard University Press, 1974.

Grotowski, Jerzy. *Towards a Poor Theatre*. New York: Simon & Schuster, 1968.

Guiraud, Pierre. *Semiology*. London: Routledge & Kegan Paul, 1975.

Handke, Peter. "Nauseated by Language." *The Drama Review* (Fall 1970), pp. 56–81.

Harari, Josué V., ed. *Textual Strategies: Perspectives in Post-Structuralist Criticism*. Ithaca: Cornell University Press, 1979.

Hartman, Geoffrey. *Saving the Text*. Baltimore: The Johns Hopkins University Press, 1981.

Hawkes, Terence, ed. *The Semiotics of Theatre and Drama*. New York: Methuen, 1980.

———. *Structuralism and Semiotics*. London: Methuen, 1977.

Helbo, Andre. *Sémiologie de la représentation*. Brussels: Editions Complexe, 1975.

Honzl, Jindřich. *Zaklady a Praxe Moderniho Divedla*. Prague: Orbis, 1963.

Hrushovski, Benjamin. "The Structure of Semiotic Objects: A Three-Dimensional Model." *Poetics Today* 1(1–2).

Ingarden, Roman. *Das Literarische Kunstwerk*. Halle: Max Niemeyer Verlag, 1931.

Iser, Wolfgang. *The Act of Reading*. Baltimore: The Johns Hopkins University Press, 1978.

———. *The Implied Reader*. Baltimore: The Johns Hopkins University Press, 1974.

Jameson, Frederic. *The Prison-House of Language: A Critical Account of Structuralism and Russian Formalism*. Princeton: Princeton University Press, 1972.

Jauss, Hans Robert. *Aesthetic Experience and Literary Hermeneutics*. Trans. Michael Shaw. Minneapolis: University of Minnesota Press, 1982.

———. *Toward an Aesthetic of Reception*. Trans. Timothy Bahti. Minneapolis: University of Minnesota Press, 1982.

Kowzan, Tadeusz. *Littérature et spectacle*. Warsaw: Mouton Publishers, 1975. PWN Editions Scientifiques de Pologne.

Kristeva, Julia. *Desire in Language*. Ed. Leon S. Roudiez. New York: Columbia University Press, 1980.

Levi-Strauss, Claude. *Tristes Tropiques*. Trans. John and Doreen Weightman. New York: Atheneum, 1978.

Lotman, Jurij. *Semiotics of Cinema*. Trans. Mark Suino. Ann Arbor: Michigan Slavic Contributions, 1976.

Lunn, Eugene. *Marxism & Modernism*. Berkeley: University of California Press, 1982.

MacLeon, Robert M. *Narcissus and the Voyeur: Three Books and Two Films*. The Hague: Mouton Publishers, 1979.

Martin, Graham Dunstan. *Language, Truth and Poetry*. Edinburgh: At the University Press, 1975.

Matejka, Ladislav, and Krystyna Pomorska, eds. *Readings in Russian Poetics*. Ann Arbor: Michigan Slavic Contributions, 1978.

Matejka, Ladislav, and Irwin R. Titunik, eds. *Semiotics of Art: Prague School Contributions*. Cambridge: MIT Press, 1976.

Molinari, Cesare, and Valeria Ottoleoghi. *Leggere il Teatro: Un Manuale per l'analisa del fatto teatrale*. Firenze: Vallecchi, 1979.

Mounin, Georges. *Sémiologies des textes littéraires*. London: The Athlone Press, University of London, 1977.

Mukařovský, Jan. *Aesthetic Function, Norm and Value as Social Facts*. Trans. Mark E. Suino. Ann Arbor: Michigan Slavic Contributions, 1979.

———. *Structure, Sign, and Function*. Trans. and ed. John Burbank and Peter Steiner. New Haven: Yale University Press, 1977.

———. *The Word and Verbal Art.* Trans. and ed. John Burbank and Peter Steiner. New Haven: Yale University Press, 1977.

Nadin, Mihai. "Sign Functioning in Performance." *The Drama Review.* 23 (December 1979): 105–20.

Pavis, Patrice. "Notes toward a Semiotic Analysis." *The Drama Review* 23 (December 1979): 93–104.

———. *Problèmes de sémiologie théâtrale.* Montreal: Les Presses de l'universite du Quebec, 1976.

Pettit, Philip. *The Concept of Structuralism.* Berkeley and Los Angeles: University of California Press, 1975.

Poetics Today 2:3 (Spring 1981).

Reeder, Roberta. "An Encounter of Codes." *The Drama Review* 23 (December 1979): 81–92.

Robey, David, ed. *Structuralism: An Introduction.* Oxford: Clarendon Press, 1973.

Schmid, Herta. *Strukturalistische Dramentheorie.* Kronberg: Scriptor Verlag GmbH, 1973.

Scholes, Robert. *Semiotics and Interpretation.* New Haven: Yale University Press, 1982.

———. *Structuralism in Literature.* New Haven: Yale University Press, 1974.

Slawinska, I. *La sémiologie du théâtre in statu nascendi: Prague 1931–1941.* Warsaw: Roczniki Humanistyczne. 25 (1977): 53–75.

Steiner, Peter, ed. *The Prague School: Selected Writings, 1929–1946.* Austin: University of Texas Press, 1982.

Sypher, Wylie. *Rococo to Cubism in Art and Literature.* New York: Vintage Books, 1960.

Temkine, Raymond. *Grotowski.* New York: Avon Book, 1972.

Thody, Philip. *Roland Barthes: A Conservative Estimate.* London: MacMillan Press, 1977.

Todorov, Tzvetan. *The Fantastic: A Structural Approach to a Literary Genre.* Trans. Richard Howard. Ithaca: Cornell University Press, 1975.

Trabant, Jürgen. *Zur Semiologie des literarischen Kunstwerks.* Munich: Wilhelm Fisk Verlag, 1970.

Ubersfeld, Anne. *Lire le Théâtre.* Paris: Editions Sociales, 1977.

Veltruský, Jiří. *Drama as Literature.* Lisse: The Peter de Ridder Press, 1977.

———. "Theatre in the Corridor." *The Drama Review* 23 (December 1979): 67–80.

———. "Man and Object in the Theater." In *A Prague School Reader on Esthetics, Literary Structure and Style.* Washington, D. C.: Georgetown University Press, 1964.

Volosinov, V. N. *Marxism and the Philosophy of Language.* Trans. Ladislaw Matejka and I. R. Titunik. New York: Seminar Press, 1973.

Wellek, René. *The Literary Theory and Aesthetics of the Prague School.* Ann Arbor: Michigan Slavic Contributions.

Zich, Otokar. *Estetika drametickeho umeni.* Prague, 1931.

Meyerhold

Alexandrova, Vera. *A History of Soviet Literature.* Trans. Mira Ginsburg. New York: Doubleday & Co., 1963.

Barna, Yon. *Eisenstein.* Bloomington: Indiana University Press, 1973.

Barron, Stephanie, and Maurice Tuchman, eds. *The Avant Garde in Russia, 1910–1930.* Cambridge: MIT Press, 1980.

Billington, James H. *The Icon and the Axe.* New York: Vintage Books, 1957.

Bowlt, John E. ed. and trans. *Russian Art of the Avant-Garde: Theory and Criticism 1902–1934.* New York: The Viking Press, 1972.

Bradshaw, Martha, ed. *Soviet Theaters 1917–1941.* New York: Research Programs on the U.S.S.R., 1954.

Braun, Edward. *The Theatre of Meyerhold.* New York: Drama Books Specialists, 1979.

Brown, Edward J. *Mayakovsky: A Poet in the Revolution.* Princeton: Princeton University Press, 1973.

Carter, Huntley. *The New Spirit in the Russian Theatre, 1917–1928.* London: Brentano's Ltd., 1929.

――――. *The New Theatre and Cinema of Soviet Russia.* New York: Arno Press, 1970.

Deák, František. "The Agit Prop and Circus Plays of Vladimir Mayakovsky. *The Drama Review* March 1973: 47–52.

――――. "Blue Blouse." *The Drama Review* (T-57): 40–46.

Eisenstein, Sergei. *Film Form.* Ed. and trans. Jan Leyda. New York: Harcourt, Brace, 1949.

――――. *The Film Sense.* Ed. and trans. Jan Leyda. New York: Harcourt, Brace, 1947.

――――. *Notes of a Film Director.* London: Laurence & Wishart, 1959.

Fuchs, Georg. *Die Schaubuhne der Zukunft.* Berlin, 1906.

――――. *Revolution in the Theatre.* Ithaca: Cornell University Press, 1969.

Gibian, George, and H. W. Tjalsma, eds. *Russian Modernism: Culture and the Avant-Garde, 1900–1930.* Ithaca: Cornell University Press, 1976.

Gorchakov, Nikolai A. *The Theater in Soviet Russia.* Trans. Edgar Lehrman. New York: Columbia University Press, 1957.

Gordon, Mel. "Meyerhold's Biomechanics." *The Drama Review* (September 1973): 73–88.

Gorelik, Mordecai. *New Theaters for Old.* New York: E. P. Dutton & Co., Inc., 1962.

Gregor, J., and R. Fulop-Miller. *Das russische Theater.* Zurich, 1928.

Hoffman, L., and D. Wardetzky, eds. *Meyerhold, Tairov, Wachtangov: Theateroktober.* Leipzig, 1967.

Hoover, Marjorie. *Meyerhold: The Art of Conscious Theater.* Amherst: University of Massachusetts Press, 1974.

――――. "The Meyerhold Centennial." *The Drama Review* (September 1974): 69–72.

Houghton, Norris. *Moscow Rehearsals: The Golden Age of Soviet Theatre.* New York: Grove Press, Inc., 1962.

――――. *Return Engagement.* New York: Holt, Rinehart, and Winston, 1962.

――――. "Russian Theatre in the 20th Century." *The Drama Review* (March 1973): 5–13.

Huppert, Hugo. *Wladimir Majakovski.* Reinbeck bei Hamburg: Rowohlt Verlag, 1965.

Law, Alma H. "Meyerhold's *Woe to Wit.*" *The Drama Review.* (September 1974): 89–107.

Lenhoff, Gail. "The Theatre of Okhlopkov." *The Drama Review* (March 1973): 89–104.

Leyda, Jan. *Kino: A History of the Russian and Soviet Film.* London: George Allen and Unwin, Ltd., 1960.

Macleod, Joseph. *The New Soviet Theatre.* London: George Allen & Unwin. Ltd., 1943

Mayakovsky, Vladimir. *The Complete Plays.* Trans. Guy Daniles. New York: Simon & Schuster, Inc., 1968.

Meyerhold, V. E. *Meierkhol'd V. E. Stat'i Pis'ma Rechi, Besed'i 1917–1939.* Moskva: Izdatel'stvo Isysstvo, 1968.

――――. "Meyerhold Speaks: Observations on Acting and Directing." *The Drama Review* (T-63): 108–112.

――――. *Meyerhold on Theatre.* Trans. and ed. Edward Braun. New York: Hill and Wang, 1969.

Proffer, Ellendea, and Carl R. Proffer, eds. *The Ardis Anthology of Russian Futurism.* Ann Arbor: Ardis Publishers, 1980.

Roose-Evans, James. *Experimental Theatre from Stanislavsky to Today.* New York: Universe Books, 1973.

Ripellino, A. M. *Majakovskij und das russische Theater der Avant-Garde.* Köln, 1964.

Ruhle, J. *Theater und Revolution.* Munich, 1963.

Rudnitsky, Konstantin. *Meyerhold, The Director.* Trans. George Petrov. Ann Arbor: Ardis Publishers, 1981.

Schnitzer, Ludu, and Jean and Marcel Martin, eds. *Cinema in Revolution.* New York: Hill and Wang, 1973.

Seton, Marie. *Sergei M. Eisenstein.* New York: A. A. Wyn, Inc., 1952.

Slomin, Marc. *Soviet Russian Literature.* New York: Oxford University Press, 1964.

Stanislavsky, Constantin. *An Actor Prepares*. New York: Theatre Arts, Inc., 1936.

Stepanian, Juliette R. *Mayakovsky's Cubo-Futurist Vision*. Houston: Rice University Press, 1986.

Symons, James M. *Meyerhold's Theatre of the Grotesque: The Post Revolutionary Productions 1920–1932*. Coral Gables: University of Miami Press, 1971.

Tairov, Alexander. *Notes of a Director*. Trans. William Kuhlke. Coral Gables: University of Miami Press, 1969.

Tertz, Abram (pseud). *On Socialist Realism*. New York: Pantheon Books, 1960.

Vendrovskja L., ed. *Vstrechi z Meirekhol'dom*. Moskva: Vserossiiskoe Teatral'noe odshchestvo, 1967.

Volkov, Solomon, ed. *The Memoirs of Dmitri Shostakovich*. Trans. Antonina W. Boucs. New York: Harper & Row Publishers, Inc., 1979.

Williams, Robert C. *Artists in Revolution: Portraits of the Russian Avant-Garde 1905–1925*. Bloomington: Indiana University Press, 1977.

Woroszylski, Wiktor. *The Life of Mayakovsky*. Trans. Boleslaw Taborski. New York: The Orion Press, 1970.

Worrall, Nick. "Meyerhold's Production of *The Magnificent Cuckold*." *The Drama Review* (March 1973): 14–34.

Brecht

Abel, Lionel. *Metatheater: A New View of Dramatic Form*. New York: Hill and Wang, 1963.

Arvon, Henri. *Marxist Aesthetics*. Trans. Helen Lanel. Ithaca: Cornell University Press, 1973.

Arendt, Hannah. *Benjamin Brecht: Zwei Essays*. Munich: Piper, 1971.

Axer, Erwin. "Brecht o wspolczesnym dramacie." *Teatr* 5 (1952).

———. "Dialogi Berlinski." *Teatr* 16 (1954).

———. *Listy ze sceny*. Warszawa: Czytelnik, 1957.

———. "Skok na Schiffbaurdamm." *Teatr* 12 (1961).

Barnas, Kazimierz. "Brecht odmlodzony." *Zycie Literackie* 49 (1958).

Benjamin, Walter. *Illuminations*. Ed. Hannah Arendt. New York: Schocken Books, 1969.

———. *Lesezeichen: Schriften zur deutschsprachiger Literatur*. Leipzig, 1970.

Bentley, Eric. *The Brecht Commentaries*. New York: Grove Press, Inc., 1981.

———. *In Search of Theater*. New York: Vintage Books, 1954.

———. *The Playwright as Thinker*. New York: Meridian Books, Inc., 1946.

———. *The Theatre of Commitment*. New York: Atheneum, 1967.

———, ed. *The Theory of the Modern Stage*. New York: Penguin Books, 1968.

———. "Are Stanislavski and Brecht Commensurable?" *TDR* Fall (1964).

Berwinska, Krystyna. "Kaukaskie Kredowe Kolo." *Nowa Kultura*. 4 (1955).

Bloch, Alfred. "Literary Letter from Warsaw." *The New York Times Book Review* (March 31, 1965).

Bloch, Ernst. "Entfremdung, Verfremdung, Alienation, Estrangement." *TDR* Fall (1970).

Braun, Kazimierz. "Modern Acting Theory and Practice." In *Beyond Brecht*. The Brecht Yearbook, Vol. II, 1982. Eds. John Fuegi, Gisela Bahr, John Willett.

Brecht, Bertolt. *Brecht: Collected Plays*. 9 Vols., eds. Ralph Manheim and John Willet. New York: Vintage Books.

———. *Brecht on Theatre*. Ed. and trans. John Willet. New York: Hill and Wang, 1964.

———. *Die Stücke von Bertolt Brecht in einem Band*. Frankfurt am Main: Suhrkamp Verlag, 1978.

———. "Notes on Stanislavski." Trans. Carl R. Mueller. *Tulane Drama Review*. (Winter 1964).

Brustein, Robert. *The Theatre of Revolt*. Boston: Little, Brown and Company, 1962.

Cohn, Ruby. *Currents in Contemporary Drama*. Bloomington: Indiana University Press, 1969.

Csato, Edward. "Nieporozumienie dyskusyjne." *Teatr* 3 (1953).

———. "O Bertolcie Brechcie." *Teatr* 22 (1956).

————. *The Polish Theater*. Warsaw: Polonia Publishing House, 1963.

————. "Uwagi o realizmie scenicznym." *Teatr* Special Stalin Issue (1953).

Czanerle, Maria. "Bertola Brechta tragedii ciag dalszy." *Teatr* 19 (1958).

————. "Wielka markietanka." *Teatr* 7 (1962).

Czerwinski, Edward J. "Dialog and the Socialist World: The Spectrum of Influence." *Comparative Drama* (Winter 1967).

————. "Twelve Years of Dialog." *Comparative Drama* Spring 1968).

Daszewski, Wladyslaw. "Aktor polski w spoleczenstwie socjalistycznym." *Teatr* 3 (1949)

Deák, František. "Structuralism in Theatre: The Prague School Contribution." *TDR* (December 1976).

Demetz, Peter, ed. *Brecht: A Collection of Critical Essays*. Englewood Cliffs, NY: Prentice Hall, 1962.

Dort, Bernard. "Epic Form in Brecht's Theater." *Yale Theater* (Summer 1968).

Eaton, Katherine. "Brecht's Contacts with the Theater of Meyerhold." *Comparative Drama* (Spring 1977).

Esslin, Martin. "Brecht: The Absurd and the Future." *TDR* (Summer 1963).

————. *Brecht: The Man and His Work*. Garden City, NY: Doubleday & Co., Inc., 1961.

Ewen, Frederic. *Bertolt Brecht: His Life, His Art, and His Times*. New York: The Citadel Press, 1967.

Frisch, Max. *Sketchbook 1966–1971*. New York: Harcourt Brace Jovanovich, Inc., 1971.

————. *Tagebuch 1946–49*. Frankfurt am Main: Suhrkamp Verlag, 1950.

Frühling, Jacek. "Das polnische Theater gestern und heute." *Theater hinter dem eisernen Vorhang*. Basel: Basilius Presse, 1964.

————. "Brecht na Wybrzezu." *Swiat* 12 (1955).

————. "Brecht o teatrze amerykanskim." *Teatr* 5 (1952).

————. "Brecht po raz pierwszy po polsku." *Swiat* 5 (1955).

————. "Jeszcze o teatrze Brechta." *Nowa Kultura* 7 (1953).

————. "O wlasciwe proporcje." *Nowa Kultura* 7 (1953).

————. "Prawdziwa cena strachu." *Nowa Kultura* 5 (1961).

————. "Spotkanie z Brechtem." *Przeglad Kulturalny* 34 (1956).

Fuegi, John. *"The Caucasian Chalk Circle* in Performance." *Brecht Heute, Brecht Today*. Frankfurt am Main: Athenaum Verlag, 1971.

————. *The Essential Brecht*. Los Angeles: Hennessey and Ingalls, 1972.

————. "Russian Epic Theatre Experiments and the American Stage." *The Minnesota Review* (Fall 1973).

Gajek, Konrad. *Bertolt Brecht na Scenach Polskich (1929–1969)*. Wroclaw: Wroclawski Towarzystwo Naukowe, 1974.

Gassner, John. *Directions in Modern Theater & Drama*. New York: Holt, Rinehart & Winston, Inc., 1966.

Gawlik, Jan Pawel. ''Dwie Opery.'' *Zycie Literacki* 44 (1962).

Giese, Peter Christian. *Das Gesellschaftlich Komische: Zu Komik und Kömodie am Beispiel der Stücke and Bearbeitungen Brechts*. Stuttgart: J. B. Metzlersche Verlagsbuchhandlung, 1974.

Gombrich, E. H. "Meditations on a Hobby Horse of the Roots of Artistic Form." *Aspects of Faith*. Ed. L. L. Whyte. New York, 1951.

Gorelik, Mordecai. "Are Stanislavski and Brecht Commensurable?" *TDR* (September 1959).

Gray, Ronald. *Brecht the Dramatist*. Cambridge: Cambridge University Press, 1976.

Gren, Zygmunt. "Brecht po raz pierwszy." *Zycie Literackie* 4 (1955).

Grimm, Reinhold. *Brecht und die Weltliteratur*. Nurnberg: Verlag Hans Carl, 1961.

————. *Brecht und Nietzsche oder Geständnis eines Dichters*. Frankfurt: Suhrkamp, 1979.

Grossvogel, David I. *Four Playwrights and a Postscript: Brecht, Ionesco, Beckett, Genet*. Ithaca: Cornell University Press.

Haas, Willy. *Bert Brecht*. Trans. Max Knight and Joseph Fabrytians. New York: Frederick Ungar Publishing Co., 1970.

Handke, Peter. "Brecht, Play, Theatre, Agitation," *Theatre Quarterly* (October–December 1971): 89–90.

Hartmann, Karl. "Bertolt Brecht auf den polnischen Bühnen." *Osteuropa* 11 (1960).

————. "Neue strömungen in der polnischen Literatur seit 1956." *Osteuropa*, 9 (1959).

————. "Polens Schriftsteller sagen sich los vom sozialistischen Realismus." *Osteuropa* 5 (1957).

————. *Das polnische Theater nach dem Zweiten Weltkrieg*. Marburg: N. G. Elwert Verlag, 1964.

Hecht, Werner, ed. *Sieben Studien über Brecht*. Gottingen: Vandengoeck & Ruprecht, 1960.

Hinck, Walter. *Die Dramaturgie des späten Brechts*. Gottingen: Vandenhoeck & Ruprecht, 1971.

Ihering, Herbert. "Brecht—tworczy rewolucjanista teatru." *Dialog* 2 (1957).

————. "Der Dramatiker Bert." *Sinn und Form: Beitrage zur Literatur, Zweites Sonderheft Bertolt Brecht*. Berlin: Rutten & Loening.

————. "Dramaturg Ludowy." *Pamietnik Teatralny*.

Jablonska, Leonia. "*Pan Puntila* na Wybrzezu." *Teatr* 13 (1955).

Jarecki, Andrzej. "Nie boje sie tego co mnie smieszy." *Nowa Kultura* 18 (1958).

"Jeszcze o nieporozumieniach dyskusyjnych." *Teatr* 13 (1953).

Kaluzynski, Zygmunt. "Miedzy rewolucja i neurastenia." *Nowa Kultura* 5 (1953).

————. "Problemy powojennego teatru." *Teatr* 1 (1948).

Keler, Jozef. "Brecht u Rotbauma." *Przeglad Kulturalny* 22 (1957).

Kirby, E. T., ed. *Total Theater: A Critical Anthology*. New York: E. P. Dutton & Co., 1966.

Klossowicz, Jasn. "Szkola Brechta." *Przeglad Kulturalny* 28 (1962).

Koenig, Jerzy. "O Brechcie na trzewo." *Dialog* 34 (1960).

————. "Brecht czyli teatr." *Przeglad Kulturalny* 5 (1962).

————. "Eichlerowna i inni." *Przeglad Kulturalny* 8 (1962).

————. "Rozmowa z Erwinem Axerem." *Nowa Kultura* 11 (1961).

Kolakowski, Leszek. *Toward a Marxist Humanism*. Trans. Jane Zielenko Peel. New York: Grove Press, Inc., 1968.

————. "Z czego zyja filozofowie?" *Nowa Kultura* 3 (1956).

Knopf, Jan. *Bertolt Brecht: Ein kritischer Forschungsbericht Fragwürdiges in der Brecht Forschung*. Frankfurt: Atheneum Verlag, 1974.

Korsch, Karl. *Revolutionary Theory*. Ed. Douglas Kellner. Austin: University of Texas Press, 1977.

Kott, Jan. "Mutter Courage." *Przeglad Kulturalny* 46 (1957).

————. *Theatre Notebook: 1947–1967*. Trans. Boleslaw Taborski. Garden City, NY: Doubleday & Co., Inc., 1968.

————. "Zywy czlowiek i bogowie." *Przeglad Kulturalny* 5 (1956).

Kral, Andrzej Wladyslaw. "Zapiski o Matce Courage." *Teatr* 3 (1959).

Krawczykowski, Zbigniew. "Spojrzenie Wstecz." *Teatr* 22 (1956).

Lacis, Asja. *Revolutionar im Beruf*. Munich: Rogner & Bernhard, 1971.

Lichtheim, George. *Georg Lukacs*. New York: The Viking Press, 1970.

Lukacs, Georg. *Realism in our Times: Literature and the Class Struggle*. New York: Harper & Row Publishers, 1962.

————. "The Sociology of Modern Drama." *TDR* (Summer 1965).

————. *Solzhenitsyn*. Cambridge: The MIT Press, 1971.

————. *Studies in European Realism*. New York: Grosset & Dunlap, 1964.

Lyons, Charles R. *Bertolt Brecht: The Despair & the Polemic*. Carbondale: Southern Illinois University Press, 1968.

Mayer, Hans. *Bertolt Brecht und die Tradition*. Pfullingen: Neske, 1961.

————. "Jarmarki, metaforia notatki o Arturo Ui." *Teatr* 5 (1962).

————. "Tradycja plebejska o niektorych motywach tworczosci Bertolta Brechta." *Pamietnik Teatralny* 1 (1955).

_____ . "Wystepy Berlinskiego Zespolu." *Tworczosc* 2 (1953).

Mittenzwei, Werner. *Brechts Verhältnis zur Tradition*. Berlin: Akademie Verlag, 1972.

Natanson, Wojciech. *Godzina Dramatu*. Poznan: Wydawnictwo Poznanskie, 1970.

_____ . "Wystepy Berliner Ensemble." *Teatr* 16 (1962).

Needle, Jan, and Peter Thompson. *Brecht*. Chicago: The University of Chicago Press, 1981.

Owczarenko, Aleksander. "Realizm socjalistyczny jako metoda artystyczna." *Socjalistyczeskaja Literatura i Sworiemiennyj Literaturnyj Process*. Moskwa, 1973.

Panski, Jerzy. "Zagadnienia pracy artystycznej teatrow na rok 1953." *Przeglad Kulturalny* 7 (1953).

Pike, David. "Brecht and Stalin's Russia: The Victim as Apologist." *Beyond Brecht*. The Brecht Yearbook, Vol. II, 1982.

Piscator, Erwin. *The Political Theatre*. Trans. and ed. Hugh Rorrison. New York: Avon Books, 1978.

Piscator, Maria Ley. *The Piscator Experiment: The Political Theater*. Carbondale: Southern Illinois University Press, 1967.

Pomianowski, Jerzy. "Majcher i spolka." *Swiat* 48 (1958).

Puzyna, Konstanty. *Burzliwa Pogoda: Fielotony Teartralne*. Warszawa: Panstwowy Instytut Wydawnyczy, 1971.

_____ . "Szkola Dramaturgow: Polityka, Historia i Fakty." *Dialog* 6 (1956).

_____ . "Szkola Dramaturgow: Utopia i Nauka." *Dialog* 2 (1957).

Roztorowski, M. "Tak szybko i tak przez strumien." *Dzis i jutro* 7 (1955).

Rudnicki, A. "Swiatlo aktora." *Swiat* 45 (1962).

Schiller, Leon. "Teatry Berlinskie." *Pamietnik Teatralny* 3 (1953).

_____ . "Z zagadnien repertuarowych." *Teatr* 3 (1948).

Schmidt, Dieter. *Baal und der Junge Brecht: Eine Textkritische Untersuchung zur Entwicklung des Frühwerks*. Stuttgart: J. B. Metzlersche Verlagsbuchhandlung, 1961.

Schumacher, Ernst. *Brecht-Kritiken*. Berlin: Henschelverlag Kunst und Gesellschaft, 1977.

_____ . *Brecht: Theater und Gesellschaft im 20 Jahrhundert*. West Berlin: Verlag das Europaische Buch, 1973.

Shaw, Leroy. *The Playwright & Historical Change*. Madison: The University of Wisconsin Press, 1970.

Sinko, Grzegorz. "Brecht a literatura angielska." *Dialog* 5 (1964).

Sokel, Walter H. "Brecht's Concept of Character." *Comparative Drama* (Fall 1971).

Strelka, Josef. *Brecht, Horvath, Dürrenmart: Wege und Abwege des modernen Dramen*. Wien: Forum Verlag, 1962.

Stryjkowski, Julian. "Matka Courage i jej dzieci." *Przeglad Kulturalny* 3 (1953).

Strzelecki, Zenobiusz. *Kierunki Scenografii Wspolczesnej*. Warszawa: Panstwowe Wydawnictwo Naukowe, 1970.

Stupinski, Zbigniew. *Die Funktion des Songs in den Stücken Bertolt Brechts*. Poznan: Uniwersytet im. A. Mickiewicza, Wydzial Filologiczny, Seria Filologia Germanskia, 1972.

Surina, Tamara. *Stanislavskij i Brecht*. Moskva: Iskysstve, 1975.

Swinarski, Konrad. "Z notatnika rozmow z Brechtem." *Nowa Kultura* 12 (1957).

Szczepanki, Jan Alfred. "Jeszcze o teatrze Bertolta Brechta." *Teatr* 7 (1950).

_____ . "Panstwowy nagrody artystyczne i Leon Schiller." *Teatr* 2 (1949).

_____ . "Rok przelomu w teatrze polskim." *Teatr* 3 (1949).

Szewczyk, Wilhelm. "Bertolt Brecht i jego teatr." *Teatr* (April 1950).

Szydlowski, Roman. *Bertolt Brecht in Polen*. Warsaw, 1969.

_____ . *The Theatre in Poland*. Warsaw: Interpress Publishers, 1972.

_____ . "Krytyki teatralne Brechta." *Dialog* 2 (1962).

Tarn, Adam. "Teatr Brechta." *Teatr* 5 (1955).

Toeplitz, K. T. (KTT). "Propozycja Brecht." *Nowa Kultura* 47 (1958).

Treugutt, Stefan. "Dobry czlowiek z Seczuanu." *Teatr* 8 (1956).
_____. "Matka zabitych dzieci." *Przeglad Kulturalny* 29 (1957).
_____. "Matti i jego pan." *Przeglad Kulturalny* 39 (1958).
_____. "Stara madrosc i nowa." *Przeglad Kulturalny* 5 (1955).
_____. "Wygladaja tak samo jak ludzie." *Przeglad Kulturalny* 4 (1955).
Volker, Klaus. *Bertolt Brecht: Eine Biographie.* München: Deutscher Taschenbuch Verlag GmbH & Co. KG, 1978.
Willett, John. *Brecht in Context.* London: Methuen, 1984.
_____. *Expressionism,* New York: McGraw Hill Book Company, 1970.
Wilska, Urszula. "Bert Brechts dramatische Kunst im polnischen Theaterleben." *Deutsch-polnische Hefte* 4 (1960).
Wirth, Andrzej. "Beitrag zur Brecht-Rezeption in Polen." *Theater der Zeit* 6 (1956).
_____. "Brecht & Grotowski." *Brecht Heute, Brecht Today: Jahrbuch der Internationalen Brecht Gesellschaft.* Frankfurt am Main: Athenaum Verlag, 1971.
_____. "Brecht in Polen." *Akzente* 5 (1965).
_____. "Brecht jest Brechtem." *Nowa Kultura* 6 (1961).
_____. "Granice realizmu." *Nowa Kultura* 23 (1956).
_____. "Konfrontacja czyli:ilu jest Brechtow." *Nowa Kultura* 28 (1962).
_____. "Ludowa sztuka Brechta." *Nowa Kultura* 12 (1955).
_____. "Moda czy przelom." *Nowa Kultura* 10 (1956).
_____. "Na przykladzie Brecht. Powiesci za 3 grosze." *Nowa Kultura* 23 (1956).
_____. "Oniesmielenie Brechtem." *Nowa Kultura* 9 (1962).
_____. "Pan H. jako gangster." *Nowa Kultura* 4 (1962).
_____. "Proba kredowego kola." *Teatr* 5 (1955).
_____. "Problematyka formalna sztuk Brechta." *Dialog* 2 (1957).
_____. "Przyszlosc teatru." *Nowa Kultura* 29 (1963).
_____. *Teatr jaki moglby byc.* Warszawa: Wydawnictwo Artystyczne i Filmowe, 1963.
_____. "Uwagi o teatrze w niemcach." *Dialog* 38 (1957).
Witt, Hubert, ed. *Brecht as They Knew Him.* Trans. John Peet. New York: International Publishers, 1974.
Wolff, Phillipp. "Das psycho-dynamische Theater." *Theater hinter dem Eisernen Vorhang.* Basel: Basilius Presse, 1964.
Wolicki, Krzysztof. *Wszystko jedno co o 19:30.* Warsaw: PIW, 1966.
Wroblewski, Andrzej. "Opera Brechta rowniez." *Nowa Kultura* 14 (1963).
Wygodzki, Stanislaw. "Strach i Nedza Trzeciej Rzeszy." *Teatr* 2 (1949).
Wysinska, Elzbieta. "Konfrontacje: Rewia gangsterska w wielkim stylu." *Dialog* 3 (1962).
Zeromska, Olga. "Teatr w kraju." *Kultura* 4 (1952).
Zolkiewski, Stefan. "Is 'Socialist Literature' Enough?" *The Modern Polish Mind.* Ed. Maria Kuncewicz. New York: Grosset & Dunlap, 1962.
Zytomirski, Eugeniusz. "Brecht i Gorki czy Rotbaum i Zamkow?" *Teatr* 7 (1961).

Witkiewicz

Aisenman, Leslie. "Aspects of Society in the Plays of Stanislaw Ignacy Witkiewicz." *The Polish Review* 18(1–2): 121–35.
Artaud, Antonin. *Anthology.* Ed. Jack Hirschmann. San Francisco: City Lights Books, 1965.
_____. *The Theater and Its Double.* New York: Grove Press Inc., 1958.
Asermely, Albert. "Directing Pure Form: The Pragmatists." *The Polish Review* 18(1–2): 136–38.
Baker, Stuart. "Witkiewicz and Malinowski: The Pure Form of Magic, Science and Religion." *The Polish Review* 18(12): 77–93.

Becker, Peter, "Herz Zwei, Die Welt geht in Trümmer. *Theater Heute*. 2 (1986): 1–9.

Berman, Paul. "Acting Witkiewicz." *The Polish Review* 18(1–2): 19–24.

Bersani, Leo. "Artaud." *Partisan Review* 3 (1976).

Beves, Stanislaw. "Czarny sygnalista i jego nie istniejuce potwory." *Tworczosc* 1 (1978): 103–6.

Blonski, Jan. "Powrot Witkacego." *Dialog* 9 (1963): 71–84.

―――. "Teatr Witkiewicza i Forma Formy." *Dialog* 12 (1967): 69–83.

―――. "Trzy Apokalipsy w Jedney," *Tworczosc* 10 (1976): 65–78.

―――. "U Zrodel Teatru Witkacego," *Dialog* 5 (1970): 81–90.

Bolecki, Wlodzimierz. "Witkacy: fatalne terminy (Uwagi wstepne)." *Teksty* 6 (1976): 73–81.

Breton, André. "First Surrealist Manifesto." *Avant-Garde Drama*. Ed. Bernard F. Dukore and Daniel C. Gerould. New York: Thomas Y. Crowell, 1976.

Camus, Albert. "An Absurd Reasoning." *The Myth of Sisyphus*. New York: Vintage Books, 1955.

Czerwinski, E. J. "Witkiewicz on Witkacy." *The Polish Review* 18(1–2): 10–13.

Degler, Janusz. "Witkacy's Ideas and Theories." *Le Theatre en Pologne* 12(3): 5–17.

―――. "Witkacy in Poland: Finding a Style for *The Mother*." *Theatre Quarterly* 5(18): 74–79.

―――. "Witkacy Worldwide." *Polish Perspectives* 20(12): 29–37.

Derrida, Jacques. "The Theater of Cruelty and the Absurd of Representation." *Theater* 9(3). 1978.

Dukore, Bernard F. "Spherical Tragedies and Comedies with Corpses: Witkacian Tragicomedy." *Modern Drama*. XVIII (September 1975): 291–315.

―――. "Who Was Witkacy?: Witkiewicz East and West." *Theatre Quarterly* 5(18):62–65.

―――. "Witkiewicz's *The Beelzebub Sonata* in Hawaii." *Theatre Quarterly*. 5(18): 80–94.

Esslin, Martin. "The Search for a Metaphysical Dimension in Drama." In Stanislaw Ignacy Witkiewicz, *Tropical Madness. Four Plays*. New York: Winter House Ltd., 1972.

―――. *The Theatre of the Absurd*. Garden City, NY: Doubleday & Co., Inc., 1961.

Falkiewicz, Andrzej. "Witkacy, Artaud, Awangarda." *Dialog* 6 (1960): 121–29.

Folejewski, Zbigniew. "The Theatre of Ruthless Metaphor: Polish Theatre Between Marxism and Existentialism." *Comparative Drama* III (Fall 1969): 176–83.

Galassi, Frank S. "Slapstick in Witkiewicz's *The Crazy Locomotive*." *Polish Review* 22(4): 49–57.

Gerould, Daniel C. "Introduction: Witkacy." *Twentieth-Century Polish Avant-Garde Drama*. Ed. Daniel Gerould. Ithaca: Cornell University Press, 1977.

―――. "Witkacy." In Stanislaw Ignacy Witkiewicz, *Tropical Madness. Four Plays*. New York: Winter House Ltd., 1972.

―――. *Witkacy*. Seattle: University of Washington Press, 1981.

―――. "Witkacy: Theater Outside the Theater." *The Polish Review*. 18(1–2): 14–16).

Gerould, Daniel C., and Durer, C. S. Introduction. In Stanislaw Ignacy Witkiewicz, *The Madman and the Nun and Other Plays*. Seattle: University of Washington Press, 1968.

Hoffman, Paul, and Jack W. McCullough. "Visual Images in Witkiewicz: *They* in Production." *The Polish Review* 18(1–2): 52–57.

Ionesco, Eugene. *Notes and Counternotes*. Trans. Donald Watson. New York: Grove Press, Inc., 1964.

Iribarne, Louis. "Revolution in the Theater of Witkacy and Gombrowicz." *The Polish Review* 18(1–2): 58–76.

―――. Translator's Introduction. In Stanislaw Ignacy Witkiewicz, *Insatiability*. Urbana: University of Illinois Press, 1977.

Iwaszkiewicz, Jaroslaw. "Dramaty Stanislawa Ignacego Witkiewkza." *Tworczosc* 2 (1963): 116–22.

Kijowski, Andrzej. "Samobojstwo przez parodie." *Tworczosc* 9 (1960): 40–53.

Klossowicz, Jan. "Teoria i dramaturgia Witkacego (1)." *Dialog* 12 (1959): 81–93.

―――. "Teoria i dramaturgia Witkacego (2)." *Dialog* 1 (1960): 97–111.

Kott, Jan. "Witkiewicz and Artaud: Where the Analogy Ends." Trans. Joanna Clark. *Theatre Quarterly* 5(18): 69–73.

Krasinski, Andrzej. "Leon Chwistek et ses 'Palais de dieu.'" *Perspectives Polonaises* 10 (1969): 36–39.

Krzyzanowski, Jerzy R., "Witkiewicz's Anthroponymy." *Comparative Drama* 3 (Fall 1969): 193–98.

Mencwel, Andrzej. "Witkacego jednosc w wielosci." *Dialog* 12 (1965): 85–98.

Micinska, Anna. "Na marginesie 'Narkotykow' *Niemytych dusz* St. I, Witkiewicza." *Tworczosc* 11 (1974): 30–47.

———. "U brzegow tropikalnej dzungli." *Tworczosc* 7 (1965): 101–10.

Milosz, Czeslaw. "The Pill of Murti-Bing." *The Captive Mind.* New York: Vintage Books, 1955.

———. "Stanislaw Ignacy Witkiewicz, a Polish Writer for Today." *Tri-Quarterly* 9 (Spring 1967): 143–54.

Morawski, Stefan. "Na Witkacodromie jasniej i . . . ciemniej." *Tworczosc* 5 (1977): 65–83.

Parker, James W. "Witkiewicz's *Gyubul Wahazar* and Ribemont-Dessaignes' *L'Empéreur de Chine:* Fairy Tales for Adults." *The Polish Review* 18(1–2): 25–52.

Pomian, Krzysztof. "Witkacy: Philosophy and Art," *Polish Perspectives* 13(9): 22–32.

———. "Witkiewicz zredukowany do absurda." *Dialog* 3 (1970): 106–15.

Pruska-Munk; Malgorzata. "Wyspianski's *The Wedding* and Witkiewicz's *The Shoemakers.*" *Polish Review* 22(4): 40–44.

Puzyna, Konstanty. "Pojecie czystej formy." *Tworczosc* 4 (1971): 67–74.

———. "Porachunki z Witkacym." *Tworczosc* 7 (1949): 100–8.

———. "Witkacy." In Stanislaw Ignacy Witkiewicz, *Dramaty.* 2 Vols. Warsaw: Panstwowy Instytut Wydawniczy, 1972.

Sokol, Lech. "Droga Witkacego do Teatru," *Dialog* 3 (1972): 104–13.

———. *Groteska w teatrze Stanislawa Ignacego Witkiewicza.* Wroclaw: Ossolineum, 1973.

———. "S. I. Witkiewicz and Strindberg." *Die Welt der Slaven* 12(2): 391–400.

———. "Witkacy in World Theatre, I: On European Stages." *Le Theatre en Pologne* 1 (1974): 16–20.

———. "Witkacy in World Theatre, II: In America." *Le Theatre en Pologne* 2 (1974): 26–29.

Szpakowska, Malgorzata, "Filozofia Spoleczna St. I. Witkiewicza." *Tworczosc* 11 (1974): 48–71.

Szymanski, Wieslaw Pawel. "Uczty skazanych." *Tworczosc* 1 (1966): 87–97.

Tarn, Adam. "Witkiewicz, Artaud, and the Theatre of Cruelty." *Comparative Drama* 3 (Fall 1969): 162–68.

Terlecki, Tymon. "Polski dramat Awangardowy." *Kultura* (Paris) 11 (1977): 20–30.

Wazyk, Adam. "O Witkiewiczu." *Dialog* 8 (1965): 70–75.

Wellworth, George. *Modern Drama and the Death of God.* Madison: University of Wisconsin Press, 1986.

Weyhaupt, Angela. "Death and Resurrection in Witkiewicz's *The Madman and the Nun. The Polish Review* 22(4): 45–49.

Wirpsza, Witold. "*Kurka Wodna.* czyli Marionetki." *Dialog* 2 (1964): 98–103.

Wirth, Andrzej. "Brecht and Witkiewicz: Two Concepts of Revolution in the Drama of the Twenties." *Comparative Drama* 3 (Fall 1969): 198–209.

———. "Avant-Gardist as a Classical Author of the Period." *The Polish Review* 18(1–2): 17–19.

Witkiewicz, Stanislaw Ignacy. *The Anonymous Work* from *Twentieth-Century Polish Avant-Garde Drama.* Ed. and trans. Daniel Gerould. Ithaca: Cornell University Press, 1977.

———. *Czysta forma w teatrze.* Warsaw: Wydawnictwo Artystycznei Filmowe, 1977.

———. *Dramaty.* 2 Vols. Ed. Konstanty Puzynu. Warsaw: Punstwowy Istytut Wydawniczy, 1972.

———. *Insatiability.* Trans. Louis Iribarne. Urbana: University of Illinois Press, 1977.

———. *The Madman and the Nun and Other Plays.* Ed. and trans. Daniel Gerould and C. S. Durer. Seattle: University of Washington Press, 1960.

————. *Tropical Madness. Four Plays.* Ed. and trans. Daniel Gerould. New York: Winter House Ltd., 1972.

————. *W malym dworky.* Ed. Lech Sokol. Warsaw: P.I.W., 1977.

Wyka, Kazimierz. "Trzy legendy tzw. Witkacego." *Tworczosc* 10 (1958): 122–35.

Wysinska, Elzbieta. "Konfrontacje: Witkacy jako klasyk." *Dialog* 5 (1966): 113–14.

Index